NEW INFORMATION TECHNOLOGY IN THE EDUCATION OF DISABLED CHILDREN AND ADULTS

New Information Technology in the Education of Disabled Children and Adults

DAVID HAWKRIDGE,
TOM VINCENT
and GERALD HALES

COLLEGE-HILL PRESS, INC.
San Diego, CA 92105

© 1985 David Hawkridge, Tom Vincent and Gerald Hales

College-Hill Press, Inc.
4284 41st Street,
San Diego, CA 92105

Library of Congress Cataloging in Publication Data

Hawkridge, David G.
  New information technology in the education of
disabled children and adults.

    Bibliography: p.
    Includes index.
    1. Physically handicapped children — Education —
United States. 2. Educational technology — United
States. 3. Physically handicapped children — Education —
Great Britain. 4. Educational technology — Great
Britain. I. Vincent, Tom, 1935-   II. Hales,
Gerald. [DNLM: 1. Education, Special. 2. Technology.
LC4215 H394n]
LC4231.H39   1984   371.9   84-23684
ISBN 0-88744-125-4

Printed in Great Britain

CONTENTS

PREFACE

New information technology is in the news in all Western countries. Politicians pin their hopes on its potential to revive economies and improve the quality of life. Manufacturers and retailers, bureaucrats and entrepreneurs, broadcasters and publishers all want to exploit it. It is the latest technological revolution.

In education, new information technology is greeted with mixed feelings. Educators, too, would like to take advantage of what it offers. Incorporating new information technology into existing educational institutions is far from easy, however, particularly during a period when their financial base is shrinking.

Disabled people have a special interest in new information technology. Other forms of technology have helped them to overcome their disabilities, of course, but new information technology promises even greater help, beyond their dreams of a few years ago. It can help many disabled people to overcome barriers of time and space, and to a much greater extent it can help them to overcome barriers of communication. Since communication is at the heart of living for human beings, new information technology offers opportunities to neutralise the worst effects of many kinds of disablement and to change the lives of many individuals.

Education of disabled people can also be improved greatly through new information technology, and that is what this book is about. The three of us who wrote this book had in mind a volume that would describe the state of the art, so to speak, and that would inform disabled people and all those who teach or help them, including not least policy-makers and professionals.

We start, in Part One, from the learning problems faced by disabled people, children and adults. What are their special difficulties? Without some understanding of these problems, advocates of new information technology may make serious mistakes. We also feel it is important to explain the technology and what it can do: in Part Two we provide some understanding of the general principles underlying it.

We assess in Part Three the benefits, and some problems, of new information technology in the course of describing and analysing how it is actually being used for the education of disabled students, particularly in the United Kingdom and the United States. Why these two countries? They happen to be the ones we know best, and are countries in which much research and development is going on in this field. During 1983 we were able to survey this work.

Our cautious optimism about new information technology shows as we discuss, in Part Four, many of the problems and constraints. If disabled students are to exploit the technology extensively for their own benefit, contentious issues must be debated and then resolved in the best way possible.

Finally, in Part Five we look to the immediate and longer-term future. We suggest what may happen in this field, basing our comments on our earlier analyses.

Perhaps we should say that this is *not* a book about uses of new information technology outside formal and non-formal education. For example, we do not discuss how microprocessor-controlled heating systems can benefit physically-disabled people. Others have written about these uses (for example, Perkins, 1983; Schofield, 1981). Nor is this book about all forms of disability. We have included disabilities related to physical and sensory handicap but not mental handicap. We do not cover, therefore, the whole span of 'special education', which includes children who are categorised as epileptic, maladjusted, educationally subnormal, autistic, dyslexic, slow learning, remedial and so on. We recognise that many disabled children (and adults) have to cope with multiple disability.

We came to this study with varying backgrounds. Tom Vincent is widely known in the United Kingdom for his research and development work on synthetic speech applications for blind children and adults. In recent years, apart from what he has done for Open University students, he has been involved in many projects funded by the Department of Trade and Industry. Gerald Hales is also widely known in the United Kingdom for his work on learning problems of deaf and dyslexic students, particularly in the Open University. David Hawkridge is the author of *New Information Technology in Education* (Croom Helm, 1983) and other books concerned with using technology for education. All three of us feel we have learned a great deal in carrying out our surveys and in writing this volume.

At the Open University, Mr L. Melton did a computer search for us of recent literature in this field. It yielded a large number of references, mainly in academic journals such as *American Annals of the Deaf, Education of the Visually Handicapped, Learning Disability Quarterly, Journal of Visual Impairment and Blindness, Teacher Education and Special Education* and *Journal of the British Association of Teachers of the Deaf.* The field is developing so fast, however, that much work reported only two or three years ago has been superseded. We decided to use the references to locate researchers and others, so that we could contact them personally, either on the telephone or face-to-face, and thus obtain their latest reports. As we extended our surveys, we found ourselves joining a generous network in both countries. We could not have written this book without the help of many people, some of them disabled, who kindly gave their time to talk to us, send us papers and show us how they were adapting and using new information technology. Their names make up a roll of honour of those engaged in this work.

We would like to thank the following people in the United Kingdom: Mr J. Anderson, Microelectronics Education Programme, Newcastle-upon-Tyne; Dr R. Baker, Dept. of Electronics, University of Southampton; Mr J. Bate, Putney; Ms C. Bennett, St Francis School, Lincoln; Mr R. G. Bignell, Exhall Grange School, Coventry; Dr M. P. Bolton, Dept. of Biomedical Physics, University of Aberdeen; Mr A. Brown, Chailey Heritage Hospital School; Mrs N. Bruce, Rosslyn Special School, Kirkcaldy; Mr D. M. Chaplin, Dept. of Physics, University of Oxford; Dr B. Chapman, School of Education Research Unit, Bristol University; Mrs J. Critchell, Oval Primary School, Croydon; Mr D. Child, the Open University, Milton Keynes; Dr R. J. Damper, Dept. of Electronics, University of Southampton; Mr P. Deakin, Neath Hill Professional Centre, Milton Keynes; Mr R. Dyke, Special Education Microelectronics Resource Centre, Manchester; Mrs A. Dicks, Graysmill School for the Physically Handicapped, Edinburgh; Mr A. Eyles, Foundation for Communication for the Disabled; Dr G. Flanagan, Dept. of Medical Physics, University of Newcastle-upon-Tyne; Mr M. Fountain, Stoke Mandeville Hospital Spinal Injuries Unit, Aylesbury; Dr D. Fraser, Western Information Technological Services, Clevedon; Mrs P. Fuller, Ormerod School for the Physically Handicapped, Oxford; Mr G. Fussey, District General Hospital, Barnsley; Dr J. Gill, Brunel University; Dr R. Gill, Dept. of Cybernetics and Computing, Brighton Polytechnic; Mr Robert Hinds, Hereford; Mr Roger Hinds, RNIB, London; Mrs J. Holdsworth, Thorn Park School for the Deaf,

Bradford; Mrs Mary Hope, Council for Educational Technology, London; Prof J. A. M. Howe, Dept. of Artificial Intelligence, Edinburgh University; Mrs J. Kell, Buckinghamshire County Council, Aylesbury; Mr M. Kirk, Scunthorpe; Mr R. Lambert, Fairfields School, Northampton; Mr T. Layden, Manpower Services Commission, Sheffield; Mr J. M. Leonard, Lichfield; Mrs L. Lloyd, South Lodge School, Leicester; Mr P. B. Lowe, Hereward College, Coventry; Mr J. McCann, Dept. of Trade and Industry, London; Miss M. I. F. Markes, Chorleywood College, Herts; Mr B. M. Morgan, Ysgol Penybont, Bridgend; Mrs M. Morgan, Ysgol Penybont, Bridgend; Prof A. F. Newell, University of Dundee; Dr J. P. Odor, Godfrey Thomson Research Unit, Edinburgh University; Ms E. M. C. Pantekoek, Wimbledon; Mr A. Pearce, Headmaster, Mary Hare Grammar School, Surrey; Mr C. Richards, Special Education Microelectronics Resource Centre, Newcastle-upon-Tyne; Mr G. Rochester, Queen Elizabeth Foundation Training College, Leatherhead; Dr A. Rostron, Dept. of Psychology, Hull University; Mr J. Sanderson, Siscroft Ltd, Beckenham; Dr J. Sandhu, Handicapped Persons Research Unit, Newcastle-upon-Tyne; Dr J. Schofield, Twickenham; Dr D. Sewell, Dept. of Psychology, Hull University; Mr T. Southgate, Ormerod School for the Physically Handicapped, Oxford; Mr Ian Staples, Educational Development Centre, Walsall; Mr S. Syme, District General Hospital, Barnsley; Dr W. Tagg, Hatfield Polytechnic; Dr L. Thomas, Northeast Wales Institute of Higher Education, Flint; Mr J. Tillisch, Sensory Information Systems, London; Dr A. Tollyfield, King's College, University of London; Mr B. Turner, Kirkby Springfield School; Dr R. Ward, Dept. of Psychology, Hull University; Mr J.M. Watson, Castlecroft Primary School, Wolverhampton; Mr P. Watts, Medical Engineering Unit, UMIST., Manchester; Ms D. Williams, Dept. of Trade and Industry, London, and Mr M. Wright, Rotherham.

We would like to thank the following people in the United States: Dr M. R. Barker, Children's Hospital, Stanford, CA; Mr R. F. Bergamini, Pinehaven School, Concord, CA; Dr M. A. Berthiaume, Jackson County Intermediate School, MI; Dr D. Beukelman, Dept. of Speech Pathology, University of Washington, Seattle, WA; Dr V. Casella, Dept. of Special Education, San Francisco State University, CA; Ms C. Cohen, Schneier Communication Unit, Cerebral Palsy Center, Syracuse, NY; Ms S. Dashiell, Huntington Beach, CA; Director and Staff, John Tracy Clinic, Los

Angeles; Dr J. Eulenberg, Artificial Language Laboratory, Michigan State University, East Lansing, MI; Dr R. A. Foulds, Tufts-New England Medical Center, Boston, MA; Ms R. Gertzulin, Santa Cruz County Office of Education, Capitola, CA; Dr D. Gilden, Smith-Kettlewell Institute of Visual Sciences, San Francisco, CA; Dr C. Goodenough-Trepagnier, Tufts-New England Medical Center, Boston, MA; Dr G. Goodrich, Veteran's Administration Medical Center, Palo Alto, CA; Ms R. Griese, De Anza College, Cupertino, CA; Dr L. Grimm, The Learning Company, Menlo Park, CA; Mrs M. Irwin, California School for the Deaf, Fremont, CA; Dr D. Jaffe, Veteran's Administration Medical Center, Palo Alto, CA; Mrs L. Jenkins, California School for the Blind, Fremont, CA; Ms M. Jost and Mr R. Brawley, California School for the Deaf, Riverside, CA; Dr L. Leifer, Rehabilitation Research and Development Center, Palo Alto, CA; Mr S. Longacre, Los Angeles County Schools, CA; Dr L. Meyers, Speech and Communication Research Laboratory, University of Southern California, Los Angeles, CA; Mr L. Mohr, Cotting School for Handicapped Children, Boston, MA; Mr J. Moore, Chandler-Tripp School, San Jose, CA; Mr R. Murray, Fairport, NY; Mrs P. Neu, Theuerkauf School, Mountain View, CA; Dr L. Palmer, California State University, Northridge, CA; Dr A. Piestrup, The Learning Company, Menlo Park, CA; Principal and Staff, particularly Mr E. Savannick, Gallaudet College, Kendall Green, Washington DC; Principal and Staff, Model Secondary School for the Deaf, Washington DC; Principal and Staff, Kendall Demonstration Elementary School, Washington DC; Dr T. Redburn, Artificial Language Laboratory, Michigan State University, East Lansing, MI; Dr B. Russell, County Office of Education, San Mateo, CA; Dr H. Shane, Children's Hospital Medical Center, Boston, MA; Mrs K. Spychala, Glanker School, Fremont, CA; Dr C. Stauffer, Apple Computer, Cupertino, CA; Dr R. E. Stepp, Regional Center for Hearing Impaired, University of Nebraska, Lincoln, NE; Mr and Mrs D. Steward, Monte Vista High School, Cupertino, CA; Dr E. R. Stuckless, National Technical Institute for the Deaf, Rochester, NY; Mr G. Turner, Wayne County Intermediate School District, MI; Ms J. Teekell, Pinehaven School, Concord, CA; Dr D. Uslan, California State Dept. of Education, Sacramento, CA; Dr G. C. Vanderheiden, Trace Research and Development Center for the Severely Communicatively Handicapped, University of Wisconsin, Madison, WI; Mr E. Vitu, Telesensory Systems Inc., Mountain View, CA; Dr S. Weir, Artificial Intelligence Laboratory, Massachusetts Institute of Technology, Cambridge, MA; and Dr Frank Withrow, US Department of Education, Washington DC.

We acknowledge with thanks financial support from the Nuffield Foundation and the Open University. We are particularly grateful to our consultants: David McConnell visited or telephoned many centres in the United Kingdom on our behalf, and in the United States Oscar and Sarah Roberts did the same. Together with the visits and calls we made ourselves, their efforts enabled us to achieve reasonably good coverage in both countries.

Lastly, we recognise that some of our chapters will stand the test of time better than others; a new edition will probably be needed in three or four years from now. If by any chance we do not write it, we hope somebody else will inform disabled people and those who help them about the latest developments in this exciting field.

David Hawkridge
Tom Vincent
Gerald Hales
Institute of Educational Technology
The Open University, Milton Keynes

PART ONE
Learning Problems of Disabled People

1 COMMUNICATION, LEARNING AND DISABLED PEOPLE

The Basic Issues

For many disabled people, communication problems are at the heart of their disablement and central to their personal struggle to learn to overcome their disabilities. This is true whether they are young or old, whether they are male or female, whether they are disabled from birth or became disabled later in life. They are often left isolated, powerless and dependent. They are deprived of important ways of expressing their individuality.

For humans generally, being able to communicate means being able to send, transform and receive information. Sending, transforming and receiving information depend on a wide range of human abilities. 'Disablement' frequently implies loss or lack of some of these functional abilities, and the degree of disablement is often related to how many remain. 'Handicap' is sometimes used as a synonym for 'disability' in the literature, but elsewhere and in this book it is used to refer to the disadvantage actually caused by the disability.

Of disabled people, those who are speech-impaired, blind, deaf or who have certain motor disabilities also have particular difficulties in sending information. Those whose speech is impaired cannot articulate the words and sounds they wish to. This is distressing whether it is congenital, due perhaps to cerebral palsy, or when it occurs later in life through a stroke or multiple sclerosis. Blind people are hampered in sending written information. Deaf people may have difficulties in enunciating words, especially if they are congenitally deaf. Those who cannot move their upper limbs properly may struggle to write, type or even to use a simple word board. Blind and deaf people also have immense difficulties in receiving information, of course, because they cannot see or cannot hear. Unfortunately, blind people may misunderstand despite their often acute hearing, and deaf ones despite their lip-reading.

Difficulties in sending and receiving may also hinder transforming of information, that is, the process by which information is changed into different symbols, codes, languages and modes (see

3

Chapter 7). This transforming process underlies communication between humans, and between humans and their machines.

Education of disabled children and adults depends on communication. Without communication, others cannot pass on their knowledge and skills to disabled people through the two-way processes of teaching and learning, in classrooms, workshops or at home.

Types of Communication Disability

Who are the people with communication disabilities and how many are there in a country like the United Kingdom? Nobody can answer these questions precisely because different categories of disability overlap and the statistics differ according to the categories used. One classification (see the *Royal Society of Health Journal*, February 1975) uses nine categories to cover the full range of disability (in this document termed handicap), with a total of 41 components or sub-categories. Of the main categories, one is actually labelled 'communication handicap' and its four sub-categories are impaired hearing, talking, reading and writing. Visual handicap is shown separately, and incorporates sub-categories of total loss of sight, impaired (uncorrectable) visual acuity, impaired visual field and perceptual defect. A third main category, locomotor handicap, includes one sub-category, impaired manual dexterity, that has vast implications for communication. Other main categories such as visceral handicap (for example, disorders of excretion), invisible handicap (for example, metabolic disorders) and senescence handicap (for example, reduced recuperative powers) are somewhat remote from problems of communication. This book does not deal with them, nor with intellectual handicap (ranging from congenital mental retardation to impaired memory), emotional handicap (for example, psychoses and drug disorders) and aversive handicap (tics, skin disorders, etc.), although these last three may indeed have some indirect impact on communication.

Some American authors (for example, Vanderheiden and Krause, 1983) try to distinguish between those who are non-vocal (speech not fully functional) and those who are speech-impaired (speech functional but impaired), and similarly between the blind and visually-impaired and between the deaf and hearing-impaired.

Clearly, as in the case of physical disability, the degree and nature of impairment is what matters rather than precise labelling.

Perhaps not surprisingly, the exact numbers of disabled people are difficult to determine and there may well be some double counting. For example, from a 1968-9 survey, Harris and others (1971) estimated that there were about three million *handicapped* people aged 16 and over living in private households in the United Kingdom and suffering from some physical, mental or sensory impairment, but their categories included only those who considered that their impairment actually handicapped them in their work, in getting about or in taking care of themselves. Counting numbers of people with particular disabilities is made more difficult by lack of agreement among authorities on what constitutes 'official' disability. For instance, if there are about 100,000 registered blind people in England and Wales, this means that each of these has failed a particular sight test. There may be other blind people, unregistered, who have never taken the test, or if the test were slightly different, the number registered would be higher or lower. Distinguishing blind from partially sighted people may be important in certain contexts, but the problems in doing so are so well known as to inspire little confidence in the statistics. Few people are completely blind, and those who cannot perceive forms can usually sense light. People with the same measured visual acuity may be able to do quite different things. Low (1983) quotes a 1981 figure of only about 3000 blind or partially-sighted children attending schools in England and Wales. The numbers of people of all ages with disabilities of the kinds discussed here, however, probably amount to roughly one million or about 2 per cent of the United Kingdom population, with a similar percentage in other Western countries, including the United States. In other words, in the United Kingdom up to a million disabled children and adults may be able to use information technology to improve their education, should they so wish.

In the United States, recent estimates suggest there are nearly two million speech-impaired people (Gibbons, 1982), of whom about 60,000 are non-vocal cerebral palsied children (Meyers, 1982). Again, two million people are blind or visually-impaired (Jampolsky and others, 1982); about 120,000 can make virtually no use of visual information. About four million handicapped children are at school: many of these do not have communication disabilities (US Department of Education, 1982).

Examples of Communication Disabilities

The harsh realities of being disabled are disguised in statistics but not in personal case histories, of which there are many in this book. George became progressively deaf after an illness at about 14. He managed to complete his schooling at a local grammar school, then, in the 1920s, using a hearing aid with a large battery which he carried around in a special case, with great difficulty he trained as an accountant. Despite increasing deafness, he held down a Civil Service job until retirement, by which time he had been profoundly deaf for a decade. At work or at home, he could never use the telephone; everyone had to communicate with him either in writing or by depending on his lip-reading. His speech deteriorated with age, although it never became completely unintelligible. For his colleagues, explaining new procedures to him was particularly trying. He died after a long decline during which he became increasingly withdrawn and socially isolated.

A few years ago, Tony was a young officer in the Army. By accident, he was blown up and blinded at 24 by a land-mine while on manoeuvres. He came out of hospital and started studying braille, which he found far from easy. He persisted, however, and two years later registered for an Open University degree, having to depend on braille or tape-recorded versions of the texts and on his girlfriend reading aloud to him. He attended the residential summer schools, where he needed much assistance, particularly with laboratory and field work. He took his examinations through dictating to somebody who wrote down what he said.

Rachel received serious head injuries in a car accident when she was ten, write Hall and Turner (1983). She is now spastic, a quadriplegic with very badly impaired mobility and no speech. Her left hand is reasonably effective, but not the right. The family expected that her speech might be restored and apparently did not encourage her to learn to communicate through symbols and signs. At any rate, her interest in doing so was low. Before the accident, however, she had acquired basic literacy skills, and after it was very frustrated by having to resort to very crude communication techniques, such as 'air writing' and gestures. Chapter 9 describes how Rachel overcame these communication problems to a remarkable extent with the help of new information technology.

In each of these cases, and in hundreds of thousands of others, communication was difficult or nigh impossible between the disabled person and those around him or her. Learning depends on good communication, therefore disabled people with communication problems are at a double disadvantage, when learning first to overcome their disability by substituting other abilities and then to learn what other people learn, whether in the formal education system or informally.

To compensate for congenital communication disabilities, children need help most urgently before and during primary school, but both they, and adults who are disabled through illness, accident or old age, need some help for the rest of their lives. Can technology provide it?

The Challenge to New Information Technology

People who have never been disabled look to new information technology to improve communication and to solve all kinds of communication problems. They are not being disappointed, as a spate of devices and systems comes out of laboratories and onto the market, backed by powerful political and economic forces.

The challenge to new information technology from people who are disabled is similar: can it improve communication and solve communication problems for *them*? Can the same devices and systems, or perhaps others developed specially for disabled people, meet their needs? The answer is beginning to emerge, and it has particular implications for the education of disabled children and adults.

Consider, for example, the case of Michael Rogers (reported by Mahon, 1983). When he was 23, Michael was self-employed and a sportsman. He contracted a viral infection which left him paralysed from the shoulders down, a tetraplegic. He is able to use a variety of mouth-sticks, but in recent years has been experiencing excessive wear of his neck joints due to this activity. With the sticks he operates a microcomputer with a printer. To cope with the need to press two keys simultaneously for some operations on the computer, he has three extra switches to hold down the shift, control and repeat keys when he wants to. He has complete control of the computer and even changes discs (see Chapter 9) with his mouthsticks. He uses a tape dictating machine and an electric typewriter, which he operates with mouth-sticks. With his word processing program, he has written one book about paraplegia and is completing another, as well as using the program in his domestic life to communicate with those around him. He suffers less physical strain because some of the effort is taken out of his typing and, like many able-bodied people who start word processing, he finds his writing has improved because of the ease of re-formatting and correcting text.

A different example is quoted by Duncan (1983). This man, whom we shall call Mr F, is middle aged. He had a stroke several years ago, which paralysed his right side and arm and severely impaired his speech. He could use a typewriter before his stroke, but now can only type with his left hand. Mr F now has a small typewriter-like device which he carries in a satchel on a strap over his shoulder. Its keyboard is like a typewriter's but with extra keys, about 50 in all. The device incorporates software (programs) that allow Mr F to use a kind of shorthand. By typing in various two-letter codes, devised by himself, he can made the device speak names of family, friends, items of food and drink ('GT' for 'Gin and tonic, please!'), everyday activities ('DT' for 'Shall I take the dog out or will you?'), in fact, anything he wishes to code in this way. Mr F is so keen to express himself that at first he used to hit two keys simultaneously, the spoken result being gibberish. This problem was solved by fitting a keyguard. He is happy taking his device with him to the corner shop and will show it off. He does not mind its peculiar computerised voice as long as people under-stand it (after repetition if necessary). He wants to communicate and the device helps him to do so. Mr F has retrained himself to use his device in everyday life.

These two examples show that using new information tech-nology to improve communication for disabled people is already possible. In neither is education the prime purpose of the par-ticular innovation, yet clearly in each case it can be immensely use-ful in enabling disabled users to gain access to education.

Summary

In this first chapter, we looked briefly at the basic issues con-cerning communication, learning and disabled people. We reviewed types of communication disabilities and their extent in the population, illustrated by several case histories. From disabled people, the essential challenge to information technology is, 'Help us with our communication problems'. This challenge is already being answered in significant ways, as a few examples show, with important implications for the education of disabled children and adults.

2 LEARNING PROBLEMS OF PHYSICALLY-DISABLED PEOPLE

Causes of Physical Disability

Physical disability can arise from early disorders, possibly congenital, of the nervous, skeletal and muscular systems, such as cerebral palsy or spina bifida. Since students with this kind of disorder are likely to have been at a disadvantage since birth, their problems are often less tractable than those who become physically-disabled later in life.

Many people become physically-disabled by damage to the nervous, skeletal and muscular systems due to accidents, for example, involving brain and spinal injury. Others contract diseases, for example, tuberculosis of the spine, motor neurone disease, multiple sclerosis, myasthenia gravis, brittle bone disease. Still others, not all old, have disorders such as Parkinsonism, muscular atrophy, progressive muscular dystrophy and cerebral vascular accidents (strokes).

Physical disability is no respecter of age or person. The type and degree of handicap experienced varies from individual to individual.

Types and Degrees of Physical Disability

The basic definition of physical disability is inability to move normally or to exercise proper control over movement. Physically-disabled individuals are those with decreased range and strength of movement, or who have unwanted and uncontrolled movements. For instance, a child with cerebral palsy (paralysis and associated disorders of motor function arising from damage to the brain during birth or soon afterwards) may be unable to hold her hand still enough to write clearly. An adult with muscular dystrophy (disorders of muscle function and structure that lead to increasing weakness and degeneration of the muscles) may become quickly exhausted by writing, which demands great effort. A student with

Friedreich's ataxia, a hereditary progressive disease of the nervous system that causes increasing inco-ordination of movement, may find it impossible even to press the keys of a calculator.

The boundary between physical and mental handicap is blurred. Many mentally-handicapped people are also physically-disabled and because they have great problems in conceptualising are usually beyond the reach of formal education. On the other hand, many physically-disabled children and adults do not lack intelligence or any of the senses. With help, many can participate in education.

Most of all, physically-disabled students need help to communicate. Many cannot write or type. Some can only do so slowly, very poorly or for short periods at a time. Their writing may be almost illegible, even when it has cost them much exhausting effort. Not all students are as badly off as Scott, who learned after four years of therapy to open his hands and can now use a modified keyboard. For a few, poor hand-eye co-ordination is due to visual handicap as well as lack of fine muscle control (athetosis, or uncoordinated involuntary movements associated with brain damage). Some cannot reach very far. Others have impaired speech or even none at all. Physically-disabled people with good speech are at a disadvantage, but those without good speech are doubly so.

As anyone knows who has dealings with disabled children or adults, their needs vary greatly, from person to person and in the same person over time, depending on both the nature of the disability and the stage of intellectual development. This is particularly true for those who are physically-disabled. As Carter (1983) reminds us, each student may have different needs. A single switch (see Chapter 9) that has to be pressed fairly hard for 'on' is unsuitable for a young child with weak muscles or poor control. Each individual has to be assessed and, ideally, provided with appropriate hardware and software.

Fitting Information Technology to the Disability

It is important to adapt technology to meet the needs of particular forms of disability, and fortunately computer technology does not require great physical strength to operate it or even very much mobility (Pollan, 1982). One British device in particular, the

Microwriter, has been adapted to many forms of physical disability.

Students with muscular dystrophy may find they can only use one hand, although the good hand may function quite well. For them, keypads may be better than single switches or full keyboards. If both hands are weak, or arm movement is limited, then the hands can be placed one on each side of the keypad, to spread the effort of keying in. The Microwriter has been adapted to provide right- and left-handed keypads (see Chapter 9).

Cerebral palsy may be accompanied by a rhythmic tremor. Students with this tremor may need slightly stiffer keys. They may also have difficulty in hitting a single switch at the right time to select an item from an array scanned by a light or cursor (see Chapter 9), but on some machines, including the Microwriter, students can vary the scanning speed to suit their own rhythm or speed of movement.

Physically-disabled students who are also blind or partially-sighted can be helped to use an array scanned by a cursor if there is an audible signal as well. In the case of the Microwriter, they hear a rising tone.

Cerebral palsied and other physically-disabled students with poor control over their movements may need a keyboard or keypad which allows them to 'set up' their input, probably through using a stick to press a sequence of keys, and then enter it into the device or computer. They can thus be sure they have it right before actually entering the 'code' (see Chapter 7). Again, the Microwriter has been adapted in this way.

Some students have rather small hands, often through thalidomide or brittle-bone disease; for them, standard keypads and keyboards may present difficulties. One student with brittle-bone disease has problems reaching keys, but she can use a modified Microwriter keypad in the form of a strip of keys.

Students who cannot easily move need a display, on a screen or in some other form, the angle of which can be adjusted so that they can see it well and avoid awkward reflections. Some may also need a separate keyboard rather than one integrated with other parts of a system. Thus one lecturer with tuberculosis of the spine has a Microwriter keypad at his side and a separate display overhead where he can see it while lying on his side.

A severe haemophiliac cannot write or use a standard keyboard because the pressure causes bleeding, but he can use the keypad of a Microwriter, which requires only light pressure.

One severely physically-disabled university student used her nose to operate a Microwriter keypad and took lecture notes in this way while seated in her wheelchair. She now has a job.

For many physically-disabled students it is important that any technology they use for learning should be portable: it should be light, small and robust, as in the case of the Microwriter.

A few disabled students have poor spatial perception, which causes them to write badly and they find it difficult to control their movements on a typewriter keyboard. They can often cope quite well using a Microwriter or similar keypad on which one hand rests all the time.

Thus the Microwriter is very adaptable and copes with students' interface difficulties as well as providing word processing and access to computing on a microcomputer. It is, of course, also possible to use one microcomputer in place of the Microwriter and another run by the first as a conventional computer with, say, word processing. We shall have more to say about this later.

Some Specific Learning Problems Caused by Physical Disability

At the most basic level, many physically-disabled students cannot write or can only do so very slowly and clumsily. Their rate of response is often so slow that remedial drill and practice becomes very time-consuming for them and for staff who help them. The cost in staff time is high, as Vanderheiden (1982b) points out. Such students fall further and further behind other students. For instance, as Foulds (1982) suggests, they get less spelling practice and cannot use a 'scratch pad' or 'rough notebook' in mathematics. Nor can they take notes in lectures or on a field trip. For these students, using a single switch, keypad or keyboard (see Chapter 9) to operate new information technology is a great advance, making it possible for the younger ones to do normal school work, although still not at the pace of able-bodied children, and for older ones to study too. The technology amplifies abilities of disabled individuals.

Some physically-disabled students cannot manipulate objects or draw. Vanderheiden (1982b) notes how difficult chemistry, physics and other experimental sciences become for them, and that studying mathematics may require them to draw geometrical figures. Computers enable these students to 'handle' experimental equipment on the screen and thus to carry out, through simulation, studies they could not otherwise undertake. Drawing on the screen becomes possible for them, too, and they can manipulate their drawings electronically in exactly the same way as an able-bodied student can on the computer.

Papert and Weir (1978) suggest that 'the computer can become an extension of the operator who can then do anything a computer can do, such as draw, compose music, gain access to information libraries, put text on permanent file and so on'. They state that 'in particular the computer enables someone who has never manipulated concrete objects to manipulate abstract objects drawn electronically on a TV screen in a simulated but physically and geometrically veridicial world'.

Papert and Weir have explored, among other things, how students with almost no capacity for the overt manipulation of objects in physical space develop spatial thinking. How does the notion of 'cube' in the head of someone who has never touched one differ from the notion of 'cube' in the head of someone with full motor abilities? With one cerebral palsied youth, they found that his rate of learning of Logo turtle geometry (see Chapter 9) showed no impairment that could be attributed to weakness of spatial representation. Similarly, they ask how linguistic structures develop in individuals who have acquired comprehension competence with almost no experience in production of structured speech. They point out that severely physically-disabled individuals cannot engage in motor activity that will provide explicit confrontation between actions performed and the consequences of such action in the physical world. Logo provides opportunities for such confrontation to occur.

Papert and Weir also state that 'the critical education problem for physically-handicapped persons is the restriction in their expressive power, so that such mental activity as does go on is trapped within the individual's own head'. Information technology can overcome this problem. In using Logo, Papert and Weir's subjects show that by communicating with and through a computer they can undertake much more complex tasks than would otherwise be feasible for them.

Summary

The causes of physical handicap are disorders of and damage to the nervous, skeletal and muscular systems. They occur at birth and later in life, and in varying degrees. Physically-disabled students cannot move normally or exercise proper control over their movements. Most of all, to learn they need help in communicating. New information technology can provide this help, if it is fitted to the user. It can also help them to overcome specific learning problems caused by their disabilities, such as developing spatial thinking.

3 LEARNING PROBLEMS OF BLIND AND PARTIALLY-SIGHTED PEOPLE

Nature and Implications of Visual Handicap

Blindness is a severe handicap. Loss of this dominant sense requires use of the other four senses, which gives a less integrated impression than sight. Enhancement of the tactile and auditory senses, however, combined with considerable ingenuity, often leads to attainments that most sighted people would not predict. Efforts made by both teachers and students to overcome what at first may appear to be an insurmountable barrier are highlighted in an article (Flather, 1983) about the Royal National College for the Blind, where blind and partially-sighted students play cricket and practise archery. For cricket the ball is filled with ball-bearings so that the visually-handicapped cricketers can listen for the ball. Such experiences are related by Raffle (1970) who enjoyed these games at school and, later, actively encouraged students to participate.

The term 'visually-handicapped' covers the two medical categories of 'blind' and 'partially-sighted'. Although it is a term too wide for precise definition, the apparent visual efficiency shown in a classroom does not always relate discretely to the two medical categories.

Much learning is dependent on vision. In the lecture theatre or the classroom, teachers generally assume that a student can see clearly in the near environment and at a distance, maintaining binocular vision for reading, drawing or experiments, and then switching to the blackboard or a screen for various visual presentations. Clearly, this assumption has many implications for visually-handicapped people being taught by conventional teaching methods.

Partially-sighted children go through a difficult process of discovery, diagnosis and assessment to determine whether they need special education either in a special school or in a mainstream school with additional support services. This process is examined in detail by Chapman (1978) in an account primarily intended for

16

those who teach or who are training to teach visually-handicapped children.

Visual impairment may become evident through developmental screening provided by health services on a regular basis from infancy through to later school years. This screening may include determination of a child's level of functioning in sensory, physical, intellectual and communication areas. Then the effects of these have to be carefully assessed and related to the nature of any special education.

Chapman (1978) discusses the implications of visual handicap in school learning. They are numerous and include: presentation of learning material, discovery by touch including tactile drawings and diagrams, learning to listen, reading and writing in braille, reading speeds and comprehension, teaching mathematics and number concepts, recording of work, mobility orientation and movement training and personal independence. Harley and Lawrence (1977) present guidelines for regular classroom teachers with visually-handicapped children among their students. They concentrate on the education of low vision children, vision screening, the visual environment, optical aids and visual perception.

Developing communication skills is of prime importance for visually-handicapped people, and has become even more essential as technological advances have resulted in rapid and inexpensive methods of reproducing text. This applies to almost all areas of the curriculum but there is the need also to consider special subject adjustments and the acquisition of alternative skills. This latter aspect is considered by Napier (1974). In general terms, he indicates how educational material may be classified as (a) usable in original form, (b) requiring some modification or adaptation, (c) designed specifically for the visually-handicapped, and (d) substitute experiences. He gives examples in a wide range of subjects.

Teaching science and mathematics to the blind was the subject of a study at Worcester College for the Blind in 1965. An updated report (1973) gives many examples of practical methods that have been used to overcome problems in these subject areas. An example is drawn from the contribution to the study by Tapton Mount School concerning the introduction of the Cubarithm method for the recording of mathematics in braille. Although the Perkins Brailler could be used for recording in a linear form, this was not considered the most suitable for mathematics. The Cubarithm method is based on a small cube with raised dots on five surfaces and a raised line on the sixth. Selected orientations of the faces enables numbers and arithmetic signs to be represented. The cubes can then be placed on a frame to record a mathematical expression. For example:

Figure 3.1: The Cubarithm Method

$$\frac{1}{2}+\frac{3}{4}=1\frac{1}{4} \ :$$

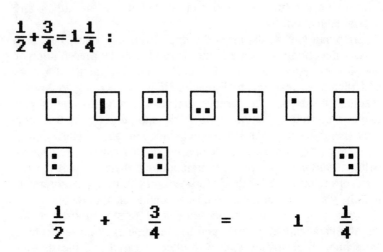

$$\frac{1}{2} \quad + \quad \frac{3}{4} \quad = \quad 1 \quad \frac{1}{4}$$

Once children had learnt to manipulate the cubes, the speed of operation became as fast as previous methods. The system has the important advantage that the same braille symbol is used to denote a number as with braille notation.

The laboratory presents other problems. In Hadary's introduction to *Seeing Through the Dark* (Weiss, 1976), she invites the reader to enter her science laboratories where sighted students are working side by side with blind students. The example of two students 'observing' a physics experiment indicates how other ways of seeing are used: in this case the raising of paper-clips by a magnet were 'observed' by touch. Alternative ways of seeing is the theme of the book, which tells how children in the science laboratory learn to 'hear' changes in the colour of light as changes in the pitch of a sound with the aid of a photoelectric device attached to a buzzer. One application described is the detection of how iodine changes a colourless solution of starch to a dark blue colour. Further examples relate to how the other senses can provide information that would usually be acquired visually.

Problems of visually-handicapped students in higher and further education in the UK are outlined by Butler (1978) in a survey based on data collected over a period of nine years. The survey covers 485 students and provides information on admission, the student environment and work methods. The statistics show that on average, seven visually-handicapped students attended each university during 1969-78. This small number highlights the relative isolation of any student, and the need to be able to study independently in a university department that only infrequently has a visually-handicapped student on a course. The survey concludes with a review of employment.

Communication Skills

In educational terms, the most difficult problems for blind and partially-sighted students are associated with reading and writing. They cannot depend on speech and hearing for all educational activities, and there have been numerous developments to overcome communication problems caused by loss of sight.

Reading

Students must have access to printed material. In addition to the printed word, diagrams, pictures and models are used in many subjects to convey information in a concise and often interesting form. For example, a simple graph can replace a paragraph or more of words. A blind person is denied immediate access to printed material, and must use the tactile and auditory senses.

Tactile sense

Blind people depend a great deal on braille to convey information. Braille is a sequence of cells (each cell is a 3 x 2 matrix of raised dots) which can represent words, numbers and punctuation. Individual cells can represent the letters of the alphabet and simple words: with punctuation signs added, this is known as grade 1 braille.

Grade 2 braille is similar to shorthand. Grade 1 symbols together with contraction signs (other cell arrangements) represent whole or part words. Complete words can be abbreviated to single or reduced numbers of grade 1 symbols (for example, 'k' for 'knowledge' and 'abv' for 'above'). One of the advantages of grade

Figure 3.2: The Alphabet in Grade 1 Braille

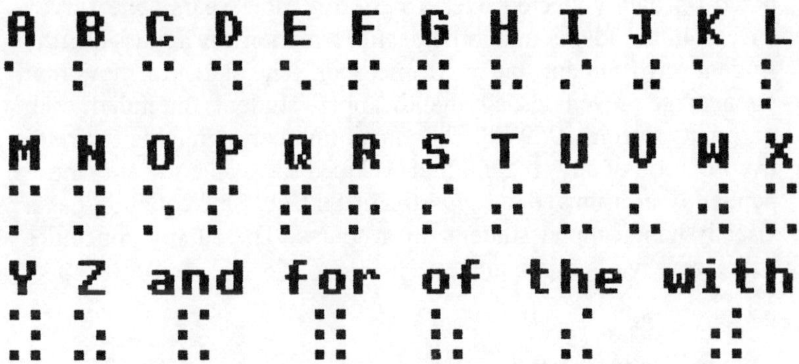

2 braille is that the physical space required for the sequences of raised dot cells is reduced. For example, the word 'comforting' can be represented by four cells rather than ten if each individual character required a cell:

COMFORTING = (COM) (FOR) (T) (ING) = ⠉⠕ ⠿ ⠞ ⠬

The meaning of each cell is enclosed in brackets.

The use of grade 2 braille is very important in relation to reducing both the amount of embossed material required, and the time involved in converting text to braille. Traditionally, it has needed skilled braille transcribers to convert text to braille. Even with the contracted form of braille, this is very time-consuming and it is one of the reasons for the limited number of texts that are available.

The sheer bulk of books produced in braille is also a limiting factor: in many cases the volume can be increased by a factor of 15 to 20 compared to printed text. In the classroom, this has resulted in text books being used as occasional reference sources, and a greater dependence on class dictation with pupils producing their own notes in braille.

The teaching of braille reading is reviewed by Harley and others (1979). They include a section on 'reading readiness', and demonstrate the importance for blind children of the need for tactile readiness materials just as seeing children need visual readiness materials. The tactile discrimination of a braille cell requires a special preliminary readiness programme. Several approaches to reading instruction are compared but no single method is identified as superior. An important conclusion from this survey of research is that the teacher can help greatly by being constantly diagnostic and prescriptive.

Diagrams are an invaluable aid in many subject areas. Methods have been developed to produce special embossed diagrams for the blind. Not only are these diagrams used to supplement text, they also have an important role in compensating for the lack of a blackboard or other visual aids. A common technique is to create a master copy of a diagram with solid items such as metal strip or wire, mounted on a flat surface. Plastic sheets can then be vacuum thermo-formed on to the master copy; a process which can be repeated many times to produce multiple copies of the original. A great deal of attention has to be given to the format and structure of the diagrams, however, as they will be 'seen' through touch. 'Drawing' them requires special techniques, different from those used in visual diagrams, and the pupil must be given additional training in interpretation. Despite these difficulties, tactile diagrams are successfully used in teaching many subjects including geography and electrical circuitry.

Auditory Sense

A very important development in recent years has been the 'talking book' with text being transcribed on to audio cassettes which are played back through conventional or adapted (variable speed) cassette players. Learning to study by audible techniques requires new skills. It may initially appear as an attractive alternative to reading braille, as only listening is required, but study by cassette needs to be active rather than passive. Combining listening with note-taking is one way of increasing concentration in a medium that lacks visual or tactile stimuli.

Access to recorded information should be carefully organised. Although the audio cassette has the advantage of containing a large amount of text in a small volume, it has the disadvantage of being in a linear format. Indexing techniques are necessary to overcome the disadvantage of not being able to access randomly the information as a sighted person would when reading a book. To facilitate this, cassette players have been enhanced to improve access by tone indexing and variable speed.

The 'reader' who first produces a cassette recording needs considerable skill. Accurate reproduction of the text, transmission of the author's message, and quality of the sound recording are all important in producing satisfactory material. For these reasons, it is unlikely that an academic subject can be satisfactorily transcribed by someone who is unfamiliar with the field. Illustrations and diagrams cannot be 'read'; they must be interpreted for the listener. Style and pace are important, as is the inclusion of non-linear features such as footnotes and references. Once the final version is recorded, making copies and distributing them are relatively easy.

Using Residual Vision

Most visually-handicapped people have some residual vision, and this applies to many of those who are registered blind. In this context, two groups are often distinguished: (a) those who have poor central vision but who have a full peripheral field, and (b) those who have good central vision but have a restricted peripheral field (tunnel vision). Students with poor central vision, have difficulty in distinguishing fine detail such as the individual letters of printed materials. Those with tunnel vision have little difficulty with individual letters but have problems maintaining a place on a line, and find it even harder to move from one line to another.

With poor central vision, some form of magnification is often appropriate. There are two groups of aids which can be hand-held or spectacle mounted: microscope aids (basically magnifying lenses), and telescopic aids. The former have a relatively short working distance but a wide field of view; the latter have the inverse of these features. Therefore, microscope aids with their short working distance and wide field of view might be acceptable for reading.

For those with a restricted field of view, magnification does not help with reading. Indeed, it can make the situation worse. As the major problem with tunnel vision is orientation within text, aids which assist in maintaining or changing position are often used.

Writing

In an educational environment there are two activities where there is a fundamental need to produce written material: note-taking and essay writing. Clearly the use of a pen and paper by a blind person is very difficult, and other methods have emerged to suit individual needs.

Braille is widely used in this context and has a complementary relationship to reading. Numerous devices have been developed to aid braille writing, from simple hand-held aids to more substantial desk top equipment. One of the simplest is a braille slate and stylus, which can be carried around for note-taking and does not produce any disturbing noise. The slate has a matrix of 37 cells in 4 rows cut-out in a metal guide which can be moved vertically on the slate. Each cell is shaped to guide the stylus when the dots are punched through the paper from the reverse side. This requires working from right to left in order that the embossed braille can subsequently be read from left to right with the standard dot configuration. An easier, but noisier, method is with the Perkins Brailler. This device is popular in schools, and has changed little since its introduction in the 1940s. It has six main keys for the braille dots plus paper feed, space, and back-space keys. It embosses the dots upwards as the keys are pressed (one cell at a time) which has the advantage that the braille can be read as soon as it is produced; a helpful feature which makes it easier to correct mistakes.

One of the problems experienced by teachers in the early stages of teaching use of a Perkins Brailler is that they must check what has been brailled by the students until tactile reading skills are developed. A teacher needs to give individual attention to each student for a substantial period, and this may not always be possible in a class.

Preparing essays or similar written material throws up another common problem that is often experienced: the need to communicate with a sighted person. In many cases, an essay in braille may be the appropriate medium for the student but a totally inappropriate one if the essay has to be read by a sighted person with no knowledge of braille. In public examinations it may be necessary to provide intermediaries who can transcribe a brailled examination paper into handwriting or typescript for the examiners. Typically, a three hour examination paper may take up to seven hours to transcribe in this way. Blind students studying at a distance with the Open University must send essays to a tutor who cannot read braille. Some students type essays a second time on a conventional typewriter as well as a brailler. This places considerable demands on students' keyboard skills, and they lack a facility to check the final text that they send for assessment.

Summary

As indicated earlier, loss of sight is a severe handicap. In education, it affects the majority of activities associated with learning both in or out of the classroom or lecture theatre. Numerous compensatory methods have been developed which draw on the enhanced use of auditory and tactile skills to ensure that the widest possible curriculum is available, but many learning problems still remain.

Braille is established as an important communication medium for blind people, but there are problems in producing it to meet all of the demands for study material. This is true also of tactile diagrams which are very necessary in mathematical and science subjects.

Communication problems are highlighted in integrated schools, and in further and higher education where students have to produce essays and scripts for teachers who may have little knowledge of braille. Public examinations can present a similar problem.

Developments in information technology are likely to have very important implications for visually-handicapped people. First, there will be the opportunity to examine how they might be used to overcome some of the difficulties that have been identified earlier with printed material, braille preparation, essay writing and note-taking. Second, as the widespread use of computers in schools is likely to change teaching methods, and to introduce new teaching material, visually-handicapped students could be placed at an even further disadvantage. At a time when the design of systems is dominated by visual output, access to computers by blind people raises the question: how? These and other factors will be considered in subsequent chapters.

4 LEARNING PROBLEMS OF DEAF PEOPLE

Types and Implications of Deafness

The term 'deafness' covers several dimensions of a serious communication handicap which impairs many aspects of an individual's life. Education is not least among these.

A deaf person suffers from not being able to hear, which is both a considerable inconvenience in social and interactive relationships, and an obstacle in participating in any system of which communication is a major part. There are far more serious consequences, however, of a hearing handicap, whether this be complete loss of hearing ability, a partial loss, or reduction in efficiency. These consequences arise from the social and communicative isolation experienced by the people concerned: they are unable to take part (or in some cases, take part fully) in many human situations that would otherwise have been natural for them. This is particularly true in the context of education, where not only may the individual have to cope with general problems arising from not being able to hear or participate fully, but, if the handicap existed from an early age (or birth), there will also be problems of becoming educated while a significant channel of communication is closed. In combination, these problems may be very serious.

Thus the learning problems of deaf people amount to far more than simply whether or not their hearing 'works'. The whole structure of language perception and comprehension is involved, as well as the extent of socialisation, degree of success of socialisation, ability to interact with the social world and degree of efficiency of communication.

All deaf people are not, of course, identical in their deafness. One distinction is between those who are *profoundly deaf* (that is, have no usable hearing), and those who are *partially hearing* (that is, have some usable hearing, perhaps with the assistance of a hearing aid). The difference is largely one of mode of communication, particularly the extent to which the disabled individual relies on systems unfamiliar to able-bodied people. It may also be a difference in the type of hearing problem. People with conductive deafness may find a hearing aid of some benefit, while those with nerve deafness will not do so. The type of deafness affects the type of communication used for education and the extent to which normal speech and hearing can be used.

Another distinction is between those people who are *pre-lingually* and *post-lingually* deaf. This distinction is of vital importance in education. Pre-lingually deaf people lose their hearing before they acquire language, often being hearing-impaired from birth, and this affects profoundly their storage and use of language and language-related skills. This distinction is reflected in differences in the structure of sign languages and normal lexical language (see for example Deuchar, 1979).

Such differences make education of the hearing-impaired a problem of considerable complexity. Not surprisingly, some educational institutions are more successful in solving it than others. To date, almost all the resource and endeavour has been devoted to the education of deaf school-age children, with a very small proportion in the tertiary sector, but this situation is now changing.

Deaf children and adult people therefore come to education with previous experience which may be quite different from that of their hearing classmates. This will colour the way they approach their schooling and it affects the ways in which they should be taught. Hanner and others (1971) put forward the premise that every student brings a set of traits to every learning activity, and these are reflected in, and pervade, his or her general educational behaviour.

Language Differences

Problems of language differences between the hearing and the hearing-impaired form one of the few consistent and central findings surrounding research with deaf people. Furth (1964) points out that the term 'language' is frequently used in different senses. It can mean covert or 'inner' language, which is difficult to observe or define. The term is often used, however, to cover practically all the domain of cognitive or symbolic behaviour. Furth makes the point that language behaviour may coincide with symbolic behaviour, but it does not necessarily always do so.

It is very difficult to identify these differences in language between the deaf and the hearing. The original learning of language, in babyhood, is normally initiated by aural channels, and intake of information by this aural channel is, for people with good hearing, relatively effortless. Indeed, it is physiologically impossible to stop it, and hearing people have to use internalised techniques, not visible to observers, when they do not wish to attend to a sound.

For hearing-impaired people, quite the opposite situation pertains. During their normal 'at rest' state, they receive nothing, or perhaps attenuated, distorted and inadequate parallels of the auditory world. This makes taking in information, in particular, very difficult, and such activity is obviously a substantial part of becoming educated.

Conrad (1970) studied differences in thinking patterns between the deaf and the hearing. Using memory to represent thinking, he suggests that some deaf people rely on articulatory coding (that is, speaking the words to themselves), others rely on non-articulatory coding. The latter group performed poorly in tests when reading aloud, since reading aloud was incompatible with their coding procedure. Conrad (1971) further argues that it may be possible that some deaf children may be handicapped by a strong emphasis on speech training, and that problems may arise if their coding procedures are different from those of their teachers (and their teachers' expectations). Factors like this affect the quality of school experiences for hearing-impaired children, though teachers may not realise what is happening, and indeed may be powerless to modify their teaching if they do know.

It is common to find a large language retardation in deaf school-leavers, and this cannot be easily rectified. Conrad (1977b) wrote:

> At first sight, and possibly at last sight also, deaf children leave school with what appears to be appallingly poor reading comprehension ... But because this discrepancy is so great it is unlikely that even the most radical changes in teaching methods will eliminate it. More realistic goals may be needed, and these have never been defined in a pedagogically useful way.

Yet it is known that, even in children with no sensory defect, the effects of training can be substantial. Lowenthal and Kostrevski (1973) found improvement on verbal test performance and quality of written descriptions after training procedures, and Heber (1977) found that language training improved the performance of children on seriation tasks. The particularly crucial part of this latter work was the finding that progress was much more rapid among children with a greater descriptive command of language.

The effects of a language deficiency are rapidly cumulative. Since deaf children are less able to participate in all manner of educational activities, their experiences do not add sufficiently to their skills. Lack of skills then affects performance of the next task, and the accumulated deficiency may eventually be very great. In addition, each deaf individual is isolated from the considerable auditory background which forms a substantial part of usual everyday experience. This is not only important in matters pertaining to personal health, welfare and safety, but also means that deaf people's cumulative experience of the world is lacking in certain respects.

Oral Communication vs. Signs

Deaf people's problems arising from linguistic and cognitive deficiencies are further complicated by practical problems of communication, for there is little standardisation of methods of communication. The two main but differing traditions are represented by teachers who prefer oral communication and those who prefer manual systems. There has been much controversy, over many years, about the relative merits of each.

Exponents of manual signs suggest that, as the receptive mode of hearing is absent and the expressive mode of speech is therefore very difficult to acquire, it is irrelevant to expect hearing-impaired children to learn skills in these modes. The obvious alternative is use of an unimpaired function, manual ability. The individual does not experience the trauma of being forced into an inappropriate context, they say, and is able to communicate freely and happily.

Supporters of the oral tradition argue that being able to use manual signs is not quite as advantageous as it seems. Deaf people who 'sign' are able to communicate only with those who can understand the manual language used, usually their parents and close friends, and perhaps teachers and social workers. If instead they learn adequate speech and reasonable lip-reading, deaf people can communicate with anyone, and their horizons are greatly expanded. To which manualists retort that *if* this actually happened in the majority of cases, there would be some logic in the argument, but that in fact very many deaf people have such great difficulty in acquiring skills of speech and lip-reading that, if not taught any sign communication, they are eventually unable to communicate adequately with anyone at all!

The argument about which system is 'better' has persisted over many years, although it is now diminishing. It has raged without much objective assessment. Furth (1973) thought that the emotional tone of the debate had more to do with psychological perceptions of those working with deaf people than with educational considerations, and wrote:

> It is difficult to convey adequately the issues that are implied by the phrase 'the oral-manual controversy'. This controversy, which is as old as deaf education, colors all educational considerations; any major decision or change concerning educational practices implies some stand on the controversy. It is much more than a difference in teaching methods; it touches the very core of deaf people's existence. Indeed, in its extreme form oralism is nothing less than the denial of deafness.

The history of the teaching of communication among the deaf has been fraught with arguments about the relative merits of various approaches. As studies of communication have been extended, so there have been many attempts to take into account the widely differing needs of deaf people. More attention has been paid, too, to preferences and skills of individuals. In recent years more effort has been directed to establishing better communication, irrespective of the method. This has led to systems intended to support and maximise those skills and abilities which the deaf person can utilise most effectively and is happiest to use. One successful result of this approach is cued speech, developed by Dr Orin Cornett, which uses special signs to supplement lip-reading. There are far fewer mouth shapes than phonemes in English, and thus for lip-readers confusion can be great. On the lips, 'm', 'p' and 'b' look identical, making it almost impossible to distinguish between words such as 'mummy', 'paper' and 'baby'. Cued speech has specific signs, held near the mouth using one hand, which signal which consonant is being used.

In dealing with deaf children, the first and greatest problem is providing them with language. If deaf children are to stand any chance of taking a reasonable place in modern society, development of their language is essential. This development is extremely difficult, for by far the largest part of a language concept is normally acquired aurally, and this channel is blocked to the deaf child, who is forced to tread the arduous path of learning language through other media, often virtually by rote.

Developing language is very time-consuming and few deaf children are as competent in educational terms as their hearing peers by the time they reach normal school-leaving age. Estimates of the extent and significance of their disadvantage vary, although there is substantial agreement that it exists. Levine (1960) stated that deaf pupils show a three to four year retardation, and claims that the basic cause is the difficulty of verbal language development. Retardation in this area is, of course, carried over into other school subjects.

Hamp (1972) investigated reading attainment in deaf and partially-hearing children and confirmed previous accounts of low performance. He found that at the normal school-leaving age very few had achieved a reading age of nine years, the point which may be defined as the borderline of literacy. He reports that severely deaf children made approximately one year's progress during their last five years at school; partially-hearing children in a residential school made approximately two to two-and-a-half year's progress in the same period. His general conclusion was that at school-leaving age these children were approximately seven years retarded.

The use of concepts like 'reading age' and 'retardation' should not imply that the deficit experienced by hearing-impaired children is either simple or unitary. Experience of language, communication and education is different for deaf children, and considerable social and psychological differences must be taken into account. Furth (1965) stated:

> The deaf are often insecure in an unstructured situation of intel-
> lectual discovery and are accordingly slow in seeing what may
> be more readily obvious to the hearing peer. I have not found
> that the deaf were less capable of understanding or of applying
> a principle as well as the hearing, once it was understood. But in
> some cases the deaf find it hard to discover the basis or reason
> for thinking.

For many deaf children, opportunities to participate successfully in post-school education have been very limited until recently. Programmes of tuition at the higher academic levels are still relatively few in number and scope, although most institutions are becoming more ready to accept, and make specialist provision for, students with hearing difficulties. This trend may be seen in a British analysis of school leavers from the Mary Hare School for the Deaf: it was reported that between 1850 and 1950 only five or six students were known to have followed university courses, and from 1950 to 1969 only 37 students went on to degree, or degree-equivalent, courses (Askew, 1971).

Historically, general lack of opportunity was apparent not only in Great Britain. The Conference of Executives of American Schools for the Deaf, in 1972, saw fit to 'reaffirm its commitment to the right of all deaf students to quality education, and to their right to seek and engage in post-secondary education and training' (Stuckless, 1973). This need had been emphasised in the previous year by the President of Gallaudet College, an American institution committed to serving deaf students: he claimed that the issues were identical to those affecting hearing students, and that arguments about communication methods and techniques obscured the real task (Merrill, 1972). He said that the problems of isolation and communication make access to higher education more important to the deaf student, not less.

Communication and New Technology

Thus one of the most crucial aspects of life for deaf people is the ability to communicate effectively, efficiently and accurately with those around them. The rapid rise in availability of communications technology has enabled hearing-impaired people to participate where previously they were excluded. For example, teletext equipment provides captions for television programmes. These captions are a boon for deaf people, because in many television programmes important information is carried by the sound-track rather than the picture. As one deaf man put it, 'Do they realise how boring it is to watch television year after year and not hear what it is about?'

Easier access to information technology has also enabled greater and more efficient use of print as a channel of communication. Conrad (1977a) reports that during a study of lip-reading abilities he discovered that the performance of both deaf and hearing subjects improved significantly when information was presented to them in print. Use of the printed word (usually on television screens) as a communication aid in educational contexts has been, and continues to be, investigated in a number of institutions, including the National Technical Institute for the Deaf in America, and the Open University in Great Britain (Hales 1976, 1978).

Applications of new information techology have extended beyond the merely communicative mode into using the systems for teaching communication and language skills. Technology is making it easier to give deaf children the vast amount of organised practice they need to reinforce the basis of language they have acquired with such difficulty. Only through such practice can they avoid accumulated deficits, which not only affect education. Hine (1970) found that measures of social adjustment indicated significant differences in a hearing-impaired group with hearing norms, and Bowyer and others (1963) suggested that partially-hearing children would have more social-emotional problems than either the profoundly deaf or the hearing, because they 'belonged' to neither group.

The learning problems of deaf people affect every aspect of their lives. For them, acquisition of language skills is extremely difficult through non-aural channels, and the ability to use and practise those skills may be very limited. Poor communication abilities socially isolate deaf people, and they cannot easily participate in education. If the problems of the deaf had to be summed up in one word, that word would probably be 'isolation', with all of the frustrations implied by a disability that cuts the individual off entirely, or nearly entirely, from the communicative and social intercourse of fellow human beings.

Summary

Some types and degrees of deafness present greater problems in education than others, and individualised solutions are often called for. Deaf people develop language differently from hearing people, often with serious consequences for their education. The debate over oral communication or manual signing is not finished, but preferences and skills of deaf individuals are now being taken into account more than previously. Deaf people need to develop language for reasoning if they are to progress educationally. New technology may assist deaf students in a variety of ways, as described in Chapter 11.

5 LEARNING PROBLEMS OF SPEECH-IMPAIRED PEOPLE

Nature of Speech-impairment

In many ways, problems confronting hearing-impaired and speech-impaired people may be considered as two sides of the same coin. Both groups have difficulties caused by their inability to communicate, or at least to communicate effectively. If hearing-impaired people have problems in receiving meaningful human communication, then speech-impaired people have problems in sending it. One is 'passive', the other 'active'.

Communication between people is a critical part of the maintenance of individual identity. Those people with handicaps which affect their communication ability are probably therefore at greater psychological risk than those with disabilities that do not mar communication. Blind, deaf and speech-impaired people are all seriously handicapped, but, of the three, speech-impaired people are at a special and different disadvantage. This is because blind and deaf people have a dysfunction in receptive (passive) modes, whereas speech loss involves a dysfunction in expressive (active) modes.

This aspect of the problems of speech-impaired people has been emphasised by Broder and Hinton (1984). In discussing psychotherapeutic measures, they say:

> Selecting and providing the means to communicate are only the first steps in rehabilitating the speechless. The clients and their significant others must have an established avenue to share their feelings regarding adaptation to this new aspect of the clients' identity.

Thus the initial difficulty for those with speech-impairment, or no speech at all, is their inability to establish adequate and meaningful contact with those around them. As with almost all disabilities, this functional handicap is only the outward aspect. Many other less visible and much less obvious factors must also be taken into account.

Educational Implications

For example, how can a person with virtually no speech demonstrate, easily and quickly, that learning has taken place? Teachers and students usually exchange information very rapidly, but a speech-impaired student can only provide feedback slowly and cumbrously. This problem affects not only the speed at which the teaching and learning process progresses, but the quality of that process as well. It is difficult, or even impossible, for many speech-impaired students to use speech as a reinforcing medium. Nor can they use speech as a *self*-reinforcing medium. This, of course, is particularly crucial during early stages of language learning, for much of the teaching of symbol/object relationships is through repetitive copying of sounds.

For the person without speech, therefore, the relationship between symbol and reality becomes direct, whereas for most people there is mediation through the process of speech. Physical (muscular) movements must be learned, and these patterns, as well as language-based components, serve to establish links by which the relationship between symbol and object becomes reinforced.

Speech-impaired people are obliged to use a mode of expressive communication which is different from that employed by others and probably not well understood by them. Much depends, however, on whether the individual has *no* speech or *imperfect* speech.

A person with no speech has no choice but to use non-vocal means of communication. Success in doing so varies with the individual's physical skill and with receptive ability among those with whom he or she wishes to communicate. Unfortunately, speech-impairment is often accompanied by other physical disabilities. For those who can use their hands, sign language is possible, or fingerspelling. In both cases, little or no communication occurs unless those around the disabled people can understand the system. Those with only limited use of the hands are restricted to using, perhaps, a simple alphabet pointer board, unless, of course, they have access to new information technology.

Many speech-impaired people are able to make sounds, and further, such sounds are often controllable and repeatable. This means that a sound may be attached permanently to a particular word, or represent a specific need (such as 'I am hungry' or 'I need a toilet'). The principal difference between such sounds and 'normal' speech, therefore, is that the sound-symbol attached to the particular reality it represents is different from that utilised by everyone else. It is just as necessary for those around a speech-impaired person to understand the 'code' being used as it is for them to know sign language or finger-spelling in communicating with those who cannot make controllable sounds.

In Wayne County, Michigan, an experimental classroom project has been set up for seven non-speaking pupils with cerebral palsy (Turner, 1981). The classroom includes a full range of support, both in terms of hardware, systems and staff, and has attempted to establish models, methods and strategies. The class tries to structure its day as closely as possible to the pattern of general education, covering the whole syllabus. Extra work has been necessary, however, in the field of expressive speech, and consideration has been given to the teaching of the linguistic skills involved, in much the same pattern as that adopted in teaching English as a foreign or second language. The matter is a complex one, and extends into consideration of communication roles; for much of their lives, such pupils have played only a passive role in communication, and they cannot be expected to adopt the positions and functions of communication producers simply because they have been provided with a piece of hardware or some new software. Staff have had some problems, for it is too easy to 'do it all' for the students, anticipate their requests and work out communication consisting of no more than very limited vocal sounds coupled with clear context and high redundancy. Encouraging spontaneous speech is the goal, followed by development of linguistic and expressive competence.

Interaction between the students is sparse and sometimes non-existent, because of the same lack of experience of participating in events of this nature. Teachers develop this participation in 'conversation time', in which students tell each other about themselves and are guided into other forms of language play. The project team reports that 'the play therapy component of the project also exercises the peer group function, requiring the students to introspect and share their feelings about family, self and others, and about their responsibilities and duties'.

Not all the problems concern interaction with other learners, or technological factors. Speaking before the joint committee on Science and Technology in America, Renuk (1982), who uses a voice-output communication aid, stated that:

One of our major problems is in trying to get a good education. The teachers and other professionals most of the time misunderstand the communication handicapped child. This misunderstanding often leads these people to assume the child is much less intelligent. The price of this assumption is the loss of human mind power.

Renuk went on to say that many of the less fortunate are mistakenly thought to be severely mentally impaired. They are sometimes institutionalised and often abused, physically and psychologically. The latter is perhaps worse, because it leaves no telltale signs.

Speech-impairment and New Technology

For speech-impaired people, new information technology offers a great step forward. Programs now exist that recognise specific controllable sounds and translate them for the understanding of others, with the output as synthetic speech or a visual display. This choice of output also makes it possible for speech-impaired people to communicate with deaf or blind friends. Nicola Murray, a disabled ten-year-old, uses a Votan recognition and synthesiser module with an IBM computer (*The Times*, 22 November 1983), which has greatly widened her horizons. Chapter 12 provides other examples.

For those with no handicap, new information technology is completely external and additional to physical functioning, and may be regarded as a useful adjunct, enabling certain things to be done more efficiently, or faster, or with a higher degree of reliability or precision. Disabled people use the technology differently, as a principal and sometimes only way of interacting with their environment.

The technology is not yet well-adapted to the learning problems of speech-impaired students, however, because it is not sufficiently portable, the programming as yet limits severely the range of recognition and vocabulary production and the process is still too slow. The technology will not, and cannot, function on its own, and is only worth having if it fits the individual person and relieves the handicap of that person. It must be seen as helpful by that person, and that perception may not match the perceptions of those who designed and provided the system. There is much to be said for involving speech-impaired people in the design of systems for their use, as occurs at the Trace Research and Development Center for the Severely Communicatively Handicapped, at the University of Wisconsin, although what is suited to one individual may have to be adapted for another.

Application of the technology to learning problems of speech-impaired people normally comes after basic communication needs have been satisfied. Most technological development work has been in response to these needs, which naturally vary somewhat according to the social and psychological development of the individual. In education, too, the relationship of the technology to the individual becomes important. Students (of whatever age) can use new technology to gain access to information and to interact with their peers, thus learning social processes and structures. 'Education' is expanded beyond limits of an academic curriculum. The technology enables speech-impaired students to function on a wider basis, and takes on a different, and rather more expansive, role. It is not just an addition to the individual, something which allows him to do something that cannot otherwise be done; it is potentially part of the person, and becomes an extension of the relationship between the person and the environment.

Thus we see problems faced by speech-handicapped people as by no means confined to the practical problems of being unable to 'speak'. They are unable to participate in a wide range of communication contexts, including those which support the mental health and personal identities of individuals and those which relate to education. Aids and systems based on new information technology are beginning to make possible access to the 'real person' inside the disabled body, overcoming the barrier which speechlessness raises.

Summary

Speech impairment is particularly damaging to individuals because it deprives them of an important, perhaps the most important, expressive mode. This has serious educational implications: it affects individuals' perception of the relationship between symbols and reality, particularly for those who have no speech at all. Social interaction and learning with others, important parts of education, are greatly hampered by lack of speech. New technology may help, although it is not yet well-adapted to the needs of speech-impaired students.

PART TWO

New Information Technology for Learning

6 WHAT IS NEW INFORMATION TECHNOLOGY?

The Dawn of New Information Technology

The two words 'information technology', used together, have recently acquired special meaning. Before about 1976, technology signified materials, tools, systems and techniques. In popular parlance, information was facts, knowledge, data and news. Libraries, the printing industry, telephone exchanges, television studios, billboards, computers and sky-writing all encompassed some aspect of information technology, but scarcely anyone used these two words together in everyday conversation. As recently as 1981, a British opinion poll (reported in *The Times*, 14 January 1982) showed that 80 per cent of those interviewed then had not yet heard of information technology.

In the Western industrialised world, people have suddenly become much more aware of this, the new information technology. Governments have been telling their constituents that information technology is an important factor in maintaining and enhancing economic well-being. Whether in Britain, France, Scandinavia, Canada, the United States or the Federal Republic of Germany, leaders of many political complexions have been pressing forward plans to speed up the advent of this new technology.

Governments have been saying that new information technology is the key to economic growth. They have also been saying that it is likely to bring about substantial changes in society. Their awareness-raising campaigns are to some extent aimed at reducing what Toffler (1970) calls 'future shock'. Information technology, in its new guises, may change lives, for better or worse, within a very short time. Preparing people for change may be one way of helping them to reap advantages rather than collapsing under the strain. On the other hand, as Bowes (1980) suggests, information technology is attractive to governments not only as profitable new industry but also because it can be presented as improving the quality of life for many people. Proponents claim that information will become more accessible and that more information at low cost will increase opportunities for all, with the greatest gain being to

41

those at a disadvantage educationally and 'informationally', among them, disabled students.

To a remarkable extent, information is a source of power in Western society. Information technology becomes a means of wielding power. Robertson (1981) estimates the size of the information explosion in the United States: 30 billion original documents are created each year, with 630 billion pages of print going through the postal system and 100 billion pages coming off photocopiers. For each employed person, that is enough to fill four filing cabinets, containing twelve miles of paper. These figures will double in five years, he says, before the new technology takes effect, but the new is overtaking the old, providing more and more powerful ways to create, store, select, process, deliver and display information.

It is vital to arrive at some understanding of new information technology and of what benefits it can bring, particularly to education of the disabled. Bear in mind, however, Scriven's (1981) dictum that information is not education. Nor is information necessarily knowledge, although knowledge is based on information (see Rich, 1980, for a discussion of knowledge in society). Bell (1980) suggests that knowledge is 'an organised set of statements of facts or ideas, presenting a reasoned judgement or an experimental result', and he distinguishes knowledge from news or entertainment, though all contain information.

Institutions that produce or distribute information in some form are classed by Machlup (1980), however, as belonging to the 'knowledge industry' sector. Knowledge industries, producing and distributing knowledge *and* other information, rather than goods and services, are increasing steadily their share of the national product in Western countries (Drucker, 1969; Bell, 1980). Knowledge is arguably the most important single input into modern productive systems (Stonier, 1981). Information (including knowledge) is accumulating in many fields at rates far exceeding a worker's capacity to absorb it. Can new information technology help solve this general problem, particularly for disabled workers with their special communication difficulties?

But what is new information technology? It would be useful to have a one-line definition to throw into dinner table conversation. 'New information technology is new technology applied to the creation, storage, selection, transformation and distribution of information of many kinds'. That is more than one line and does not say very much. A more comprehensive approach takes up more space and is, unfortunately, less suitable for casual use. The definition adopted by Unesco is 'the scientific, technological and engineering disciplines and the management techniques used in information handling and processing; their applications; computers and their interaction with men and machines; and associated social, economic and cultural matters' (quoted by Raitt, 1982). Perhaps that says too much and certainly it explains very little. What is needed is a layman's introduction to new information technology, what it is and how it works. That is what Part Two of this book aims at providing.

One way of defining a new technology is to say what it can be used for, what functions it can perform, and, in the case of information technology, to describe the symbols, codes and languages that support these functions. Another way is to survey the devices and systems that have so far grown out of the technology. But first it is necessary to look at how this new technology differs from the old.

Old vs. New Information Technology

The boundary between old and new is certainly not sharp, but there are some notable differences. Stonier (1979) suggests that the industrial revolution brought devices to extend musculature, but the electronic revolution is bringing devices, such as television and the computer, that extend the nervous system. Similarly, Hubbard (1981) points out that old information technology depends largely upon mechanical means of carrying out its functions. The postal service, the press, the book publishing industry, the film industry, the sound recording industry, even the telephone system, could not have operated over the last few decades without depending upon machines that have a large number of moving parts. All, including the best, of these machines are subject to wear and tear, the more so as designers find ways to speed them up.

Why should machines be speeded up? To many people, they seem fast enough already, especially those which handle information. But to others, it is very important to obtain faster means of dealing with information, with less chance of breakdown. Higher speeds mean that much more information can be handled within a given time, and information is often a source of power. People who can get vital information first, and who can select it quickly to suit their needs, are in a very powerful position indeed in Western society. This utilitarian view applies in education as well as in industry and commerce, in politics and the military. Without information technology, disabled people may be at an even greater disadvantage than at present, in a world competing for 'fast information'. Disabled students, in particular, can make good use of faster technology to amplify their own limited capacities for writing, drawing, calculating and so on.

The new information technology depends far less on mechanical means. Instead, its machines are electronic. That is to say, the moving parts have almost entirely disappeared, being replaced by 'flows' of electrons. Desk calculators are an example. Twenty years ago, whether manual or powered by electric motors, they contained intricate systems of levers and gears which carried out the calculations. They were essentially mechanical devices. Today, desk calculators have no levers, no gears, but contain much more intricate systems of switches. Pressing the buttons sets the switches in particular patterns, guiding the flow of electrons to accomplish the calculations as commanded. 'Flow' is perhaps not quite the right term to use: it is more accurate to think of the electrons packed into the circuits from end to end, and when the current is turned on at one end, the 'push' is almost instantly felt at the other end. Thus a calculation can be done almost instantaneously once the switches have been set by pressing some keys for the numbers and others for the functions (add, multiply, subtract, or divide, for example). The function keys tell the calculator what to do with the numbers.

Electronic calculators are a rather simple example of the change from old to new. New information technology depends on three complex technologies that have recently converged: computing, microelectronics and telecommunications. In each of these technologies new materials, systems, tools and techniques are being invented at an astounding rate. The three in combination offer opportunities for use or abuse that few people ever imagined, and these opportunities are now beginning to be apparent in many fields, not least education. Can the disabled take advantage of these technologies for their education? Perhaps, but it is as well first to know something about the technologies themselves.

Computers

Jarrett (1980) offers a popular definition of the computer as a 'fast rule-following idiot machine'. It is fast because it is electronic, although the first ones were mechanical. It is rule-following because the patterns of its switches and the logic of its circuits are designed so that, when it processes information it will indeed follow rules that have been worked out beforehand, and it is an idiot machine because it has to follow these rules, incredibly complex though they may be.

Computers are surrounded by their own jargon, much of which is not essential to the level of understanding this chapter provides, but a few terms ought to be introduced here. The machine itself, with its various accessories, makes up the hardware ('everything you can touch', as somebody said). The rules or commands for the computer to follow are the software, written in one of a large number of programming languages. A set of commands is called a program (a universal spelling in English-speaking countries) and is kept in electronic or other forms either in the computer itself or elsewhere. Programs can be printed out on paper, but untrained people cannot understand them: first they must learn the appropriate language. To 'run' one of the programs to process information, a user has to make sure that the program is in the computer, or at least accessible to it electronically, before putting in ('inputting'), one way or another, the information to be processed. Processing takes place very quickly, and processed information can then be stored or displayed, or both. The display is the computer's output and can take a variety of forms, not all of them visual displays.

Computers can handle numbers, of course, but they can deal with written and spoken words, pictures, charts, music and much else too. Consider an example: this book was written on a 'word processor'. Part of the word processor was a computer already programmed to undertake a number of functions. In addition, a special 'editing' program went into the computer before the first word of this chapter was typed in. Typing was the process of input. Editing was done easily, something most writers would appreciate. The computer simply manipulated the information, that is, the words, in accordance with commands given as the text was typed or edited. Even the more complex commands, such as to move a paragraph to another page, or to another chapter, were executed very quickly indeed, with no retyping. The computer's display of the text was on a television-like screen at first, but it stored the text in coded form on a magnetic disc. When the final version was ready, the computer controlled a printer which produced a type-script automatically at a speed of about a page a minute.

Part Three gives details of many types of devices that are used by the disabled for inputting and outputting information. For the moment, note what happens inside the computer during process-ing. Like the desk calculator, the computer has intricate systems of switches and circuits inside its central processing unit. These switches and circuits differ from those of the calculator in being far more intricate and more commandable. Each switch, as in the cal-culator, can be set in one of two electronic states: on or off. It is the pattern of ons and offs, so to speak, that provides the basic code for all information processed by the computer, including the commands or programs that it needs. This code is termed binary because it employs only two symbols: 0 for off and 1 for on. Yet combinations of 0s and 1s can be used to represent numbers, letters and other symbols. In fact, the binary code is extraordinarily versatile.

The 0s and 1s that make up the binary code are called bits, the term being derived from '*bi*nary dig*its*' (Bell, 1980). Four 0s and 1s make a 4-bit 'word' (for example, 1010), and since there are 16 combinations possible using not more than four 0s and 1s, a 4-bit word, using only four switches, can represent in code any one of 16 symbols. Words of eight bits (for example, 00100110) offer 256 combinations, enough to represent all the numbers and letters on a typewriter keyboard, while 16-bit words give over 65,000 combinations. Many microcomputers now being sold are 16-bit machines. These figures provide at least an inkling of the potential of computers for dealing extremely efficiently with large amounts of information.

What does the computer actually do with all this coded infor-mation during processing? The programs, converted into binary code (switch settings of 0s and 1s) and stored in one part of the computer, act upon the information to be processed, which is coded and held in another part of the computer ready for process-ing. Nobody can see what is happening in the circuits, but imagine switches changing from off to on and from on to off. These changes represent complex changes in the patterns of states among all the switches in the set of circuits being used. The patterns of states, in turn, represent changes in the information coded into them. Thus, to take an example that does not even need the power of a computer, calculate 256 times 347: 256 and 347 are both coded into 0s and 1s (offs and ons), and the command 'multiply' (which is really 'add so many times') is put into the computer too. The answer is computed, in 0s and 1s and then converted back into figures everyone understands, giving 88,832 in the twinkling of an eye.

The same broad principles apply in much more complex processing tasks, such as arranging in strict alphabetical order all the entries under A for a new dictionary. Entries are typed into the computer's memory, where they are stored in coded form, automatically, as 0s and 1s represented by states of switches. To put them in alphabetical order, they are acted upon by the commands contained in the computer's programs. These commands rearrange the patterns of states, so that when the computer displays, on its screen or via its printer, the new patterns in the form of (decoded) typescript, all the entries are in the right order. Even extremely complex processing tasks, requiring vast amounts of information, employ similar principles. Most people have heard the often-quoted examples: how telemetry (measuring distance and position) data from spacecraft could not be processed by mathematicians with pencil and paper alone because it would take many lifetimes, or how international financial corporations process daily hundreds of millions of pieces of information regarding banking and other transactions.

Thus at the heart of the computer, in its central processing unit, is the means to use information to create new information by changing the old, whether through adding up money totals, by compiling a dictionary or by computing the new signals to be sent to spacecraft that are slightly off course. The computer is immensely powerful as an information-processing machine, better even than brains in some respects. It remembers everything it is told and works very quickly indeed: the most advanced models carry out as many as a hundred million instructions per second (Ince, 1982), although those described in this book work more slowly. Computers, available now at reasonably low cost and requiring little energy, are fundamental to the new information technology and to its use by disabled people.

Microelectronics

The real cost of computers has fallen fast in the last few years, together with the amount of energy and physical space they require. By contrast, their processing power and reliability have increased sharply, uses for them have burgeoned and they are more user-friendly (jargon: they are easier for relatively untrained people to use) than ever.

To a large extent these changes can be attributed to the development of microelectronics (Evans, 1981). Microelectronics is the result of miniaturisation, of making incredibly small the switches and circuits of processors and their accessories. Miniaturisation has been made possible by the invention of new manufacturing processes and by using new materials. Electronic elements used in today's computers serve more or less the same functions as mechanical and electrical elements in much larger machines of 20 years ago, but in those days each element was made separately and then wired to other elements. Now they are produced in microscopic form, already connected by extremely thin 'wires', on chips a quarter of an inch square. These chips, called microprocessors, can be manufactured by mass-production methods in tens of thousands, so that a single such chip may cost very little, a matter of pence, yet can contain masses of switches and circuits needed by a particular electronic device, perhaps a computer.

Miniaturisation has progressed so far that it is not easy to grasp what can now be put on a chip. Micrographs (photographs taken through a microscope) of chips reveal the complexity, but inadequately. In theory, a single chip may contain as many as a million elements and their circuits. Many chips, of varying degrees of complexity, may be used in combination or a few well-designed ones may suffice. For example, Sinclair, the British microcomputer manufacturer, reduced the 21 chips in his ZX80 model to only 4 in the ZX81.

The process of manufacturing chips begins with a slice of material, usually pure silicon, at least four inches in diameter and about fifteen thousandths of an inch thick. The circuits and electronic elements are 'printed' on to the base in a succession of layers, with insulating layers provided wherever needed. The printing is done by a series of photographic and chemical processes, leaving extremely thin lines of conducting material rather than wires as such and at the same time depositing other material that makes up the elements for that particular chip. The slice can be cut into quarter-inch squares afterwards, each one being an identical chip ready for testing. By such methods, Texas Instruments, one of the major American manufacturers, makes over 20 million chips a year of one type alone (the TMS1000), for use in digital watches, microwave ovens and other consumer items.

The circuits and elements to be printed onto each chip must of course be planned and drawn beforehand, but no longer by hand. Designing them is a difficult task now carried out with the assistance of computers. The artwork is produced on a large screen and is about 250 times the size of what goes onto the chip. With computerised controls, the circuit designer can try out very quickly a variety of layouts. In fact, the computer often selects the optimum routes for the circuits, given a set of conditions. Up to eleven layers may be needed on one chip and each has to be designed completely, down to the last detail, before photo reduction.

Where do chips fit into computers? A small computer, nowadays known as a microcomputer, needs a microprocessor for its central processing unit, designed to process or change information. It also needs electronic input and output units, often linked to keyboards and display devices respectively. And it needs two kinds of memory. The first of these is fixed: the information in it cannot be changed and it is called a ROM, short for read-only memory. The second, called a RAM (for random access memory), stores information that can be altered. It is quite feasible for one chip to contain a microprocessor, input and output units and both kinds of memory. By itself, that chip does not constitute a microcomputer, however, because it must be linked to a power supply, to various input and output devices and perhaps to other pieces of equipment, depending on its designed functions. Miniaturisation has influenced these additional items, too, therefore the whole system is likely to be small enough to fit on top of a desk or may be even smaller. Size can be important for disabled people who want to be able to handle and carry around their computer.

The next size up in computers has also been affected by miniaturisation. Minicomputers are too large to fit on a desk but only require a small room. They have become as powerful as the older very big computers. The largest computers, usually called mainframe (although this term is also applied to some minicomputers), require a large room but are very powerful indeed. They can process extremely large amounts of information at very high speed. Miniaturisation has also led to the development of networks of micro-, mini- and mainframe computers that help each other, so to speak. For example, together, a number of microcomputers can provide as much information processing power as a mainframe computer. What is more, the microcomputers can be scattered widely in different locations, thus providing a fair amount of local power as well as the greater power of the whole network.

It is easy, but wrong, to think of microelectronics only in the context of computers of various sizes, particularly the microcomputers that are widely advertised for use in education. It is wrong because the coming of the chip has revolutionised many control devices that are not strictly computers but have a place in helping students to learn. For instance, in workshops micrometers that use a chip give precise measurements in a digital readout. For disabled students, there are many specialised devices (see Part Three for examples).

Telecommunications

Computers and microelectronics are having great impact on telecommunications and developments in telecommunications have considerable significance for future use of computers. Telecommunications provide the means to deliver information over distances great and small, accurately and speedily. Each year the pace of development accelerates, meaning that more information can be sent faster and more faithfully. There is also potential for lowering the cost of telecommunications. The real cost has dropped noticeably over long distances, as in the case of Transatlantic telephone calls. Here, too, disabled people may be able to benefit.

Computers are taking their place as controllers of telecommunication systems, as well as being generators and transformers of information to be delivered via these systems. There are many well-known examples. Credit card users' credit is checked in seconds via telecommunication channels that span oceans and continents to a computer that is asked whether the credit limit has been exceeded or the card stolen. A disabled owner of a microcomputer, living in New Mexico, can use a telephone network to gain access to information of many kinds held on a mainframe computer in Virginia. Using a terminal in an office in one city, a disabled clerk can call up any of hundreds of thousands of insurance records on his or her screen, linked by telephone line to a computer, in another city, that searches optical videodiscs, each one containing 40,000 pages of information.

The most significant changes in telecommunications in recent years have been in new transmission channels and new ways of sending information through both these channels and the older ones. The 'old' channels, still extremely valuable, are those used for the past 50 years for radio and television broadcasting, and for telephone and telex. Telecommunications are being influenced by microelectronics as miniaturised components make possible more powerful satellites, including those that broadcast direct to homes and institutions such as schools. Similar components are going into switching devices and equipment to step up the strength of signals during long-distance cable transmissions.

Take the telephone network, for example. In most countries at present, messages pass through it in analogue form: that is, variations in the current in the wire are analogous to variations in the sounds spoken into the mouthpiece. New information technology will convert such networks so that messages are coded in digital form, that is, in binary code, as 0s and 1s, making the signals compatible with computers and at the same time increasing the quality and efficiency of transmissions. Converted networks will be able to handle numerical, textual and visual information, all coded digitally (see Chapter 7), and their capacity to inform will be increased greatly. Copper cables, used everywhere for decades, will be gradually replaced by glass optical fibre cables (Chapter 8) that carry signals as pulses of light instead of in the form of electrical impulses. Again, systems' capacity to inform will be increased because such cables convey many more messages than copper ones. These systems may well serve disabled people better than the old, being more adaptable to their particular needs.

Summary

This chapter has been rather technical, perhaps, to give an appreciation of the technology itself. It has explained some of the principles underlying the technology and has looked at examples of the confluence of computers, microelectronics and telecommunications.

Information technology devices and systems are explained more fully in Chapter 8. Users need to be well aware of the technology's potential functions (Chapter 7) and its technical limitations (Chapter 17). Part Three looks at experience with the technology among disabled students.

7 WHAT CAN NEW INFORMATION TECHNOLOGY DO?

Information and Communication

What can new information technology do? What functions does it serve, and does it serve them better than the old? The fundamental function served by the technology is that it enhances humans' ability to communicate information. But what is 'information' and what does it mean to communicate?

Paisley (1980) suggests two ways of defining information, structurally and functionally. Structurally speaking, he says, information is 'an encoding of symbols (e.g., letters, numbers, pictures) into a message ... communicated through any channel'. That is what much information looks like, if only it were always visible. Needless to say, these encoded symbols take many forms. Functionally speaking, in terms of what it does, Paisley suggests that information denotes 'any stimulus that alters cognitive structure in the receiver ... something that the receiver already knows is not information! Or, in the words of Stafford Beer, information is what changes us' (quoted by Knott and Wildavsky, 1981).

Information, says Paisley (1980), varies in quality, depending on its relevance, timeliness, comprehensiveness and authoritativeness. Its value depends on not only its quality but also its specifiability (distinctness of representation), locatability (distinctness of location), acquirability (ease of acquisition, including cost) and usability (suitability of form and content for intended use). In other words, much information is of no or low value to particular individuals at any one time. In education, above all, students are obliged to develop selectivity and disabled students may have to be very selective indeed.

Information has been defined even more technically. It is widely accepted among communication scholars that information is 'a difference in matter-energy which affects uncertainty ... where a choice exists among a set of alternatives' (Rogers and Kincaid, 1981). What is a difference in matter-energy? Such differences

53

appear in the physical world as differences that humans can sense. Thus we more or less imperfectly sense, by sight and touch, differences in form. We attach meanings to what we sense and construct a psychological reality for ourselves from these perceptions. If we perceive printed words, each of us interprets what they mean. If we hear music, we interpret it each in his or her own way. We use the differences in matter-energy to alter the uncertainty we possess, in whatever degree, concerning what we already know. We learn nothing from messages that contribute nothing to the resolution of uncertainty (Pierce, 1961). We want information to increase our understanding. This is as true of disabled people as it is of the able-bodied.

Clearly, it is possible for a person to *create* differences in matter-energy for others to perceive, as well as perceiving such differences, in varying ways. Human communication consists of exchanges of information, of differences in matter-energy. Education entails such communication. New information technology is ready to be used to create, store, collect, select, transform, send or display information. In particular, disabled people should be able to take advantage of this technology for their education.

Models of Communication

These functions of storing, collecting and so on, are important, but they are better understood in terms of one or two models of communication. The best-known is Shannon and Weaver's (1949), depicted in Figure 7.1. In this model, a message emanates from an information source. It is converted into a signal or series of signals by a transmitter. *En route*, this signal is mixed with or contaminated by 'noise', that is to say, various kinds of unwanted interference coming from noise sources. The received signal is decoded by a receiver, being converted back into the original message, more or less, which is what the receiver (or destination) receives.

Shannon and Weaver's model seems straightforward. It recognises that encoding and decoding occur. It takes into account the problem of interference: 'noise' is a term from electrical engineering, denoting electro-magnetic interference. Noise arriving with the signal makes it more difficult to decode accurately, as we all know from everyday experience.

Figure 7.1: Shannon and Weaver's Linear Model of Communication

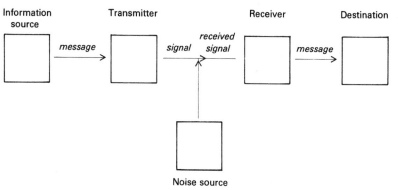

Source: Reproduced by permission from Shannon and Weaver (1949).

This model has been criticised, however, because it is linear, a one-way model, based on engineering. In fact, this was the dominant model for a quarter of a century (Rogers and Kincaid, 1981). The thinking behind it was probably reflected in the thinking of many top managers in communications organisations. Broadcasters, for example, thought of themselves as primarily responsible for sending out messages, and perhaps for reducing noise to a minimum, but not for receiving them back. Broadcasting organisations put most of their resources into production and transmission of programmes, and much less into listening to audience opinion. A one-way model like this is scarcely relevant to the education of disabled children or adults.

Shannon and Weaver's model can be converted into a two-way model of communication by adding a feedback channel, complete with transmitter, encoding, noise, decoding and receiver, all to deal with messages returning from the receiver to the sender. In this two-way model, the feedback channel may be vitally important to the original receiver as a means of seeking clarification of the original message. Feedback channels, verbal and non-verbal, continually serve this purpose in human communication, especially when disabled people are involved. New information technology, in many situations, provides better for two-way communication than did the old.

Shannon and Weaver's model, important as it was when it was first published, has also been criticised because it did not provide for the complex nature of relationships among humans, and other scholars (for example, Schramm, 1977 and Kincaid, 1979) have advanced models intended to fill this need. Although none of these has yet gained wide scholastic acceptance, they stress the danger of over-simplifying human communication processes.

What are the characteristics of a model of communication that helps to explain the functions of new information technology? First, it must be a two-way model: the channels within it must allow for two-way traffic. Second, it must include all the functions, and, third, it must show how these functions are integrated. Ideally, it should also exhibit the complexities of both human-human and human-machine interaction.

Figure 7.2 establishes four principal functions: making, sending/ receiving, storing and displaying. Making is subdivided into creating, collecting, selecting and transforming. Sending is of course complemented by receiving. We can look at each of these functions in turn and examine their interrelationships.

Making Information

Do humans make information? Or do they simply discover it? These are interesting philosophical questions. Those in the business of *creating* 'differences in matter-energy' for others to perceive as information can afford to take an empirical view and say that the answer does not really matter. People may read a book as an original 'creation', yet freely acknowledge that it and every

Figure 7.2: A Model of Functions of New Information Technology

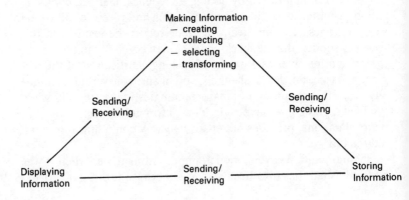

other book include amalgams of information *collected, selected and transformed.* Some books are more original than others: Shakespeare's plays, for example, owe less to others than does the *Encyclopaedia Britannica.*

Collecting information may call for channels to bring it from stores or sources of many kinds, from many places and in many forms. The rate at which information is available will depend on the capacity of these channels. The variety of information they can bring in depends on their flexibility. The quality of information they provide, including the amount of noise present in it, is determined in part by the efficiency of the channels, with noisy channels yielding noise-ridden information. New information technology increases the capacity, flexibility and efficiency of channels for collecting information. All this can be very important for disabled people, as in, say, voice recognition and synthesis.

Examples abound of new information technology being used to collect information in industry, agriculture, medicine and many other fields. The head of a manufacturing company collects sales information from retail outlets through data networks that transmit the figures at high speed over telephone lines. In the same company, the production manager collects information continuously from the automated assembly line, using remote sensors linked to computers. Even the night-watchman, one of the last of the unskilled workers, has at his service a closed-circuit television system that collects information unflaggingly and in all weathers. In agriculture, new information technology, in the shape of a satellite carrying infra-red cameras, collects information about weather and the state of crops over a very large area at frequent intervals. In medicine, new information technology monitors the condition of patients.

Selecting information precedes and follows collecting. Indiscriminate collecting leads to information overload, therefore information must be selected by setting up criteria. These are of many kinds, sometimes to include information in the collection, sometimes to exclude it, and more often to sort it into categories. In other words, people switch information through complex paths and into various stores. They merge information, too, after selecting it from different sources. As the sum of information circulating in society has increased, however, so has the need to select information efficiently. Technology has been used to help for many decades, in the form of indexes and mechanical sorting systems.

Now new information technology has the power to search and select quickly from very large stores indeed.

An example from the entertainment world: a pop group makes a recording of its music. The recording is a process of collecting information from each performer, from each instrument or vocalist, on a separate track. Afterwards, the producer uses new information technology to select what he or she wants from each track. A particular track may be enhanced electronically. On another, more sounds may be added. On another, the volume may be changed or sounds may even be eliminated. The end-result is an edited version of the original. In the television industry, producers follow similar procedures in the 'post-production' videotape editing room, again using new information technology to select information that finally makes up the broadcast. Even during live broadcasts, producers are busy selecting information by switching from one camera to another and by instructing the cameramen to take particular shots of the action.

The new technology excels at selecting information when the stores are massive and the criteria for selection are complex. It can handle with ease the task of searching among a few million items for those which belong to certain sets. For example, to select from a store of research studies all those published in the last ten years concerning the use of computers for teaching blind adults, simply specify these sets: (1) the dates, (2) computers, (3) blind persons, and (4) teaching adults. The computer counts how many there are in store within each of these sets, and how many there are in the intersection of the four sets, that is, where they overlap each other. If needed, it may be able to count those from a particular country. It will provide an instant listing on the screen or on paper of titles and summaries for any of the studies it finds. Impressive as this may sound, it is an even more remarkable use of the new technology when the search is done, as similar searches are every day, on a terminal in a European library, linked by telephone line to an earth station that sends the signals via a satellite stationary at 22,000 miles above the equator to an earth station in America, and then by telephone line to the computerised databank. The information selected comes back, by the same route, barely seconds later, at a cost of a few pounds.

Transforming information that has been collected and selected entails rearranging it, reordering it, preparing it for presentation in various modes (see below). The transforming function requires the ability to manipulate information, to analyse and synthesise it at high speed and with great flexibility. It also requires a facility for trying out transformations, so that people can see whether they fit their purposes, before they finally choose one out of a number of alternatives. Here again the new information technology is ready: they can use it to create 'mock-ups', based on trial transformations, and to compare these and refine them until they have the one they want. For example, Chapter 9 mentions computer programs that enable a physically-handicapped person to rotate, in several axes, three-dimensional engineering drawings of working mechanisms so that he or she can check whether clearances are adequate between adjacent parts.

Sending and Receiving

Sending and receiving information are further functions performed excellently by new information technology, which enhances transmission. Chapter 8 provides details of devices and systems serving these two functions, and they can be divided into three broad classes depending on the means of transmission. One class includes those which depend on electrical waves or pulses transmitted through wires or similar conductors. A second class includes all that depend on electromagnetic waves or pulses broadcast through the atmosphere, and a third class includes devices and systems that depend on transmission of light pulses, produced by lasers. Information is delivered, on its outward journey from the 'making' source, to a device or system that serves either the *displaying* or the *storing* function, but may also be returned to the source for reselection or transformation, hence on Figure 7.2 the arrows point in both directions. There can also be interchange of information between devices and systems that display or store it.

Storing and Displaying

Information is stored in many forms, and new information technology makes conversion into the most economical form very much more feasible. Thus thousands of pages of words can be stored as very dense magnetic patterns recorded on tape or disc, for display on a screen or in print. Millions of 'bits' of information can be stored in microscopic indentations in a videodisc, for display as colour television pictures and sound. Chapter 8 contains many examples.

Integration

Integration of these functions is made possible by new information technology, which combines in single systems, large or small, components for input and display, for storage and delivery, for selection and transformation of information. Technical reliability improves with greater integration and costs tend to fall. Integration is increasing as more system components use digital codes and as they become compatible with computing equipment that can process information at high speed and with great reliability.

Human Communication

Education, by any definition, depends on human communication. Many forms of human communication are enhanced by new information technology, which can increase the fidelity with which messages can be transmitted and the variety and amount of information in these messages. Fidelity improves as 'noise' is reduced. Variety increases as humans find new ways to transmit more of the full range of messages they want to send, including extremely complex messages made up of many 'bits' of information.

Humans (and machines) communicate by means of signals. A set of signals make up a message. Messages are transmitted through one or more channels or media, being encoded by the transmitter and decoded by the receiver. All messages are 'shaped' by the codes used. These codes are usually chosen by the transmitter, affected by noise and the media used, and decoded by the receiver. If the receiver is human, decoding always occurs against a context; this may even occur when the receiver is a machine.

Without technology humans communicate through, for example, auditory, visual and tactile channels. In the auditory channel, they send and receive sets of sounds that make up messages; these sounds may be verbal, musical, shouts of laughter, cries of pain, and so on. Technology extends humans senses. Some signals they can receive only with technology to help them, as when they listen to the radio. All this is elementary and much has been written on this subject (see, for example, Innis, 1951; McLuhan, 1964; Gumpert and Cathcart, 1979; Salomon, 1979).

Symbols, Codes and Languages

It is important to distinguish, however, between symbols, codes and languages, all of which are vital to transformations of information. Without transformations, there would be no civilisation based on recorded knowledge and near-universal communication. To achieve transformations, humans arbitrarily assign meanings to symbols or groups of symbols. In countries of Western Europe and North America, symbols called alphanumeric characters are used to represent numerals and letters. Groups of letters in certain combinations make up words corresponding to spoken words. Groups of numerals have certain meanings. Groups of characters by themselves cannot convey much meaning, but when combined according to a syntax they become languages, capable of expressing abstract ideas. Languages are principal tools of transformation of knowledge.

Alphanumeric characters can also be used to devise codes, in which the original 'plain language' messages are hidden, compressed or otherwise transformed. One code can be translated into another, according to a given set of rules. Codes are essential to new information technology, not to hide information but to deal with it efficiently, to carry out the functions discussed earlier in this chapter.

Binary code (in 0s and 1s, see Chapter 6) is the basis for machine language, the most primitive form of language used in the computer (Jarrett, 1980), but there are languages at higher levels. Next up the scale is assembly language, a relatively simple form used by programmers to avoid working in binary code direct. The computer translates assembly code into binary code, for the progammer, before carrying out the instructions contained in it. Almost every make of computer has to have its own assembly language, not transferable to others, therefore assembly languages are termed low-level. High-level programming languages are less exclusively linked to particular makes, although few are freely transferable. They need more translation (by the computer, not the programmer) before they are in binary code. Examples are COBOL (Common Business Oriented Language), FORTRAN (Formula Translator), BASIC (Beginners' All-purpose Symbolic Instruction Code), COMAL-80 (Common Algorithmic Language), which was developed from BASIC in Denmark (Atherton, 1981, 1982 and Bramer, 1982), and PASCAL (named after the

French mathematician, Pascal), the last three being more commonly used in education. Logo was developed by Papert (1977, 1980) with children in mind and is being used by numbers of disabled children. All these programming languages include a large number of plain language (English, for instance) words combined with abbreviations and special terms and symbols. BASIC, in various 'dialects', is the programming language most widely used for microcomputers, although it has a number of disadvantages for educators. For example, it is not very suitable for presenting text on the screen and lacks the kind of structure needed for educators' information processing. It tends to lead to the development of programmes that are extremely hard to read, modify or debug (repair), according to Bramer (1982). On the other hand, it is relatively easy to learn and is readily available.

Digital and Analogue Signals

It is also important to distinguish between two forms of electronic signal in new information technology: digital and analogue. Martin (1977) points out that information of most types (aural, visual, tactile) can be converted into one of these forms. Analogue signals can be changed into digital signals and vice versa. In old telephones (which most people still have), the strength of current in the wires directly varies with the frequency of the voice. By contrast, new digitised telephones encode voice frequencies as a stream of electrical pulses. Each group of pulses represents the binary code for a particular voice frequency. This may seem to require immensely long strings of pulses to reflect faithfully the original voice, but sampling and compression techniques reduce the actual number of pulses to be transmitted, without significant loss of fidelity.

Digital signals have the advantage of being compatible with digital computers, which now far outnumber analogue computers. They can be easily amplified for long distance transmission and are not susceptible to electrical noise in the same way that analogue signals are. Electrical noise corrupts analogue signals, but digital signals are coded as pulses therefore interference has to be very strong to overwhelm the pattern. Moreover, streams of digitised signals interfere with each other less than streams of analogue signals. The capacity of lines carrying digital signals is very much greater than those carrying analogue signals, resulting in cheaper transmission.

Digital and Analogue Information Storage

Digitised storage forms are displacing analogue forms, too. Here the word 'analogue' is in a wider context. Film records an analogue of what the cameraman sees through the viewfinder of the camera. But in using an electronic videocamera, say in a television studio, does the cameraman also record on tape an analogue of the scene? Do videocassettes contain an electronic analogue? The answer to both questions is at the moment usually Yes, although it soon may be No. Magnetic tape in videocassettes does not carry digitised information, although it can and soon will for most new cameras. The cameras on spacecraft that take pictures of Saturn, for example, convert into digital code the colour and light intensity of each of a large number of 'spots on the retina', so to speak. These digital signals are transmitted by radio to Earth, where the pictures are reconstituted.

All magnetic tapes and discs used in computers carry digitised information, however, and the 'move to digital' is almost accomplished in other parts of the electronics industry. Digital recordings of music are now on sale. When these were made, the original sounds were transformed into digital signals, then recorded on a master tape. Most people do not yet have digital players, for audiodiscs or tapes, therefore the master tape must be used to create old-style analogue pressings or tapes, suitable for our equipment. Digitising the original recording is worthwhile, however, because it eliminates one major source of noise and retains high fidelity during editing. Digital audiodiscs are esteemed by connoisseurs even though the needle still has to move along the groove, which is shaped as an analogue of the sounds it helps to produce. Other digitised information technology, such as videodiscs, is discussed in Chapter 8.

Analogic, Digital and Iconic Modes of Communication

Finally, in looking at human communication, it is important to distinguish between its analogic, digital and iconic modes. In the digital mode, people employ characters and digits, letters and figures. Each character has little meaning in itself, but strung together in particular ways and placed in context, characters convey deep meaning, as in a book. If somebody reads the book aloud, however, that person shifts into the analogic mode, since the spoken word is an analogue of the written. A digital watch has changing numerals; sweeping hands belong to an 'analogue' watch. Print without illustrations is in the digital mode. Print with illustrations is in both the digital and the iconic (pictured) mode. Radio broadcasts are in the analogic mode, but the scripts from which they may originate are in the digital mode. Television (sound and pictures) is certainly in the analogic and iconic modes, but can also be in the digital mode when titling appears. Printed tonic sol-fa music is in the digital mode, but performed music in the analogic.

In each of these modes, information is structured and conveyed differently, that is clear. Moreover, humans have become accustomed to the patterns, called symbol systems by Salomon (1979), in which information is structured in each mode. Salomon takes the view that educators overlook the potential of particular media, operating in one or more modes, to cultivate human skills of recognising complex symbols. Thus in film people become accustomed to symbol systems (music, juxtaposition of actors, etc.) used by film makers and expressed in analogic, iconic and sometimes digital modes. Some symbol systems require more 'mental translation' than others, some contain more ambiguity.

Much primary schooling, for able-bodied and disabled students, is taken up with learning how to communicate in the digital mode ('reading, writing and arithmetic'), which is the dominant mode of education generally in industrialised society. Many people value a 'bookish' education that teaches students how to excel in the digital mode. Less attention is given to learning how to communicate in analogic or iconic modes, despite the fact that numerous concepts are difficult to explain in the digital mode. The analogic mode is vital, for example, to drama and performed music; the iconic mode to design, fine art, engineering, town planning, architecture and cartography. It is possible that soon there will be more learning in analogic and iconic modes, and perhaps less emphasis on learning in the digital mode, which has actually proved difficult for large sections of the population. It is already clear that some digital modes of communication, such as writing, are becoming less essential in modern society. This is very important for disabled people, as Part Three shows.

One reason why these shifts are likely to accelerate is that new information technology is capable of handling human communication in all three of these modes, despite the challenges of the most demanding mode, the iconic. To be able to generate, select, transmit and receive information in the digital mode over vast distances, as a telex system does, is impressive. To do the same with voice or music, as radio does, is more impressive. But perhaps most impressive is the capacity to generate, select, manipulate, store, transmit and receive in iconic mode, with great speed and fidelity. New information technology can do this with ease. It can also achieve already certain transformations from one mode to another: for instance, it can change what was originally in digital mode (say, the printed word) into analogic, as in voice synthesis, and the reverse transformation is already possible, within limits that are fast disappearing, to the great advantage of many disabled students.

Summary

An understanding of symbols, codes, languages and modes is essential to an understanding of how new information technology can be used in educating disabled children and adults. Disabled students need to be able to use the technology to transform information. The power to transform information increases the capacity of individuals (and society) to store information and to select it, in one mode or another, for use in multi-media systems. This is especially important for disabled children and adults. Disabled learners may benefit from opportunities to learn in more than one mode, often in more than one medium. Each medium employs a different combination of symbols to convey information (see Lindenmayer, 1981), therefore learners who find difficulty with using one medium and learning through it may have less difficulty in another. New information technology greatly increases society's capacity to provide disabled people with opportunities to learn.

8 DEVICES AND SYSTEMS

Classifying Devices and Systems

Which are the devices and systems that belong to new information technology? What can each do? These questions are quite difficult to answer in the face of a great variety of inventions, with new ones being added every month. In general, the new technology is marked off from the old because it is electronic rather than mechanical or electro-mechanical, and the new technology often uses microelectronics: most of its devices and systems take advantage of miniaturisation, the chip and its integrated circuits. But it would be a mistake to draw too sharp a line between old and new, because devices and systems belonging to the old can be modified for use alongside the new. For example, existing electro-mechanical telephone exchanges can accommodate data transmissions between computers, and paper remains an important storage medium in many settings where new information technology is bringing substantial changes. This merging of old and new is only to be expected. To replace the old is very expensive, particularly when huge sums have been invested in, say, copper cable under the streets.

One way to classify the devices and systems of information technology is in terms of its function or functions. Chapter 7 showed, however, that the functions of new information technology overlap and it is also true that many devices combine two or more functions. Systems, made up of different devices, always combine functions, sometimes all the functions displayed in the model of Figure 7.2. This chapter looks first at devices used mainly for putting information into information technology systems, then at storage media, before going on to consider transmission devices and systems. Finally, it looks at output devices and at systems that integrate by serving most or all functions.

Input Devices

The first, and best-known, input device is the keyboard. The standard QWERTY keyboard has been fitted to typewriters and teletype machines for decades in all English-speaking countries using the Roman alphabet, with minor variations to suit different cultures. By placing much used keys some distance apart, separated by less used keys, the original designers enabled typists to work faster without jamming the key bars. In Europe other arrangements of the letters (for example, AZERTY) are in use, but the QWERTY keyboard is close to being the world-wide standard for typewriters and computers using the Roman alphabet, and Gates (1980) assumes that it will not be displaced easily, despite its inefficiency. In the United States, QWERTY keyboards are standard, although for its Sesame Place educational playground Children's Television Workshop installed teaching computers with ABCDE keyboards (*Time*, 21 September 1981), and Texas Instruments' educational game, Speak & Spell, also uses an ABCDE keyboard. The British Maltron ergonomic keyboard has a key arrangement in which 90 per cent of the letters of the 100 most used words in English are in the home row directly under the fingers (for QWERTY keyboards there are 40 per cent). The layout and height of keys are arranged to compensate for the unequal length of fingers. Computer keyboards usually have additional control keys for various functions. Often computers have a separate numeric keyboard for use when large quantities of numbers must be keyed in. Computers used for word-processing, like the one on which this book was written, have special keys for moving around the text, deleting characters, words or paragraphs, and so on. Many computers have specialised keys for use in programming. Sometimes a keyboard will have dual uses for the same keys, with the second use being written on the front of the key rather than its top. The second use is actuated by first pressing a control key. The Sinclair Spectrum, a low-cost microcomputer, maximises the use of its QWERTY keyboard by assigning up to six functions per key. This includes single key selections for BASIC programming commands, and simplified colour and graphics commands.

Keypads are small keyboards with only a few keys. Pocket calculators, remote control devices for television sets or videocassette recorders, push-button telephones and check-out tills in stores all have keypads. Keypads are usually intended for use with one hand only. A keypad recently appeared on which the user presses various combinations of keys ('chords') to produce letters of the alphabet, numerals 0 to 9 and punctuation marks. This is enough for most writing tasks. A fourteen-character line of what is being written appears in a small window above the keys. The number of keys? Only five, one for each finger. An additional control key in combination with the five keys provides a range of editing features.

Keyboards and keypads used to be entirely mechanical, with levers moving in response to each keystroke. New ones are electronic, requiring much less energy from the user. Some keys are springloaded switches, which make contact when pressed quite gently. The most advanced are touch-sensitive, requiring only that the user makes contact with them.

Touch-sensitive boards, made in several sizes, consist of a set of squares which can be coded. Input is simply by touch, therefore a young child can learn to use such a board even before learning to use a keyboard. The codes generated by touch-sensitive boards can be used to create keyboards specific to any program (see Chapter 10 for an example). If a board has 128 touch-sensitive squares it could, for example, be arranged into two large areas (64 squares each) that provided a 'yes' or 'no' input. This would require a matching overlay to indicate the responses and software to match the codes. More complex patterns of responses can be used with appropriate overlays and software modifications.

Similarly, touch-sensitive screens are available. They look like television screens but are linked to computers which are able to record the co-ordinates (the 'cross-references') of any spot on the screen when that spot is touched. Therefore even an illiterate can make an input when asked to touch a particular part of a picture shown on the screen.

Another device, the graphics tablet, combines the capabilities of touch-sensitive boards and screens. The author or artist writes or draws on it with a special stylus connected to the computer. Whatever is drawn appears on the computer's screen and can be stored in the computer's memory. The tablet works in much the same way as the screen, but is easier to draw and write on because it can be held at any suitable angle and does not have a slippery glass surface. Some tablets have additional facilities: for instance, Apple makes one accompanied by programs that enable the user to select with the stylus from a menu of functions specified by the user in advance.

In a somewhat different version, marketed by Rediffusion, a British company, anyone can write the numbers 0-9, the letters of the alphabet and 22 other symbols on the paper surface of the tablet in ball-point pen or pencil and the device identifies the characters and their position on the tablet, signalling this information to a computer, which not only records it appropriately but also flashes it back to the tablet for display in a small window. Thus the writer can check for errors.

Computer-assisted design devices go further than the graphics tablet, which they can easily incorporate. The computer's keyboard is used to instruct the computer to draw lines between different spots on the screen. Sometimes, as in designing the layout of a chip, the computer will solve intricate logic problems before 'deciding' where to draw the line. In architecture, sets of rules and lists of standard components can be programmed into the computer. In engineering, strain factors and the like can be taken into account, quite apart from the fact that the screen offers an almost limitless range of scales. If the database contains data for three dimensions, objects can be constructed and viewed from any angle on the screen. Moving parts can be 'moved' through their complete cycles to check clearances, and so on (see *Computers and Education*, vol. 5, no. 4, 1981, or *Microvision*, no. 18, Autumn 1981). But the means of input remain the keyboard and the tablet, often used in conjunction with a cursor, or pointer, on the screen.

Numerous design and graphics software packages are available for microcomputers that provide a simple means of drawing and colouring on a screen. The input device can be a 'joy-stick' which is used to indicate points where lines, triangles and circles are drawn, or areas to be coloured. An advanced system for microcomputers is the Bitstik that gives added precision through a zoom facility; an individual item in a diagram can be enlarged, details added and then returned to its original size.

Xerox Corporation has produced a versatile input terminal, with a larger than usual screen, plus the normal keyboard and a mouse. The mouse is a device for easily controlling input, rather than for making inputs itself. It fits under the user's hand and runs on the desk surface next to the terminal, being connected to it by a thin wire. In its back are two switches. The user moves it around the desk and each movement of the mouse is paralleled by a movement of the cursor on the screen, except that the cursor moves faster, therefore further, than the mouse. The user points the cursor at, say, an item in a list of commands on the screen and then presses one of the two switches to execute that command. Alternatively, the cursor can be used to define the corners of a figure to be drawn on the screen. Since the terminal is backed up by a large and sophisticated computer, experienced operators acquire great versatility in using the mouse. Other manufacturers are now producing similar systems (for example, the Apple 'Lisa').

Lightpens look like pens without nibs or points. They too are attached to computer terminals by a short length of wire, and each contains a photoelectric device responsive to light displayed on a terminal's screen. A user simply brings the pen close to the screen or even 'writes' on it. As with touch-sensitive screens, the computer is able to register the co-ordinates of the points touched by the pen. It is quite possible to use a lightpen to draw on one screen, in various colours and shadings if desired, in a way which is visible both to the author or artist and to those watching a number of screens elsewhere, linked by telephone line.

Optical character recognition devices are an important new group of input devices. They are used to scan written or printed characters, to recognise them, and, usually, to convert them into digitised code for storage, transmission and further processing. Among the simpler kinds, there are devices that read the numbers on cheques or the marks made by respondents on questionnaires and multiple-choice tests. The optical wands in stores, and recently in libraries too, to read black stripes of varying widths (bar-codes) printed on part of the packaging of goods or on a label placed inside each book, are optical recognition devices. The stripes represent coded letters and numbers, and the data from them are used for stock control. Computer programs can be published in magazines in bar-code format. 'Reading' them into a computer with a pen device avoids the time-consuming and error prone problems of retyping a listed program. More advanced devices will read several typefaces or fonts, including typescript. The most sophisticated read almost all fonts now in use, with remarkable accuracy and at very high speeds. Thus it is possible to insert into one of these machines a mixed set of magazine clippings, typescript from several typewriters, plus materials from existing books or journals, and from it will come, if desired, an edition set in whatever typeface we specify. As Gates (1980) says, such devices have the advantage of being able to transform text into digital codes for processing, at high speed.

Voice recognition devices are still being developed. The bulk of commercial products now available are isolated-word systems with strong speaker dependency. They allow limited commands to be given to a computer (such as simple numbers or keywords). Research continues into producing ideal voice recognition devices that can accommodate connected speech from any speaker. The potential of voice input is very high. It could, for example, relieve people from having to use keyboards or visual displays for long periods. Microphones are familiar as input devices, connected to other equipment, and so are optical cameras. Video or electronic cameras are new, however, combining as they do optics with electronics to turn the images entering the camera into analogue and, more recently, digital signals to be stored on tape. The size, weight, power requirements and price of these cameras have dropped sharply, while their efficiency has greatly improved (Hawker, 1981). A slowscan television camera can send pictures along ordinary telephone lines, a frame at a time, ideal for applications such as surveillance or calling up drawings from a distant archive.

Once one of these input devices has been used, how is information stored, or, to use the jargon, what are the storage media and devices?

Storage Media and Devices

Paper remains, for the time being, an important storage medium. Printed paper, product of the Gutenberg revolution, is far from being excluded by new information technology (Williams, 1982). True, the 'paperless office' has come to a few large companies and will come before long to many more, large and small. But it is not clear yet how paperless they will remain. The advent of optical character recognition actually favours retention of printed paper as a storage medium, since recognition devices form a technological bridge between our immense stores (in libraries, offices and law courts, for example) of printed paper and new forms of electronic storage. Printed paper stores information at a relatively low density, however, and for many applications is likely to be overtaken by storage media that provide much higher densities. The differences are emphasised by Evans (1981) who compares the 'data units' of print (the letter or number, two to five millimetres long) with those of computers (switches only thousandths of a millimetre in size).

Punched paper tape used to be vital to computer technology and to telecommunications by teletype. The 'ticker tape' of New

York welcomes is still in use for teletype machines, but it is a fading part of computer technology, even if some schools are still obliged to use it. Information is stored on the tape in code represented by the punched holes, which can be read back later. Punching it is a slow process and reading is not much faster. Paper tape suffers from being not very durable and comparatively bulky to store.

Similarly, punched cards used to be much more important in computer technology than they are today; they do not belong with microcomputers at all, for instance. Each card is punched with a series of holes which represent coded information, and the cards can be read by a card reader attached to a computer. This form of input is still in use for some purposes: for example, the responses to a questionnaire from one individual may be punched onto one or more cards which can thereafter be held for processing in various ways. Punched cards are again rather bulky to store although they are more durable than paper tape.

Magnetic tape is a standard storage medium in new information technology. As the tape, coated with oxide, passes over a series of drums it is magnetised by one or more 'heads' in extremely dense patterns that can later be read back by the same heads. The magnetic patterns, which can be recorded at very high speed, may represent coded information from a computer, or frequencies or pulses from a microphone or videocamera. There is audiotape, videotape and computer tape, but there is some interchangeability. An audiotape can be used to record a computer program, for example, and is indeed used in this way with several makes of microcomputer that employ an ordinary tape recorder as a storage device. Magnetic tape suffers from one or two disadvantages: the magnetic patterns can be damaged by mishandling or heat or a magnetic source, and it is quite difficult and slow to find information on a magnetic tape unless a high-speed tape drive is being used, as in mini- and mainframe computers. The reliability of this tape is signified by the numbers of magnetic tape videorecorders (about 800,000 in the United Kingdom, 1 million in the Federal Republic of Germany, 3.3 million in the US and 3 million in Japan at the end of 1981, and now greatly increased).

Magnetic discs are divided into two categories based on the flexibility of the material from which they are made: floppy and hard (sometimes called rigid). In both cases, information is stored on them in much the same way as on magnetic tape. A 'head' passes over the disc as the latter rotates at a high speed, and the disc is magnetised in extremely dense patterns that can later be read by the same head. As the head's movement across the face of the disc can be controlled with microscopic accuracy, it can 'address' any part of the disc to store information there or retrieve it, very quickly indeed. Hard discs, commonly known as Winchester discs, offer greater density and therefore greater storage capacity than floppy discs (floppies), although the latter can now store more than 300,000 characters on a single side, or over 600,000 characters on a double-density, double-sided eight-inch floppy. As a general rule, microcomputers and specialised computers such as word processors use floppies, although there is a trend towards hard discs. Both kinds can be damaged in the same ways that magnetic tape can be.

How do the different forms of storage compare in terms of capacity? Morgan (1980) suggests the *Concise Oxford Dictionary* as a standard: a five-inch floppy will hold 40 pages, a C60 audiocassette (magnetic tape) will hold 80 pages, a 15-inch hard disc two dictionaries, a 2400-foot magnetic tape four dictionaries. But optical and capacitance videodisc technology offers the most capacity, therefore it must be explained in some detail.

Optical discs, one kind of videodisc, store information as patterns that can be read by an optical device. Since such discs are attracting considerable attention, it is worth looking at the principal types. Phillips, the Dutch electronics company, are making a 12-inch disc which will store about 25,000 pages, coded into a spiral groove with 45,000 usable tracks (Klimbie, 1982). A very thin layer of a tellurium alloy is deposited on both sides of a metal base, and the groove is pressed into this layer. Every track is separated into segments, each segment having its own 'address'. To record on the disc, a laser beam melts holes at appropriate points in each segment, the holes corresponding to digital code. Each hole is less than one micron (about 35 millionths of an inch) in diameter, giving an information density much higher than magnetic discs (Schubin, 1980). Recording can be done only once. To read the disc, the same laser beam is bounced off the track. When it hits a hole it bounces back at a different angle. Since the laser can be directed to any track and any segment, immediate access to data is easy. A set of these discs held in a sort of jukebox provides a very large information store that can be consulted electronically from terminals in many places. One American system, manufactured by Teknekron Controls, is designed to store 22,000,000,000,000 bits of information.

The first optical videodisc system in public use was the MCA laser-read disc, very similar to Phillips' disc, with very small pits in an aluminised surface sandwiched between protective layers of transparent plastic. A laser beam is reflected differentially by the pits, which again represent signals encoded in binary, and the beam's position is determined by other encoded signals alongside the pits. One side of an MCA disc can carry all the signals required to record half an hour of colour television, including two sound tracks, or, if preferred, no less than 54,000 frames or over 40,000 pages of print holding about a million words.

An optical disc is durable, since the laser beam reads pits that are below its surface and ignores scratches or dust on the disc surface. There is no contact with the surface, therefore the laser 'head' lasts a very long time. Specialised equipment is needed to make the discs and it is much more expensive than, say, videocassette recording equipment. A videodisc player is rather more expensive than a videocassette recorder/player, although the prices may soon be very similar. The discs themselves are comparable in cost to videocassettes, but only when reproduced in large numbers. On the other hand, these discs are more compatible with computers and other digital information processing devices and transmissions systems than are videocassettes (Otten, 1980).

Another optical system in public use is made by Thomson-CSF. It has many of the features of the Phillips/MCA discs, but instead of bouncing the laser beam off a pitted surface, it shines a beam through the disc to a detector on the other side. The beam is modified by pits pressed into the surface of the disc. By changing the focus of the beam, it can be made to read either one side of the disc or the other.

Capacitance discs, another kind of videodisc, store information in grooves, rather like audiodiscs. The two principal types were developed by the Radio Corporation of America (RCA) and the Victor Company of Japan (JVC). In the RCA system the grooves guide the player's stylus across the face of the disc. JVC's system depends on signals in the grooves to guide the stylus, more like an optical disc. Capacitance discs are made of vinyl impregnated with carbon to make it electrically conductive. The stylus is diamond-tipped (JVC's is said to last ten times as long as RCA's) and it registers differences in electrical capacitance as it passes over pits in the floor of the groove. The discs contain one hour of video recording per side, twice what is available on optical discs. Both systems provide for some random access, although JVC's is more flexible. At present, capacitance discs carry only one sound track, although this may rise to two quite soon. The discs have a very high information density, like optical discs (Schubin, 1980), but suffer the disadvantage of being subject to wear by the stylus, especially where freeze frames are used. This problem may be serious enough to prevent much use of capacitance discs in education (Schneider and Bennion, 1981).

The chip itself can be a storage device, too. Indeed, most chips contain some storage. Within their miniaturised circuits information can be stored as electrical charges or as voltage or current levels: their switches can be set in particular ways which represent coded information. This form of electronic storage is particularly useful when relatively small amounts of information, say for control purposes, must be stored in a very small space.

One further type of storage: microform. Images (digital or iconic) can be reduced photographically to microscopic proportions and recorded on film. For several decades information has been stored on microfilm, but as optics and film manufacture have improved it has become possible to reduce the images drastically. Microfiche are pieces of film the size of an index card, each piece containing reduced images of up to 98 pages (Teague, 1980). Hyperfiche or ultrafiche are similar, but contain up to 3000 pages. Although microform storage is not electronic, it is worth mentioning here because systems exist that combine microform storage of, say, the documents of an insurance company, with new information technology. In one major system being marketed, all incoming documents are put onto microform in random order, each document being given an identifying number or address. Any document can then be called up very quickly, if not as quickly as in electronic storage, and its image transmitted elsewhere in the system as required. Moreover, 'micropublication' is possible (Otten, 1980) at the original size either on a screen or on paper. The Open University uses laser equipment which puts into microfiche computerised data, such as student records.

Terms employed for different kinds of storage or memory are, unfortunately, somewhat confusing. Let us start with serial and random access memories. Serial memories store information in sequence. They are relatively cheap per item of information stored, but finding a particular item takes comparatively long. Random access memories, by contrast, store information in rows and columns or in some other form that is instantly addressable, resulting in retrieval of an item of information with practically no delay (and are sometimes called direct access memories for this reason). Magnetic tapes and capacitance discs are examples of serial memories. Magnetic and optical discs, under the control of 'players', are random access memories. Chips are produced that have both kinds of memories. Then there are volatile and non-volatile memories. Volatile memories forget everthing if the power is cut off, but non-volatile ones do not. Most of those examined in this chapter are non-volatile, but some kinds of chips are volatile, so that, for example, many pocket calculators do not, after being switched off, remember the last answer. Finally, there are read-only and read-or-write memories. Read-only memories, known as ROMs, store data when they are first made and the data cannot be changed thereafter. Some chips are ROMs, and we could consider the optical disc as a further example of a ROM. Certainly the audiodisc or record is a ROM. Read-or-write memories contain information that can be retrieved and changed. Again, some chips are of this type, being confusingly labelled RAMs. RAM stands for random access memory, hence the confusion, although Morgan (1980) suggests that it might more appropriately stand for read and modify. ROMs in microcomputers are now of four sub-types: those on which programmes are stored during manufacture (mask-programmed ROMs), those that are programmable later, but only once (PROMs), those that can be programmed many times, called erasable programmable read-only memories (EPROMs), and, lastly, those that are electrically alterable read-only memories (EAROMs). The most important point to note here is that the distinction between ROMs and RAMs is being eroded.

Processors

Next, we consider processors, that is, devices and systems that are used to select and transform information. At the simplest level these are electronic calculators that can do no more than add, subtract, multiply and divide. Pocket-sized devices that go by the same name now carry out many more mathematical functions. Some are specialised to meet the needs of engineers, architects, navigators, businessmen or scientists. Almost all of them are designed to work with numbers, but it would be a mistake to think that this will always be so. Soon similar pocket-sized devices will be widely available to process words too; the first models are in the marketplace. In the meantime, something larger, a desktop microcomputer, may be needed to provide sufficient power and the peripheral equipment required for word processing. For very large storage and immense processing power, a mini-or mainframe computer may be necessary. To analyse a large amount of statistical data, for example, may well be beyond even a minicomputer if the statistical manipulations required are complex. To store many pages of text may not require a minicomputer, but to manipulate those pages may.

So far this chapter has looked only at the processing of numbers and text, both sets of digital symbols (see Chapter 7). New information technology can also process information in analogic and iconic modes. Computers help to edit audiotape and videotape. Sounds and images can be altered, enhanced or diminished electronically. Computer graphics is a fast-developing field, in which computers are extending the creative powers of designers and artists through giving them precise control over a graphic medium (see below).

Transmission Devices and Systems

Within the electromagnetic spectrum are frequencies used for radio and television, for conventional broadcasting. We start by considering devices and systems that use these frequencies, which lie between about 300kHz and 300MHz (Hz stands for Hertz, the unit of measurement, named after Heinrich Hertz, a German scientist, and equalling one cycle per second). Radio and television signals are broadcast by transmitters, normally through tall antennae, and picked up by much smaller antennae, which feed the signals to receivers. All this is well known. The range of transmitters varies considerably for radio, depending on the wavelength being used, while television transmitters have a maximum useful range of about 65 miles. To provide national networks for television, countries build repeater stations, which pass signals to each other, usually at microwave frequencies, above 300MHz, and along line-of-sight paths.

Satellites, which also use microwave frequencies, are bringing sweeping changes to broadcasting. Until very recently, satellites used for broadcasting were of relatively low power; indeed many of these are still operating. It is necessary to set up costly ground stations to receive signals from these satellites, in addition to the cost of building transmitters to beam signals up to them. Broadcasting companies take advantage of the services offered by satellite companies to bridge great distances, and round-the-world television broadcasts are commonplace. The most recent development in this field, however, is the direct broadcast satellite, which is very much more powerful and can broadcast signals direct to small dish antennae suitable for purchase by individual householders. These antennae require a converter, which pushes up the total cost a little, but no expensive earth receiving station is necessary. As satellites can broadcast to very large areas indeed, this is a significant development. A direct broadcast satellite is already in use in Canada, enabling television signals of high quality to be received in the remote communities of the northern parts of that country as well as in the more heavily populated south. Direct broadcast satellites are planned for several other countries, and are being adopted even in such a small and heavily-populated country as the United Kingdom, where the case for such a satellite was widely considered (Home Office, 1981) before the final decision was taken in 1982.

Other telecommunication tasks, as well as broadcasting, can be carried out by satellites. Voice and data transmissions are increasing greatly every year, and satellites are part of national and international telecommunication systems. American businesses that want immediate access to specialised market data can tune into a satellite which broadcasts market reports at regular intervals, in code, to those who have paid for the service. Similarly, specialised satellite broadcasts can supply continuous weather information over a wide area to farmers who have the equipment to pick up the signals, or to navigators at sea or in the air. Inexpensive narrow-band channels on satellites can carry signals for slow-scan television, suitable for teaching, tutoring, testing and teleconferences (Nettles, 1981).

Satellites have already proved so successful in telecommunications that the cost of sending and receiving signals has become less and less dependent on the distance they have to travel. Other terrestrial transmission systems being installed are also helping to make distance and cost less closely related so that, for instance, telephone subscribers are seeing international tariffs fall while local ones rise.

Some 20 years ago, each scattered community in countries like Canada had a tall television mast to capture signals from the nearest station or repeater, which might be 60 miles away, close to the line-of-sight limit for transmission. The signals were fed into a cable connected, for a monthly rent, to most dwellings in the community. Those on the cable were able to see very clear pictures on their domestic receivers, while their less fortunate neighbours could often see nothing but 'snow' on their screens. Often the mast captured signals from more than one station, bringing variety of programming, perhaps for the first time. The cable was of a special type, termed coaxial, and provided a one-way channel into the home for signals which occupied a fairly large amount of the Hertzian spectrum and were therefore called broadband, as opposed to the narrowband transmissions of radio or along telephone lines.

Within the past five years or so, a major change has occurred in cable systems (Smith, 1981). Businessmen and others have realised that the cable systems already installed in thousands of communities in Canada, the United States, Japan and several Western European countries, offer profitable opportunities to exploit the potential of new information technology in general, not simply television (see Large, 1982, for comment on British proposals). At the numerous 'ends' of a cable system, users may have at their disposal, within a few years, many of the devices and systems described in this chapter, plus those still on the drawing board. Most cable systems at the moment are one-way only, reminding us, perhaps, of Shannon and Weaver's model of communication, and the experimental two-way systems such as QUBE in Columbus, Ohio, are not without their problems (Kaiser, Marko and Witte, 1977). Clearly it is cheaper merely to deliver signals into homes and institutions, but two-way systems may be the norm for all new installations, at least in urban and suburban areas, within ten years. Much will depend on whether cable operators can be persuaded that the return on investment will be better than for a one-way system and that the greater capital risks are worth taking (Mason, 1977).

One of the most spectacular uses of cable has been to increase choice for home television viewers. In North America, the newest cables provide up to 120 channels, and cables with 36 and 48 channels are commonplace. Where does all the programming come from? The answer is that there has been a proliferation of specialist broadcasting. Stations aiming at relatively small groups, whether ethnic, religious, bound by language, interests or hobbies, now put out many hours of broadcasting each day. Cable operators charge these stations little or nothing to carry the signals, since they obtain cable revenues from those to whom the cable delivers. They can augment the number of channels by installing a satellite broadcast antenna to capture further broadcasts. By steering the antenna, signals from more than one satellite can be picked up (Bakan and Chandler, 1980). As each satellite may be broadcasting many or all of the channels being broadcast on another cable system elsewhere in the country, or even in another country, the potential for diversity is great indeed, although cable subscribers will have to pay more for some kinds of programming than others. In March 1981 no less than nine satellites were broadcasting on a total of over 70 channels beamed at North America. Consider, along with Mahony, Demartino and Stengel (1980), what possibilities and challenges the combination of cable and satellite transmissions open up for educational broadcasting in the United States.

The cost of installing and operating cable systems will fall, and their capacity to carry messages will rise, because expensive and bulky coaxial cable will slowly give way to fibre optics. An optical fibre is a hair-thin glass fibre, along which digitised information can pass extremely rapidly in the form of light pulses, each lasting seven millionths of a second. These pulses can now be generated by very small lasers which are manufactured cheaply in much the same way as the chip. A half-inch cable made of optical fibres can carry far more information than a four- or five-inch coaxial cable: a single pair of fibres carries nearly 2000 telephone calls simultaneously. Minute laser repeaters, installed within the optical cable, boost signals every 20 miles. Such cable systems have been installed on an experimental basis in the United Kingdom, the United States, Canada, France and Japan, and will become the new standard for terrestrial transmission systems. It is unlikely, however, that older cable systems, whether for telephone or television transmission, will be quickly replaced as there are considerable sums invested in them and it is costly to remove cables, particularly those underground. An interesting development in the United Kingdom is use of railways' rights of way for laying new cables, which can be easily placed alongside the tracks (Dineen, 1981).

The last transmission system we consider here in the context of new information technology is microwave broadcasting. The frequencies used fall outside the Hertzian spectrum and transmitters must have clear line-of-sight to the receivers. Microwave systems are particularly used to provide repeater chains between conventional television transmitters, but they also carry telephone and data transmissions over long distances between cities. Microwave towers, each in sight of the next, are now familiar in town and country.

What is vital to note about all these transmission systems is that, more and more, they provide connections between a wide variety of input, processing, storage and output devices and systems. Broadband transmission systems are usually required to link those that deal in moving pictures, because these pictures must be transmitted as a very large number of bits of information. Narrowband transmissions can be used for conveying messages that require fewer bits. Both broadband and narrowband systems are becoming more efficient, some remarkably so. The technical problems of communicating over large distances, of broadcasting to large areas, whether by television or radio, and of linking many people are no longer waiting to be solved. The combined power of devices and systems linked up in fast-reacting networks has yet to be fully exploited, but it is immense.

Even the telephone system is being transformed. For example, the United Kingdom has already a few digital exchanges. These are replacing electro-mechanical versions that have many moving parts, each worn out a little every time a subscriber places a call (Street, 1981). In a digital system, callers' voices are represented by pulses, not by a varying electrical current as in the old analogue system. The new equipment is cheaper to buy, install and maintain, and takes up much less space. Callers will be able to obtain step-by-step spoken guidance in placing difficult calls, provided by an entirely automatic computer program. The digital system will give access to both voice and data transmission services, at high speeds and without the need for the traditional modem device to convert digital signals into analogue ones. Some 200 British towns and cities will have the system by 1990, representing 5 million connections. Telephone companies in North America, Japan and other Western European countries are moving quickly in the same direction, and hope to challenge the cable companies by providing a range of services, such as electronic mail (Maddox, 1981).

Electronic mail is already present, particularly within individual large companies. *Communication News* for November 1981 reports on two systems installed by New York banking houses. Users type messages, with addresses, onto terminals. The messages are transferred via a computer to the addressee's terminal. He or she may retrieve messages by typing in an identification number. In one bank, there are now 350 users, 300 of them professional or managerial. By the end of 1983, 3000 staff will be using the system in this bank, but at the time of the report, 40 per cent of the messages replaced telephone calls, 40 per cent replaced memoranda and casual meetings and 20 per cent were judged to be new kinds of communications that had not occurred previously. In the other banking house, electronic mail is part of an integrated system, a paperless office. The system is integrated with word processors, adapted typewriters, telex machines and computers. Soon staff will also have portable terminals for use at home or when travelling. In this bank, managers were not told all the advantages of the system but have found out for themselves after basic training.

Output Devices and Systems

Next, there are the output devices and systems. Some are so familiar as to need little space here. Among the aural ones are the speaking end of the telephone, the earphones and loudspeakers that belong to radios and many other electronic devices, including now pocket calculators, clocks, microcomputers and educational games that speak or play music or emit other sounds. All of the last four contain voice or sound synthesisers, not tapes. In the jargon of the new technology, an aural display is part or all of the output. People are more accustomed to thinking of displays as being visual, but these devices provide analogic aural displays.

Many new electronic devices provide a visual display as part of their output. Visual displays are in either soft or hard copy. Soft copy is the term applied to a picture on a screen, or, for that matter, a set of letters and numbers on a screen. Soft copy becomes hard only when it is printed out, therefore teletype printers produce hard copy. A word processor produces first soft copy, which appears on its screen and can be manipulated in various ways, but then the printer attached to the processor can produce hard copy. Such a printer may be of several varieties, all the newer ones being largely electronic. Matrix printers have printing heads that consist of a matrix of, say, 9 by 7 pins that hit the paper in patterns corresponding to letters and numbers. Other printers use the old golf-ball or, more often, the new daisy-wheel, which has all the characters arranged at the ends of its 'petals'. Some form the letters through an electrostatic process, using special paper. These charge the paper in a pattern of dots similar to those produced by matrix printers, then the paper is passed through a toner solution that causes black specks to cling to the dots. More expensive ones spray a very fine jet of ink, guided electrostatically, to form the letters. Still others use heat or electricity to 'scorch' dots on specially-coated paper. All of these printers are very much faster than a human typist. Another way of describing them is as serial, line or page printers. Serial printers are like typewriters and print only one character at a time. Line printers are faster, printing a line at a time at rates of up to 3,000 lines a minute, and page printers are fastest. Perhaps the most impressive are the laser printers, working at 16,000 to 30,000 lines a minute in a wide range of fonts or typefaces (Jarrett, 1980). Printers are part of the new information technology: they have fewer moving parts each year and become faster and faster, with greater flexibility.

We should also mention phototypesetting equipment, which enables users to prepare text on a typewriter-like machine from which the output is a page that appears to have been typeset (Gates, 1980). Such machines are likely to change publishing practices.

Visual displays on television-like screens are vital for most computing, but particularly so for computer graphics. High resolution graphics is possible on screens that have more dots per square inch than those usually used. Computer-aided design equipment incorporates high resolution screens, introducing precision of control for designers and artists, as we have already noted. These screens are also becoming popular among those with microcomputers who like computer graphics as a hobby or an artform.

What is yet to come is high fidelity television broadcasting: it is noticeable that all television stations broadcast monoaural sound, unlike some radio stations. Predictions in the industry are that stereophonic transmissions will come soon, followed by high resolution on the screen. These broadcasts are technically feasible now, and one American satellite to be launched in the early 1980s will have the capacity to receive high fidelity transmissions from earth, for rebroadcast to what will be initially very small numbers of high fidelity domestic television receivers.

Adding speech output to a computer is a simple task. Many speech synthesisers are commercially available that can be connected to a computer in a similar way to a printer. When text is 'printed', the output is synthesised into speech rather than appearing on paper. The early synthesisers sounded unnatural but there have been developments that improve the quality, this includes copying the intonation patterns of human speech to remove the monotonous feature. Higher quality speech can be obtained from human speech which has been digitised, compressed, stored and re-called on demand. The disadvantage of this method is that large amounts of memory are required for only a few words.

Integrating Systems and Devices

From a layman's point of view, all these devices and systems for input, storage, processing and output may seem a bewildering array. There is a trend, however, towards integrating them. At the most miniscule level, integration, ever-increasing integration, is the target of manufacturers of chips. Above all, they want to miniaturise so that more components, more switches and circuits can be produced in integrated form on a single chip. Why? The chief reason is economic. The cost of manufacture is likely to drop still further. There is also an important technical reason: reliability is enhanced by integration. Chips that have passed the quality controllers are unlikely to fail, and if they do they fail early in their lives. Their reliability is very much better than that of wired and soldered circuits containing valves and electro-mechanical relays.

Integration is also the target of designers and makers of devices ranging from pocket calculators to large communication systems. Their desire is to increase the capacities and capabilities of these devices and systems. By integrating within a pocket translator, say, an optical character recognition device, a processor and a voice synthesiser, they may be able to market a device that actually reads aloud, in another language, the words printed in a foreign newspaper or a book. Such a technological dream device would probably do little to solve major problems of translation, as in literature, but it might be valued by those whose tasks include scanning of foreign publications. In the meantime, Sharp markets a pocket translator with plug-in modules for eight languages (for English, into German, Dutch, Spanish, Japanese, French, Italian, Swedish and Portuguese). Each module carries 2000 words and 152 phrases covering 14 of the most likely situations: air travel, customs, etc. The screen takes 23 characters; longer sentences roll across it at an easy reading speed. There is no voice synthesis, but that will surely be added soon.

On a much larger scale, systems are being installed to bring together a broad range of input, processing and output devices and to use them in conjunction with storage media and transmission systems to provide a widely distributed service, covering the whole of a single country or region. These major developments are dubbed 'The Network Nation' by Hiltz and Turoff (1978), who studied a well-known American project, the Electronic Information Exchange System (EIES) for scientific research communities, in which over 1500 people were linked through a central computer.

Teletext and videotex (viewdata) are both systems of this type, intended for regional or national implementation. Teletext systems are much more limited than videotex, being dependent on broadcast signals, either over-the-air or on cable, which can be converted into messages for display on a television set. They were pioneered in the United Kingdom, under the name of Ceefax (See Facts) and Oracle (Optional Recognition of Coded Line Electronics), by broadcasting organisations whose example was soon followed in several other countries. Technically, the signals are broadcast in the brief interval between transmission of successive pictures. A fairly cheap adaptor is necessary on the receiver before it can display the messages. The number of 'frames' or 'pages' that can be transmitted is quite limited, although Morgan (1980a) indicates that this will change. The viewer, with a keypad, can call up pages containing news, the weather forecast, market reports and other items of broad interest. The over-the-air systems are one-way, since the viewer cannot transmit back to the broadcasting company by a similar channel. It is possible, however, to broadcast programs (software) in the form of coded signals to micro-computers, as British experiments show, including those on Oracle (Hedger, 1980). New cable-borne broadcasting systems may be two-way, of course, in which case they approach videotex.

Videotex or viewdata systems, also pioneered in the United Kingdom, use a different combination of technology (Woolfe, 1980). Messages are displayed on the television screen, but they are delivered via telephone line, telephone set, modem (to convert analogue signals to digital) and an adaptor. With a keypad to select items from menus displayed on the screen, a user can search a vast library of information, much of it regularly updated by 'information providers', and can respond to any page, as the systems are two-way. Prestel, the videotex system being installed in the United Kingdom, has over 200,000 pages in its central computers. Similar systems are under development with government backing in the Federal Republic of Germany (Bildschirmtext), the Netherlands (Viditel), Sweden (Datavision), Finland (Telset), France (Teletel and Antiope), Canada (Telidon, and various project names), Japan (Captain), Switzerland (Videotex) and the United States (various private schemes). All expect to offer a wide range of information services to users in commerce and industry, with some systems adding services aimed specifically at the professions and education. Woolfe (1980) names many potential applications for videotex in the home: amenity and service listings, news, sports fixtures, weather forecasts, home education courses, welfare and consumer advice, travel and tourism, health information, advertising and selling, reservations, banking, entertainment and calculations such as tax, mortgage and discounts. To purchase goods and services, users can use the response keys, with or without credit card numbers. To date, however, domestic users in the United Kingdom are outnumbered by commercial, industrial and other institutional users. The French Teletel system seeks to offer a similarly wide range of services: in 1981-2 about 2500 households participated in a trial, with some households testing a 'smart card' for purchases, that is, a plastic card containing a microchip, and tens of thousands of these cards are being distributed for use in terminals located in shopping areas. In 1982, a special kind of videotex was installed in 300,000 French homes: the electronic directory service, as it has been called. Telephone subscribers have a new telephone, attached to a terminal with a keyboard and screen. With it, they are able to consult over 350,000 'white-' and 'yellow-page' telephone directory entries. Other services may follow.

In addition to such publicly available videotex systems, 'closed' systems, accessible only to a limited group of users but still using the public telephone lines, are being developed, such as Lawtel, a service for lawyers in the United Kingdom.

Devices and Systems for Disabled People

New information technology has many implications for disabled people. Of prime importance is the question of how the many devices and systems described in this chapter can be made accessible. For example, output devices (screen or printer) are designed on the assumption that a visual medium is appropriate; this presents an immediate barrier for the blind person. Keyboards assume a manual dexterity which may not be possessed by a physically handicapped person. Fortunately there have been many developments to overcome these barriers that have resulted in new or adapted devices and systems. Many will be described in later chapters in relation to the experiences of adults and children in education. We do not intend to describe every device and system that has been developed for disabled people as they are well documented in a number of publications dedicated to this purpose, and our prime concern has been with their use. The following are recommended as printed sources of information:

1. Electronic aids for those with special needs (1984). Handicapped Persons Research Unit, Newcastle-upon-Tyne Polytechnic.
2. Voice output for computer access by the blind and visually impaired (1983). *Aids and Appliances Review*, Carroll Center for the Blind, Issues No. 9 and 10.
3. Braille and computers (1984). *Aids and Appliances Review*. Carroll Center for the Blind, Issue No. 11.
4. Catalogue of vocational and educational aids (1983). Rehabilitation Engineering Center, Smith-Kettlewell Institute.
5. International survey of aids for the visually disabled (1983). Research Unit for the Blind, Brunel University.
6. International Software/Hardware Registry. Trace Research Center for the Severely Communicatively Handicapped, Madison, Wisconsin.

PART THREE
Experience in Using the Technology

9 EXPERIENCE AMONG PHYSICALLY-DISABLED PEOPLE

This chapter draws together information from three main sources: experience, as reported in journals and other publications and as described by contacts we made during the survey on which this book is partly based; technical details provided by researchers and manufacturers, and advice and opinions from workers in this field.

A fair number of published reports now exist about experience of use of new information technology by physically-disabled children and adults. Fortunately, some of the authors of these reports are physically-disabled people, who write first-hand. The record is not entirely about educational experience in classrooms; education, in a broader sense, comes to disabled students through using the technology in many different settings, with and without teachers. During our surveys, examples of such use frequently came up and they are quoted here, with names changed.

Besides this record of experience, researchers and manufacturers quite freely provide details of new devices and systems, some of which are only at prototype stage. A few firms publish evaluation reports or at least case studies of use of their products.

Against the background of this experience, workers in the field are critically analysing new theoretical developments, such as applications of artificial intelligence (see Chapter 19). They also offer much practical advice, an example of which follows.

Some Practical Advice

In a study at the Trace Research and Development Center for the Severely Communicatively Handicapped (University of Wisconsin), Armstrong and others (1983) compare different makes of microcomputers, assessing their suitability for use by physically-disabled people. From these comparisons it is possible to give some practical advice, in the form of a checklist of questions. Anyone thinking of buying a microcomputer-based system for physically-handicapped students will benefit from using the checklist. Some of the terms used in it are explained fully later in this chapter.

— Is the keyboard detachable (from the main system), to allow optimum positioning?

— When the keys are pressed do they provide tactile feedback, a 'click' or for certain uses speech?

— Is the keyboard the right size, neither too large nor too small for the individual?

— Is there a control key lock (to hold down the control key when required) as well as a shift lock key?

— Can the keyboard be fitted with a guard (see below)?

— Can the microcomputer accommodate a keyboard emulator (see below)?

— Does it provide for inputs from joysticks, paddles, single switches, lightpen, etc. (see below)?

— Does it have a touch-sensitive screen?

— Is the size of characters on the screen right, and are they luminous (as on a television set) or low-power (as with a liquid crystal display)?

— Are the characters upper and lower case, correctable, with a reasonable number (at least 20) per line and at least 16 lines on display at a time?

— Are computer graphics provided?

— Is the printer fast enough and paper handling easy enough?

— For processing and storage, is automation and speed provided through disc drives, especially with new 3 inch discs in sturdy plastic cartridges?

— Is the microcomputer portable or at least easily transportable?

— Is memory available that retains the program even when the computer is switched off?

— Is the memory size large enough (at least 16K for educational uses)?

— What software and hardware modifications are needed and available? For example, can a phone modem be used?

— Can the system be adapted to the individual easily? Does it have extra slots to accept additional devices or attachments?

— Is the system modular, permitting the user to purchase only what is immediately needed?

— Are there good repair and maintenance facilities?

In general, Armstrong and his colleagues advise that a physically-disabled person wishing to purchase a microcomputer should first define exactly the need, then consider whether a microcomputer-based system is the answer to that need. He or she should find out what suitable programs exist (because without them the computer is useless), and if possible should try them out on a borrowed machine. If the programs are right, there may be more than one make of machine to choose from, and the makes must be compared carefully, to match as many as possible of the individual's characteristics.

One further point of practical advice is worth mentioning here. Using a microcomputer is very much easier for disabled people if the software is able to 'boot' itself, that is to say, if it is able to work automatically, once the tape or disc is inserted, up to the point where a menu or other instructions appear on the screen. This autobooting cuts down the work required each time to get started.

A Model for Learning to Use New Information Technology

It is also valuable, in reading this chapter, to bear in mind a general model of how physically-disabled children and adults can learn to use new information technology, and Vanderheiden (1981) provides one. He suggests a four-level model. At the first functional level students learn how to make inputs through devices or systems of the kind described later in this chapter. In the second, they learn to amplify or expand information by using these devices and systems. For example, a single keypress may tell a computer to type or speak a whole sentence or more. Third, they learn to select programs appropriate to particular tasks. Finally, they learn to use functional programs for tasks such as word processing, calculation and graphics, and, if software is available to do so, to transfer data between them. With these programs they can carry out many activities in class or at work.

A British project based on this model is located at Hereward College of Further Education, Coventry. Many of the physically-disabled students there have workstations. Each workstation consits of a standard microcomputer plus extra devices and software selected on the basis of a very careful assessment of students' needs. There are two specialised input (level 1) devices as well as the microcomputer keyboard: a concept keyboard, a Microwriter, both explained in detail below. For level 2 use in workstations such as these, Pickering and Stevens (1984) say they will develop a prototype word processor that will provide better information amplification than existing devices (for example, Vocaid, below) and programs (for example, MAC, below), particularly through improving prediction of what information the user is trying to communicate. At level 3, the students will have programs for calculation and graphics as well as word processing, making up a kind of 'student's notepad', and will be able to select between them. At level 4, they will add to these a range of commercially-available programs.

A valuable modification incorporated in some programs is some sort of monitor that provides feedback on a student's progress in using the program. Sometimes the monitoring takes the form of a simple record of students' time working on the computer. In research projects, a very detailed record may be kept of how an individual student moves through the program, including when he or she backtracks and branches off, and what answers he or she gives to questions along the way.

Examples of Devices and Systems

Because formal education involves learning through symbols that must be created, displayed to others, stored, transformed and so on, new information technology can to some extent enable physically-disabled people to do these tasks, even if not as easily and quickly as able-bodied people.

Students need devices and systems that make communication possible, clearer or speedier, or all three. Most enable them to 'write' and 'draw', thus opening opportunities for communicating many forms of mental activity, ranging from writing letters to keeping accounts to writing computer programs to generating computer graphics. Being able to produce written work is clearly very important at school and other institutions of formal education, as well as for informal education.

The hardware can be divided roughly into input devices, processors and output devices. Often all three categories are combined in complete systems, and processors need not be described separately. For almost all of the devices and systems, software is necessary. Some programs are written specially for physically-disabled students.

Input Devices and Systems

Keyboards

As Hogg (1984) points out, teachers are understandably concerned that their physically-disabled students will not be able to use a keyboard. In fact, some who cannot produce legible handwriting can use unmodified keyboards with their fingers, toes or a mouthstick or headstick. If they find a manual typewriter too difficult because of the pressure needed on the keys, they may be able to type perfectly well on an electric machine. Alternatively, most models of electronic typewriters provide easy correction, a great advantage, and usually the amount of pressure needed on the keys can be varied to suit different needs. One small problem is that electric and electronic keyboards usually repeat the letter if a key is held down too long: for students who cannot remove their fingers or toes quickly enough, Vanderheiden and Walstead (1983) show how to modify the Apple IIe's circuits.

For some students the Maltron Scripta typewriter may be better. It was developed after careful study of how hands work, the positions in which they are most comfortable and the sequences of finger movements that can be made quickly (Hobday, 1983). It has a keypad for each hand, five inches apart, with special function keys (if required), in between. The keys are in scooped out sets for the fingers and two separate groups of up to nine keys for each thumb. The firm also makes a single-handed keypad, which has extra thumb keys, and one suitable for use with a head- or mouthstick.

Alan is a student who has cerebral palsy and cannot speak. With a Sharp Memowriter, which has a small conventional keyboard, a small flat screen and a printer, he works out simple arithmetic problems, using it as a calculator with a printout. When asked what year he is in, he quickly clears the screen and types in '2', and when asked his age, types '15'. He is very quick in answering, even beginning to type while the questioner is still speaking. His teacher encourages him to work out in his head the answers to the problems, before getting the calculator to print them. Alan uses the Memowriter for all his written work for school, such as English and History, and for general communication with other people. He is slow but very accurate in his typing and works well on his own (McConnell, 1983).

Jeff broke his neck several years ago but has been able to continue his Open University studies with the help of a word processing program and a Sinclair Spectrum. He finds writing very difficult but can type. He uses the program to prepare his essays in rough and then to add words and sentences or change paragraphs. He also keeps most of his notes on the computer and finds this easier than searching through sheets of paper. His chief problems are that he cannot easily handle the cassettes used for storage and searching through them is slow (Bate, 1983).

John, in his thirties, is severely disabled and unable to speak. He has some use of his left hand. With help from his wife he is able to use an Apple microcomputer for word processing to prepare his essays for the Open University, where he is taking a degree in art history and social sciences (Adams, 1983a).

Ruth is 14, but when she was 10 she received serious head injuries in a car accident. She is spastic, a quadriplegic with very badly impaired mobility and no speech. Her left hand is reasonably effective, but not the right. The family expected that her speech might be restored and apparently did not encourage her to learn to communicate through symbols and signs. At any rate, her interest in doing so was low. Before the accident, however, Ruth had possessed basic literacy skills and after it was very frustrated by having to resort to crude communication techniques, such as 'air writing' and gestures. She was provided with an Apple II, with a disc drive, printer and Votrax text-to-speech synthesiser (with memory). A program was prepared that gave her very clear spoken and visual instructions and prompts for using the system. The teachers considered carefully how they would introduce her to the system. They did not suggest that it was her voice, but that it was a substitute to help her express herself. When she was brought into the room, the teachers typed in 'Hello, Ruth, how are you?' and the system spoke the words. Ruth was surprised, impressed and a little puzzled, but after she was shown how to work the system, made it say 'Hello Phil', to her great pleasure. Subsequently, her typing skills developed markedly. Her motivation to communicate is 'colossal', according to her teachers. Her speed is improving. She understands the limits of the Votrax, tolerating its phonetic errors once she has checked her spelling. She invites people to come to speak to her. She uses the voice output for everyday requests and commands, and the whole system for word processing her school work (Hall and Turner, 1983).

Mandy is 16, and has cerebral palsy as well as being severely visually-handicapped. Meyers (1984) describes how she uses the Talking Screen Textwriting Program. Mandy had been trying for six weeks to learn the location of A and K on a school typewriter, but was frustrated by not being able to see the keys nor the typed letters. With the program, she now types letters to friends, shopping lists, and school work on an Apple keyboard, with voice synthesis.

For students with greater difficulties in hitting particular keys, a keyguard can be placed over the keys, permitting only one to be pressed at a time and then by the deliberate insertion of a finger, toe or mouthstick into the right hole. To reduce the number of errors, a time delay can be introduced into electronic keyboards, so that a key works only when it is held down for more than a fraction of a second. Accidental brushing of the keys may otherwise introduce much frustration.

Howard is twelve years old. He cannot use his arms or legs. Instead, he presses keys with a unicorn headpointer and can operate a very large keyboard this way. He succeeded, at the first attempt, in making the machine speak a sentence correctly. His intelligence also showed in that he used it to communicate his own opinions as well as factual information, and he accurately modified his spelling to obtain correct pronunciation. Because the boy is intelligent, he is able to use the device for his schooling (Duncan 1983).

Students are often so strongly motivated to use a keyboard that they find their own ways of pressing the keys, say Weir, Russell and Valente (1982), even by holding a pencil between their lips. Sometimes they show rapid improvement in control of direction and accuracy of limb movements.

The next degree of physical handicap, however, may require an enlarged keyboard, possibly again with a keyguard with holes. For example, British Possum equipment is now available with a Sinclair ZX Spectrum computer which has an expanded keyboard with spaced-out, recessed keys (see also Chapter 17).

The British SPLINK (Speech Link) system has a large touch-sensitive word board, with 1024 squares, providing for 950 common words, as well as letters. The student presses words, which appear on an ordinary television screen, and builds up sentences. He or she can also press letters to build up words, or phrase squares for basic phrases such as 'I want a'. Several boards can be used with a single screen, for groups.

Most models of boards take overlays so that the contents of the matrix can be changed for different users (children or adults) or different purposes, such as teaching different school subjects. For instance, the layout could be for the alphabet, BASIC keywords, the full range of computer codes, a chess board, coloured response areas, maps and diagrams, and so on.

The Star Microterminals concept keyboard, developed in Britain at Brays School, Birmingham, is also touch-sensitive. It consists of a matrix of 128 squares or boxes. Depending on the overlay in use, each box contains a picture, letter, word or even a phrase. Thus a box can represent a concept (hence the name). All the student has to do is press lightly the box he or she chooses, and this actuates a switch underneath. Such a board can be used for many purposes by children who cannot cope with an ordinary keyboard. For example, a child with a concept keyboard can control turtles (see below).

The Kirkby concept keyboard, also developed in Britain but at Springfield School, Kirkby, is divided into 32 squares, and, like the Star Microterminals one, can be used with different overlays and programs. Similarly, an American board, the Autocom, permits the user to select, store and display words, symbols, phrases or complete sentences by moving a pointer to the right squares. It is extremely versatile because it can be programmed at 60 different levels to suit different students and study circumstances.

Children use Bliss symbols, a 'code' of pictures, each always displayed with the relevant word, on concept keyboards and screens (see Bliss-Apple, below). They 'point at' particular symbols in turn, using various ways of pointing (see below), to convey meaning or even to build up sentences. This is valuable as those who cannot write any other way can at least prepare some 'written' work, and the output, in words, looks just like that of able-bodied classmates. In some schools children use them to communicate with each other, just as deaf children use signing. One early prototype system based on a Sinclair ZX81 enables very young physically-handicapped children to select one of four Bliss symbols displayed on a screen, by pointing a light beam at photoelectric detectors. They can 'find' 14 sets of 4 symbols each by shining the beam on two other detectors, which shift the sets from left to right or the other way across the screen. When they have chosen enough symbols to make up a 'sentence', they can print it out. Another prototype based on a BBC Micro will speak the symbols as they are chosen, in a child's voice. Yet another version will have a touch-sensitive screen, so that children will only have to touch the symbol they want (McConnell, 1983).

Arthur is only five years old. He has no speech but can control his limbs reasonably well. He uses a Bliss chart (160 symbols) and points with his fingers. The computer detects which symbol he is pointing at and speaks the sentence he puts together. If he wants to say 'I am thinking', he points to boxes for 'I/me', 'to be' and 'to think'. The computer can then work out the sentence, including its structure and intent, and is programmed with an elementary kind of grammar (McConnell, 1983).

Keypads

Other devices have keypads, not complete keyboards. In most cases, such as the Microwriter (already mentioned in Chapter 2), the keypad is part of the device, but in some it is separate.

Students can easily carry around the British battery-operated Microwriter, which was originally developed (and is still sold in large numbers) for ordinary business use. It is about the size of a large pocket calculator and has on it a keypad with only six keys, one a command key. Pressing the five main keys in various combinations produces letters, numerals and technical symbols in the device's small display window or on a television screen. As students write words and numbers these are either stored in the memory inside the device or can be transferred to external memory (directly to tape or via a computer to disc). The sixth key enables students to check, correct and edit the text or to send it to a printer. Without modification, Microwriters are useful to many physically-disabled students, partly because the keypad requires less strength and control of the fingers than a keyboard. Once resting on the keypad, a student's hand does not have to move, only his fingers. The keys require a light touch, but the amount of pressure needed can be adjusted. For some students, modified keypads can help, with fewer keys and/or voice output and/or braille output. A left-handed keypad is available. The 'Scanning' Microwriter has an array of lights instead of keys and can be controlled by a single switch (see below) of any kind. Students select the 'key' they want when it is lit. Another version can be used with an external keyboard, tailored to suit an individual student.

Edward is a severely handicapped teenager who attends Hephaistos School in Reading and uses a Microwriter to enable him to take examinations. He cannot use a full keyboard as on a typewriter but copes very well with the Microwriter keypad (Tait, 1983).

Some physically-disabled owners of Microwriters claim they can use the keypad for longer periods than they can an electric typewriter. A university teacher with spinal damage, who has to work on his side much of the time, uses the keypad at his side with the display above him on a separate lead. A physically-disabled student uses a Microwriter at school without problems because it is portable and quiet, compared to a typewriter. A haemophiliac who cannot write or type without bleeding internally, can use a keypad without difficulty. A college student with a progressive neurological condition successfully uses a specially modified keypad with both hands. A student with a neurological condition that affects her spatial perception (hence writing and typing) is using a Microwriter in taking an Open University degree. Another Open University student, who received a head injury and writes only with great difficulty, uses a left-handed Microwriter. Yet another not only used a Microwriter for his assignments but also wrote his final examinations with it. At a different university, a student who had poliomyelitis now uses the keypad adapted for use with her nose as she is athetoid and cannot use a keyboard.

Millar and others (1983) describe an intelligent keypad for physically-disabled students who cannot achieve precise positional control. It has eight keys, but when these are pressed in pairs a full set of characters can be produced. It also has a word store, and commonly used words can be accessed by pressing three keys in sequence. This enables disabled students to work faster than they could otherwise.

Single Switches

For those who cannot operate a keyboard or a keypad, single switches are available. These range from a baseball bat that must be moved to one side or the other (provided in one American school), to switches that must be pressed down by the hand, arm or foot, to puff-and-blow switches, heat switches, muscle (electromyographic) switches, eyebrow switches, cheekpads and head- or eye-movement switches. They can be used singly or in pairs.

At their most basic level, single switches have only two positions, on and off, yet with them many physically-disabled students can do a great deal, if slowly. Beukelman (1983) says that he and his colleagues in Seattle developed morse code as a communication medium for physically-disabled students, because when using it through a single switch they can still use their eyes to pick up other information. Moreover, anyone who can spell at about third grade level can learn morse code fairly quickly, and there is a hobby pay-off, because morse code users can become ham radio operators. Morse code is easily interpreted by computers, of course, and, using morse, students can select letters, words, even portions of sentences to build up what they want to write or say (speech synthesis is easy). So they can engage in word processing or programming, and the speed of input is good compared with other methods.

Lee goes to a special primary school in Manchester (Rees and Bates, 1982). He cannot move his arms or legs and cannot speak. Before using a microcomputer, he communicated mainly through eye movements. He was equipped with a headswitch and started by playing computer games, which delighted him. He moved on to a suite of programs that included schoolwork as well as play. His equipment was extended to a disc drive and printer, giving him opportunities to produce written work like other children. He is able to use all the programs and does so for a large part of the school day. His teacher can set him assignments that include spelling, making up sentences, unscrambling sentences, filling in missing letters and words, drawing pictures, doing arithmetic and answering questions in 'writing'. His programs include some for the teacher to use in setting his work: these do not require any programming skill for the teacher.

Some students have much more complex single switches with dozens of settings, which they select with great skill by, say, moving a foot. Perhaps some of these switches should not be called 'single', but they are not keyboards or keypads. Like a keyboard, they can be used to select symbols, send commands and so on.

In fact, students can use single switches to run sophisticated systems and programs, by selecting items from a matrix or menu. On a screen, a cursor usually moves around or scans the matrix or menu at a rate that can be varied to suit the student, who presses the single switch when the right item is being indicated. On a board, the squares light up in turn and the student must press the switch at the right moment. This scanning overcomes the problem of pointing, experienced by many physically-disabled students. An alternative screen method, rather slower, is for students to move the cursor one position at a time by pressing the single switch.

Thus students can select what they want from arrays of words, numbers, letters or even whole sentences. Many devices employ the same principle, usually with some form of scanning, and only a few are described here. The British Possum Scanner Input Control has a scanning light moving around the indicator panel, scanning it sequentially (not right to left AND up and down, like other Possums), which some find slow and therefore frustrating. Incidentally, Vanderheiden (1981a) suggests a way of improving selection by sequential scanning: set the device to scan very fast forwards and then, when the switch is pressed, to scan backwards slowly until the switch is pressed again. The ZYGO 100 is an American communication aid that enables students to select characters with one to five switches, from an array that is scanned by row and column. The array's characters are arranged according to frequency of use in spelling, not as a QWERTY keyboard. The ZYGO scanWRITER works in much the same way but provides a small screen display and a printer. The Chailey Communicator, developed at Chailey Heritage School and Hospital in Britain, has a blank grid of squares, each of which is illuminated in a scanning pattern, usually by holding down a single switch. Teachers enter words or letters into the squares to build a vocabulary suited to each student's needs.

Keith is six years old and has cerebral palsy. He works three times a week on an adapted Possum with an occupational therapist to help him. He uses cheekpads to operate the equipment, seated in a chair with a bar between his legs to increase his stability. He pushes the left cheekpad to track across the display from left to right and the right pad to track up and down, so that he can locate any box on the grid. The Possum display is laid out for him with coloured shapes, words, numerals and diagrams that can be changed easily. With the Possum, Keith is learning to discriminate between shapes and colours. When Keith's teacher asks him how old he is, he chooses the number 6 from the display. On some days, he has difficulty exerting fine motor control over the pads and has to start again, perhaps more than once. Changing from one pad to the other is hard for him: his head jerks from one side to the other and registers unintentional pushes. He can work more easily with only the left pad, but then scanning the display takes longer. To teach him to discriminate shapes and colours, the therapist first shows him wooden coloured shapes (for example, red triangle, yellow square, blue disc). She then hides one and asks Keith to select the box (on the Possum grid) that has a picture of that shape and colour. The exercise may not yet have much meaning for Keith, but he seems pleased with himself when he succeeds in making the right selection. He will move onto a full alphanumeric display when he is ready (McConnell, 1983).

Rhoda is studying for her O levels in Scotland. She is severely physically-disabled and has no articulation. She uses a Possum for all her school work. She started with cheekpads, one on either side of her head, which she used to select letters and symbols from the Possum display. She learned to scan the board quickly, especially when the system was later modified to operate with only one cheekpad, which she finds easier (McConnell, 1983).

Instead of a special device like a Possum, some students now use microcomputers with programs that provide a similar facility. For example, a single switch plus the British MAC-Apple program (see below) provides word processing of a special kind. Physically-handicapped students can do what they would otherwise be unable to do: produce written work for themselves and their teachers (Larcher, 1983). Gordon, with cerebral palsy, uses MAC-Apple and a single switch to select from the matrix of letters, words and numerals in the bottom half of the screen. He compiles his story in the top half of the screen. He can print it out so that his teacher can collect and check it, discuss it with him later or post it on the class noticeboard. Or he can use the output to control another computer loaded with conventional educational or game programs. Nixon (1983) quotes other examples of MAC in use. Bolton and Taylor (1981) describe their UNICAID (Universal computer and interface system for the disabled), which works along similar lines, as does MAVIS (now known as MASCOT), an earlier British system developed at the National Physical Laboratory and Loughborough University of Technology.

Like Lee, Jimmy has no speech. He can move his head to some extent, but not the rest of his body. He has been handicapped since birth. His only means of communication as a young child was through a code of eye movements. Questioners guessed what questions to ask until they got the right response. He quickly learned to use a single headswitch to operate a computer in a fairly primitive way. Programs written for him developed his scholastic skills such as reading and writing and gave him play opportunities. When he was provided with a micro of his own, plus disc drive and printer, he was able to join the class on a comparatively normal basis. He has a workbook, like everyone else in his special school.

Jane is a student in Northville, Michigan. She has cerebral palsy and is quadriplegic, with very poor motor control. She is very intelligent but has a learning disability that prevents her from learning to read. She uses a single-switch scanning system, but selects from what she hears rather than what she sees. Over earphones, the computer speaks words to her and she moves her head to operate the switch when she hears the word she wants. The computer is programmed to anticipate, to some extent, the next word in the sentence, thus speeding up selection. For example, if she chooses 'I am', the computer automatically goes next into its verb list. She can select tense, too (*Communication Outlook*, vol. 4, no. 2, 1982).

Clive is 14 years old and spastic, with no speech. He has no motor control apart from being able to raise and lower his right arm. He uses a switch with this arm to operate a BBC Micro with speech synthesis, for which software has been specially developed. His system works like a Speaking Possum, but it allows for progressively finer selections from each menu displayed. For example, after selecting 'food' from the first menu, he is offered a selection of names of foods to choose from, and so on. He only uses the system at school for 10-15 minutes a day, but it has helped him to start to read. He has another system at home for domestic communication (McConnell, 1983).

Peter is 13, with no speech and almost no controllable limb movements. He is able to operate a tilt switch on his arm: if he raises his arm, the switch tilts to on, and if he lowers his arm it tilts to off. At first he used the switch to select Bliss symbols (see below) from the computer screen but soon he moved on to selecting words and phrases. He now has access to a computer at school and another at home (Thomas, 1983).

Tim can control the movement of his head to the extent of bringing his left cheek closer to or away from a heat-sensitive switch, linked to a microcomputer. He started his education after years of being unable to do so (Nash, 1981).

Headpointers are best for some students. Adams (1983) refers to an American example, and Vanderheiden (1982a) discusses light-beam headpointers, which many individuals can use to select items much more quickly than by hand pointing, with or without scanning. Gunderson (1983) gives details of a long-range optical headpointer.

For students who have fine motor control over their eyes only, several systems are being developed. Two involve the wearing of special spectacles, with or without optical lenses (as required by the individual). In one prototype the wearer can see eight dots on the glass. Infrared sensors are able to tell which dot the wearer is looking at, and as each dot is associated with a symbol, eye movements can be used to select from among the eight symbols. Very young spastic children, however, have difficulty learning what to do and in selecting the right dot. In another prototype, developed at King's College, London, an infrared device fitted to a pair of spectacles detects eye movement and sends the data to a microprocessor, so that a cursor on the screen moves in the same direction as the eye movement, to the spot the eyes are looking at. Gazing at a character on the screen causes it to be selected, after a short delay, for use in a word. Thus students can build up words (Clarkson, 1981).

Another British eye movement system is being developed at St George's Hospital, Lincoln, for use on the BBC-B microcomputer. In this system, horizontal eye movement is measured by electrodes placed on the skin near the outer corner of each eye. Using it requires some training, of course, since the student has to keep his or her head still, as well as signalling by moving his eyes appropriately.

For students with very severe physical handicap Sutter's (1983) American work on gaze-controlled communication is particularly interesting because it involves computer recognition of wave-patterns in the visual cortex, that part of the brain handling signals from the eyes. The student does not have to keep his or her head steady. In the prototype system Sutter describes, the student selects any particular square in a matrix of 32 or 64 letters or numbers displayed on a screen, simply by looking at it for more than a fleeting moment. Each square flickers in a slightly different way, barely perceptibly. Two electrodes attached to the scalp at the back of the head pick up changes in skin potential and convey signals to the computer, which can recognise the signals coming from the square on which the student's gaze is fixed, and can put that letter onto a separate screen, print it out or speak it. The system could certainly be extended to provide words or even phrases rather than letters as output, thus speeding up communication.

An American input device that operates much as a single switch is Hansen's (1982) POS-1 prototype system. The student, who must have sufficient muscle control, touches with a fingertip a selected part of the microcomputer screen; this screen is 'touch-sensitive' in the sense that the computer can tell where it is being touched. Thus he or she can select items from the screen. This technique is likely to be used more widely soon because several manufacturers are marketing microcomputers with touch-sensitive screens.

For students with very poor muscle control, switches have been developed that depend on differences, picked up by electrodes, in electrical charges inside and outside the muscle cells. Some students use a single muscle that still works well, such as the pectoral muscle, to activate a switch. With electrodes attached to several muscles, quite complex coded signals can be sent, enabling selection of commands or characters.

What is important to realise in looking at this wide range of single switches is that the aim must be to individualise the hardware and software. One British school even has a rubber hot water bottle as a single switch that can be stamped on, and at Kirkby Springfield School (see above), the emphasis is on individualisation through tailored software.

Bar Code Readers

Bar code readers are now commonly used in libraries and supermarkets. A 'light pen' reads the code, a series of thick and thin black printed bars, and the information goes into the computer. In Britain, the Microelectronics Education Programme is developing an educational use for these readers, to enable students who cannot write to input computer programs by moving the pen over relevant bar codes. This has several advantages: it provides for error checking, it uses printing (which means that large numbers of copies are relatively cheap) and fits well into book production and distribution. Similar bar code readers could be used, of course, to input words, numbers or sentences.

Joysticks

Joysticks, available with many makes of microcomputer, are useful for some physically-disabled students, although many do not have sufficient control over their hand movements even when the joysticks are placed in their grasp. If they can select each of the four directions, perhaps to guide a cursor 'up', 'down', 'left' and 'right' on the screen, that is very useful, but they still need to be able to operate almost simultaneously a 'fire' switch, to command the computer to carry out something when the cursor is in the right position.

With a joystick called a BITSTIK, plus the accompanying programs developed by Robocom, a physically-disabled student with reasonable manual control can draw on the screen, manipulating a cursor in freehand, or using buttons on the device to join up points with straight lines of varying types and to draw curves. The cursor can be used to pick up 'pieces of line' from the margin, or to select from a menu of about 15 commands that includes 'erase' and 'colour', with 16 colours available. The student can 'zoom in' on parts of the 'drawing' where more detail is required, and can call up other parts, apparently moving around it. The image can be copied, saved and changed. There is a library of ready-made pictures that can be called up. Mudge (1984) calls it 'word processing with pictures'. This is a very user-friendly and comparatively inexpensive computer-assisted design device, available for Apple II and BBC-B microcomputers.

Rolling Ball

A rolling ball input device has been developed by the University of Manchester Institute of Science and Technology for athetoid children at a school in Walsall. Using this, such students can draw lines and construct geometric shapes, something they could probably not do by other means. They use gross forearm or hand movements to turn the rolling ball. The ball controls a cursor, which leaves a trace, thus enabling students to draw on the screen. The ball has different degrees of damping of its movement, to take into account differing degrees of athetosis.

Voice Entry

For students who have at least some speech, several voice recognition devices are available, with vocabularies of 40 or more words. They attach to popular makes of microcomputer. A user is 'trained' by the device to say the words (in any language) in a certain way to get results. Spoken words that are fairly unintelligible to a casual listener, but are spoken consistently that way, can be recognised by some of these devices (Barker, 1983). Students get 'voice on' experience rather than 'hands on'.

For example, the Voice Recognition Module is an American voice input device, capable of using a vocabulary of up to 100 words or short phrases. Its manufacturers, Interstate Electronics Corporation of Anaheim, California, claim that voice entry of data is 99 per cent accurate, higher than manual keyboard entry, for able-bodied operators, who require less training than for keyboard operations. Clearly, using the device has advantages for physically-disabled students who have speech.

The Voice Entry Terminal made by Scott Instruments of Denton, Texas, functions in a similar way when linked to an Apple II microcomputer. Software is available to help teachers prepare appropriate educational material, so that, for instance, a disabled student can take a multiple-choice test by reading the test item on the screen and speaking the answer. The computer will immediately tell the student whether the answer is correct. The same system can be used with commercially-available programs for drawing graphs and carrying out calculations. The computer can even be programmed by voice entry.

In the United Kingdom, the Department of Trade and Industry has subsidised development of VADAS (Voice Activated Domestic Appliance System), which disabled adult students will undoubtedly use for their own informal education. A large cabinet contains a VOTAN voice recogniser (made by Voice Input of St Ives) plus several 'domestic appliances', including television, stereo radio and audiocassette player, microcomputer, printer and voice synthesiser.

Output Devices and Systems

Screens

Microcomputers, without exception, use a screen as their main output device. The smaller flat liquid crystal screens on portable devices are useful, but larger video display units (VDUs, sometimes called monitors) and television screens are more versatile in that they can carry more information in larger script. Physically-disabled students may manage with fewer books and papers, which they find awkward to handle, by working on one or more screens. A particularly good British exploitation of the possibilities, for training of disabled computer programmers, is at Neath Hill (see Chapter 15).

Printers

For educational purposes, a printer of some kind is nigh essential. Physically-disabled students are gratified to see their work clear and correct on a screen, but they also need the satisfaction of providing their teachers and others with properly typed work, which a printer enables them to do.

Specialised printers are required for Bliss symbols. One prototype, developed in Britain at Chailey Heritage, is portable and self-contained, but capable of printing all the symbols on the United Kingdom Bliss charts.

Voice Output

For physically-disabled students who are also unable to speak, many systems now have speech output (see also Chapters 10 and 12). For example, the American Vocaid, developed by Texas Instruments, has a touch-sensitive matrix of 36 squares, for which several overlays are available. It was developed from Touch and Tell, a Texas Instruments educational aid, and uses the same keyboard, case and some of the original circuits. It produces four basic sets of 35 spoken letters, numbers, words or phrases, in an American-Dalek kind of accent. New memory modules can be fitted to provide further sets. Eulenberg and Rosenfeld (1982) say it is best suited to people with short-term speech loss, perhaps after an operation on the vocal tract, who have fair to good dexterity, as well as good sight and hearing.

Other Devices and Systems

Logo Turtles & the BBC Buggy

Physically-disabled students like Logo turtles, but these are not toys. They were designed by Papert (1980) to serve a serious educational purpose. Papert shows how Logo gives able-bodied children an opportunity to construct drawings in a particularly conscious way, which he called 'turtle geometry', and physically-disabled children benefit similarly, as at the Cotting School for Handicapped Children in Boston, Massachusetts, where students spend two 30-50 minute sessions each week using Logo (Roberts, 1983a). They operate the original screen version of the turtle, which, as it moves, leaves a trace or line. By changing the values for input variables, students can discover how to draw many shapes and, by combining sets of commands to repeat designs, learn Logo programming. The relationship between programming actions and their consequences is very explicit.

Papert also developed a floor version of the turtle, powered by electric motors. Floor turtles are now produced in several models by different companies. They run around the floor, or on a board covered with white paper, in response to Logo commands from a microcomputer controlled by the child. They go backwards, forwards and turn at various angles, draw with a pen, and play a tune to reward a student's efforts.

On the floor or on the screen, the Logo laboratory is, among other things, a place where concepts of physical space and shape can be explored. Weir (1981) claims that, in turtle geometry, students use their 'intuitive body knowledge about moving around in space' to gain understanding of certain mathematical ideas. This kind of learning by doing is particularly important for individuals who have been prevented by physical handicap from manipulating concrete objects.

Logo concentrates control in the hands, disabled or not, of the student. To teach the computer to carry out a particular task, the student has to instruct it precisely. To instruct it precisely, he has to understand what he is trying to do. In constructing a program, the student constructs a mental model too, and understanding increases. Logo provides ways in which physically-disabled students can carry out a programming action, see its immediate consequence and change it if they wish.

Weir, Russell and Valente (1982) note:

A severe physical handicap imposes a dependent, passive role on its victim. The uncompromising way in which Logo places initiative and control in the hands of the users allows them to have a direct effect on their environment. The Logo experience is often the first in which disabled students tackle problems which require them to initiate solutions, try them out, respond to feedback and decide whether to change track or to persist — all those things that tend not to happen in the dependent situations that typify their lives and most of their schooling.

The same team also mentions a remarkable example of a physically-handicapped student progressing through Logo to computer programming. Mike has cerebral palsy and is quadriplegic, with poor speech. He cannot use a pencil, but at the age of 17 started to spend six to nine hours a day working at a school computer. He used a Logo computer during school holidays. He became a competent programmer and went on to study for a degree in computer science at the University of Massachusetts.

Sprites, which appear on the screen in different colours and shapes, are like screen turtles in that they can be moved around. Emmett and Johnson (1983) report on using Logo turtles and sprites in Shawfold, a British special school at Stockport and say that the sprites caught the children's imagination first, because of the movement, colour and shape. The children learned to move them around the screen, using appropriate commands. In due course, they began to write their own short programs of commands. Next, they began looking at turtles during a mathematics class on shape. They soon learned to control turtles, too, and then to combine them with sprites. The teachers say that the children were learning about directionality, orientation, colour recognition, letter discrimination and fine motor co-ordination. Hogg (1984) lists other possibilities.

The BBC Buggy is a turtle-like robot developed in Britain for the BBC. With a BBC-B microcomputer and a small set of programs, a physically-disabled student can give the robot instructions and then observe how it behaves, in much the same way as with the turtle. The Buggy is a three-wheeled vehicle with several sensors, including a light-sensor. It can be fitted with a bar code reader, an up/down pen, and a grab arm that picks up and puts down small objects. Thus it has more potential functions than most floor turtles, although Papert's prototype had several of these features.

CAD/CAM Systems

CAD/CAM (Computer-Assisted Design/Computer-Assisted Modelling) systems enable physically-disabled engineering draughtsmen who can use a keyboard to 'draw' just as well as able-bodied colleagues using the same equipment, and, similarly, they can write programs for computer-controlled production equipment. In Britain, Queen Elizabeth's Training College for the Disabled, at Leatherhead, is pioneering this application with its students. Rochester (1984) reports that students are introduced to the Marconi Quest Quadrant system for computer-aided draughting in about their 23rd to 26th week of training. They spend about four weeks on the system, followed later by another two weeks on learning how to program a computer-controlled training lathe. Students can greatly increase their productivity through using the system. Rochester says that it takes the average student two days to become familiar with the keyboard and its functions, then another three days training is needed to produce simple drawings. After that, progress is more rapid. The College will in due course no longer use conventional equipment.

Toys

It is sometimes difficult to distinguish between devices that teach and toys from which disabled children can learn. Toys that respond can motivate children to do what they might not otherwise be interested in doing. At a sophisticated level, toys that react to electrical signals by moving, lighting up or making sounds can be linked to computers and used to motivate children to answer questions or carry out activities suggested through the computerised teaching system.

   Much simpler toys can also be useful. For example, the Sound Bubble, developed in Britain at the Handicapped Persons Research Unit at Newcastle-upon-Tyne Polytechnic, looks like a toy and helps very young physically-handicapped children to learn simple hand-eye co-ordination, which is rewarded with a tune.

Enabling Software

Disabled students gain access, through new information technology, to the best educational software accessible to able-bodied students. In addition, however, much software prepared for use by physically-disabled students consists of what Head and Poon (1983) call 'enabling programs'. These programs make it possible for students to become less constrained in the classroom by their disabilities, and to achieve a substantial degree of autonomy. For instance, software can be developed to increase the range of what a student with cerebral palsy can do with only a few keypresses. A board being used at Michigan State University has the usual standard set of words, but also has a set of 'strategies'. Thus the student presses the key for 'stomach' and by pressing the 'action with' function key he can get 'digest'. Another function key provides synonyms. All these words are spoken by a voice synthesiser, under software control.

Through enabling software, students may be able to work through conventional, non-computerised teaching material as well as gaining access to ordinary computer-assisted learning. Here are some examples:

For Writing

Wordscan, developed in Britain by Head and Poon (1983), offers students and teachers a kind of 'authoring system' into which they can enter their own choice of words, without any programming skills. This means that the system is adaptable to different students' needs and different subject matter. Once the words are entered, students can work through a series of multiple-choice tests, the answers to which are embedded in word lists from which students choose (with a single switch or other input device) the right answer. Poon has also developed Sentence Scan, which lets students build sentences on the screen in large letters, and speaks them.

Another British enabling program, called Microprocessor Assisted Communicator (MAC), was developed by Poon for use with first a NASCOM 2 and then an Apple II microcomputer (Head and Poon, 1982). Physically-handicapped students select what they want with a single (or double) switch from an array of letters, punctuation and/or words on the screen. The word lists can contain up to 1,500 words and can be altered without difficulty by teacher or student. The program provides word processing and students can draw line diagrams with it. For arithmetic, students may enter their answers from right to left, units column first. MAC-Apple can be linked to another microcomputer so that letters and words selected on it are sent to the other computer, thus enabling students to run ordinary programs, including games and computer-assisted learning.

Abraham is almost entirely deaf and mute, although he wears two hearing aids and does occasionally make sounds. He walks with an awkward gait, but has good eyesight. He signs well now, except that the finer points of some signs he may miss because of his athetosis. Because signing by the teacher is always accompanied by the spoken word, this encourages Abraham to lip-read. There are some distinctions, fundamental in English grammar, that cause problems, however, such as use of 'has' and 'have' with the correct number, as in 'the dog has' and 'cows have'. Abraham shows that he has grasped these distinctions and can use them correctly in making up his own sentences from a selection of whole words supplied on the Kirkby keyboard. He can use the conventional QWERTY keyboard, normal size, to get the Apple microcomputer started and to type in commands, and knows well the routines.

Abraham can also use the MAC-Apple to compile a sentence for his news, a diary of events. He consults his teacher to obtain her approval, first for the general topic and then for each word. Most of the words he finds in wordlists built up for him previously by his teacher. To find a particular word he needs two keypresses; once found, the word is selected with one more keypress. Some words he knows how to spell, but he still seems to prefer to use the wordlists. Some said he and other children would never learn to spell, but the teacher thinks they are learning, and meantime they have a much richer vocabulary to work with. Many of Abraham's diary entries are long, over 100 words, and perfectly comprehensible and interesting. His work seems slow compared to that of an able-bodied child of that age, but his progress is quite phenomenal compared with that of children with the same disabilities who have no computer assistance. His own attempts at writing and drawing by hand are pitiable.

Likewise, at Claremont School, Avon, another athetoid boy with a severe speech disorder and very poor fine motor control uses MAC-Apple to give himself almost total independence when preparing, correcting, storing and printing out all his 'written' school work.

Kathy, a girl with cerebral palsy, aged 12, who can use only one hand, who cannot walk and who has no speech at all, wrote for the first time a complete sentence on the screen using only two switches and the MAC-Apple program. She then gave the 'print' command. Her teachers were very moved to see the delight on her face as she heard the clatter of the printer and watched the script being handed to her (Griffiths, 1983).

Physically-disabled students in Britain also have Autotype, a program developed by Leonard (1983) for the BBC-B microcomputer and printer. It enables them to produce typed output. Input is via any single switch, such as the spacebar on the keyboard or a pressure switch. Letters and numerals appear on the screen in a matrix 11 × 6. One press of the switch moves a cursor along the columns at a speed that may be varied. Another press causes the cursor to descend, and a third selects the letter or numeral on which the cursor is resting. If a letter is selected, the student has three choices: the letter itself (upper or lower case), 'no' (which returns him to the start), or asking for a list of words that start with that letter. If he chooses the list, he can then choose a word from it, by further use of the cursor and switch presses. The program has many other word processing features, some specially adapted for single switch operation.

Another British program for these students is Disc Words, developed at a school in Manchester (Rees and Bates, 1983). The program is content free, in the sense that the teacher or the student can decide what words to put into it. It comes close to enabling the student to use a paper and pencil, the screen being treated as a page on which the student (or his teacher) can write, draw or move characters about. Rees and Bates give seven examples of its use: to display pages of text and to 'turn' them at the press of a switch; to provide complete words for sentence building; to copy sentences, fill in missing words or letters, and rearrange jumbled sentences; to match and sort characters on the screen; to draw pictures, trace outlines and complete shapes, and to play games with other students.

In Newcastle-upon-Tyne, Flanagan (1983) developed a suite of programs called Handisystem for use on the Apple II. Handispell is in four versions. Handiwriter enables physically-disabled students to select words from lists, for use in writing BASIC programs or for word processing. Handidraw is for drawing pictures and colouring them. Handiexam provides a simple system for taking exams through multiple-choice questions entered by the teacher.

The Combat Authoring System is a British authoring system for use in preparing computer-based training. Physically-disabled students at Stoke Mandeville Spinal Injuries Unit have tried it, with suitably adapted hardware, but the programs are now being modified and improved (Fountain, 1984).

Bliss-Apple is a suite of programs for writing in Bliss symbols (created to enable speech-impaired people to communicate) with Apple II computers. Pre-programmed symbols can be selected from a library of 1400 to make up a user-specific set, and the user can create new symbols or modify those from the library. A complete message can be displayed on the computer screen and up to four physically-disabled children can use Bliss-Apple to communicate with each other. With a matrix printer, the symbols can be printed out, too.

For Drawing

We have already mentioned the BITSTIK and its programs (Mudge, 1984), which together probably offer the best drawing facilities for physically-handicapped students who can control their hand movements sufficiently well to use the joystick and buttons.

Logo turtles can draw (see above), but several other drawing programs are available. Wigley (1983) reports on a British program called Etch-A-Sketch (one of a series produced by Poon) which enables students to draw simple pictures on the screen by using six switches mounted in a board as squares that must be pressed. Each switch produces a musical bleep to aid recognition.

Cage is a British program, originally developed for the Sharp MZ80K microcomputer, but adapted for the BBC-B at Woolley Wood School. It is a teaching program generator, with 14 subroutines that allow teachers to draw and present learning tasks. Young physically-disabled children interact with the program by drawing shapes on the screen, using the keyboard or switches.

A graph drawing program has been developed at Hereward College, Coventry, for use with a BBC-B microcomputer. Physically-disabled students can use it, with a keyboard or single switches, to draw graphs and print them out.

For Composing Music

Wigley (1983) also mentions two other British programs designed to enable physically-disabled students to create sounds and compose music. Organ attaches a sound effect, musical note or tune to each of six switches, and Composer uses the same switches to allow students to compose and then play any simple tune.

For Speaking

Two American programs for either speaking or printing output are available from the Schneier Communication Unit, Cerebral Palsy Center, Syracuse. Say It is an enabling program to help physically-disabled students. Inputs are via any kind of single switch. Quick Talk requires students to use the number keys on a microcomputer. Each one can generate his or her own vocabulary of words or sentences, stored by the computer in categories organised by number or letter (for example, H for holidays).

American software prepared specifically for physically-disabled students is catalogued by Vanderheiden and Walstead (1983). They describe other enabling programs for writing/editing, drawing, mathematics, English language and vocational guidance, as well as for general communication.

Summary

Some of the information technology mentioned in this chapter has been available for quite a long time, as in the case of the Possum range. The latest microelectronic devices and systems are smaller, easier to use and carry, faster and more powerful. They offer a wider range of options for learning to physically-disabled students, whose input and output problems can now be more easily reduced or overcome. In many cases, the result is greatly improved communication between teachers and their students, and between students themselves, in fact, better education.

10 EXPERIENCE AMONG BLIND AND PARTIALLY-SIGHTED PEOPLE

Recent developments in technology create the most promising possibilities yet available for solving or mitigating the problems of visually-handicapped people. Significant advances have been made already with microelectronic devices that can assist in both reading and writing. Paradoxically, the technology which offers this potential can also widen the gap between those with and without a visual handicap. This possibility exists in relation to employment where the number of computer-related jobs has increased rapidly, and in education with the wider use of computer-assisted learning. In drawing together experiences of new technology among visually-handicapped people, we refer to developments that seek to overcome both the long-standing problems associated with reading and writing, and the more recent problem of keeping abreast of the use of computers in education.

Access to Printed Material

Braille has been a very important medium in making printed material available to blind people. One of the limitations of this medium for the production of the wide range of material in education, has been the need for skilled people to transcribe the text into contracted (grade 2) braille. An acute shortage of such people, and the length of time associated with manual transcription, has meant that the demand has always exceeded what can be produced. In this context, the development of automated methods has made a significant contribution. Several computer-based systems are now available which translate text to braille. Typically, such a system will consist of a microcomputer, printer and embosser. Software facilities will be available on the microcomputer for the entry of text from a standard QWERTY keyboard, editing of the text, and the subsequent translation of the text into braille. The edited text can be printed out for verification or for a sighted person, and the braille version embossed. A significant advantage of this type of system is that the operator does not need to have any knowledge of braille.

A British Pilot Study

The translation of text to braille is a complex process as the braille used by most people is a natural language, context sensitive, being made up of letters, numbers, punctuation, and a set of about 200 abbreviations and contractions. A typical British microcomputer-based system is the one developed by the University of Warwick Research Unit for the Blind (Gill, 1983). Although it was first used for the internal needs of the Unit, the system became commercially available (BITS system). It was included in an educational pilot study, entitled 'Information Technology Driven Direct Braille Translation in Schools', at Chorleywood College.

Chorleywood College (for girls with little or no sight) was chosen for the pilot study as it had been involved in the use of computers since 1969. The College maintains a very varied curriculum, and has an excellent record of high academic achievement. In order to support the wide range of subjects offered, girls frequently attend local secondary schools. In these cases, the College assists by providing class material that has been transcribed into braille. The Royal National Institute for the Blind (RNIB) provides brailled examination papers and text books; however, most of the class material is brailled by the College staff. In this context, there is clearly the need for a large amount of educational material to be produced in braille; hence, the establishment of a pilot study to examine the role of automated braille transcription within an educational environment (Markes, 1983). Three principal reasons were given for the study:

1. It would provide a system where an ordinary typist could prepare class material without knowledge of braille.
2. It would release more staff time which could be used in teaching rather than in preparing braille material.
3. It would lead to a clearer understanding of what technology might provide in the future.

A preliminary report (Crosby, 1983) on the first phase of the pilot study on the introduction of the microcomputer based transcription system indicated that it had been used in a variety of ways:

Teachers have used it to prepare examination papers and work for the girls; braille for the blind and print for the partially-sighted. One of the most significant uses was the recent production of poems for the English Department by our CSV (Community Service Volunteer), who has no knowledge of braille. It is planned to produce a larger collection of ballads in the near future.

This represented an important breakthrough with, for the first time, the involvement of a non-braillist in the production of braille material at Chorleywood College. However, it was at the braille embossing stage that a limitation of the transcription system was experienced. At an embossing rate of 15 characters per second, 20 copies of typical class material (five pages of braille) could take up to one and a half hours to produce. This limitation can now be overcome with embossers that operate at 160 characters per second which significantly increases the output rate of the braille, but at present the cost might be a limitation for an individual school.

Alternatives for Text Entry

Typing in large amounts of text for braille transcription remains a time-consuming activity, hence, other methods that can replace this feature are important to consider. Two methods that are relevant to this need are Optical Character Recognition (OCR), and the transmission of text from other digital sources that have been used to create original text. The use of OCR is important for text that is already in a printed form as the text can be 'read' by the OCR device, converted to a digital form, and stored on magnetic tape or disk. The digitised text can then be input to a braille transcription system directly without the need for it to be typed again. As an OCR device can be 'trained' for a wide variety of typefaces, it can accommodate most needs. However, this technique would seldom be necessary if all printed text was prepared by computer typesetting. In this case, the text is digitised at the start of the printing process then, potentially, it is available for other processes including transcription and embossing. If, as we hope, transferability of such information can be successfully achieved the amount of brailled material will be increased substantially, as well as produced in a much shorter time.

Automated braille production has important implications for

education as with it the range and amount of course material could be increased. The semi-automated process with text entry from a keyboard provides a complementary facility for a teacher preparing class material. Not only does it ease the preparation of the braille copy, but the simultaneous output of a printed copy means that the material can also be used by sighted or partially-sighted students.

Non-braille Devices — the Optacon

One device which gives access to printed material without using the medium of braille is the American Optacon. It is a compact, portable reading system which gives an immediate and independent means of reading print. The Optacon converts regular print into a large vibrating image in a tactile form. To 'read', a miniature camera is passed across a line of print. As the camera passes a letter, the image is simultaneously reproduced on a tactile array (approximately 1 ½″ × 1″) of vibrating miniature rods on which the index finger rests.

The camera has a silicon integrated circuit with 144 light-sensitive phototransistors; there is a corresponding number of miniature rods which vibrate in relation to the independent outputs of each phototransistor. Collectively, this produces a vibrating image. As the Optacon will display any image under the camera, it can be used for all types of printed material. Not surprisingly, it requires a significant amount of training to master the skills demanded by the Optacon for effective reading. Once mastered, it provides a blind person with an independent and non-linear means of reading text and, very importantly, it does not require any modification to the source material. Terzieff and others (1982) undertook research into the development of alternative training methods that could increase reading rates. They found marked increases with instructional material based on structural and functional aspects of language, cloze procedures and auditory pacing.

The Optacon has played a significant role in two extensive school programmes: one in Italy, and the other in the United States. In Italy, the emphasis is on providing support to mainstreamed students. Students (36 in one year) are integrated into regular schools with special support from a group of teachers and social workers. This integration includes daily living skills, mobility and typing in addition to training in the use of the Optacon. Each student is provided with an Optacon with the help of regional government funds. The scheme is operated through the David Chiossone Institute (DCI) whose director, Dr Massimo Campo (1980), reports:

> Our alternative experience of deinstitutionalisation and social integration of the blind has grown with the Optacon and, in many cases, has been made possible by the Optacon ... Young people of Liguria now attend normal schools, using the Optacon for reading the usual text books while continuing with braille for personal use on the rare and lucky occasions when relative text exists.

Teaching methodologies associated with this project have been developed and evaluated as part of a research programme. Testa and Venturini (1980), the researchers, say that 'children in the fifth grade, after four weeks of Optacon training, showed an increase in their desire for independence, cognitive progress, and socialisation'.

In the United States there have been several years of Federal Government funding of Optacons. This has included equipment for teacher training sites at universities, student training sites at residential and public schools, and for students declared independent readers. The programme has served over 1000 school students, with ages ranging from four to twenty.

In the United Kingdom, the use of Optacons in schools has been limited. This is, at least in part, due to the lack of government funding in schools, although the Manpower Services Commission has provided blind adults in employment with these devices. An evaluation study (Tobin, 1974) at the Research Centre for the Education of the Visually Handicapped indicated some caution for the use of the Optacon in schools. The report suggests that

> ... with letter-by-letter presentation of an unstable image (unstable because of the vibrating nature of the stimulus and the distortions produced by fluctuations in the reader's fine-motor co-ordination), the reader is having to hold information in store while locating, identifying, and integrating the additional information needed to bring about correct labelling of the whole word or phrase.

In employment, adults are benefiting from using the Optacon, and the adaptation of its use with a VDU enables blind people to work as computer programmers.

Koyanagi and others (1981) report a study of tactile reading training with the Optacon for the Japanese language. Initially, it was expected that Katakana and Hiragana characters could be read as the shapes of letters are similar to the alphabet. It was later shown, however, that the more complex shapes of Kanji could be accommodated, and it is reported that a 5th grade elementary schoolchild learned to read Kanji correctly.

The Optacon heralded a new era for blind people as it was one of the first attempts at applying 'new technologies' to overcome reading problems. By December 1983, 9462 Optacons had been distributed worldwide, as shown in Table 10.1

Non-braille Devices — the Kurzweil Reading Machine

For some time, visually-handicapped people have used the auditory sense to receive information that sighted people receive visually. There has been widespread use of 'talking books' (audio cassette recording) with recent enhancements including compressed speech which can be replayed at high speed whilst, at the same time, maintaining normal pitch. It is in the area of synthetic speech that many innovations and advances have been made. One such American development has been the Kurzweil Reading Machine (KRM).

The KRM can read a book to a blind person by tracking over the pages, reading the characters optically, assembling the characters into text and converting the text into synthesised speech. The tracking and page selection can be controlled by the user. Central to this device is an Optical Character Recognition (OCR) system

Table 10.1: World-wide Distribution of Optacons (Telesensory Systems Inc., 1983)

Western Europe	2831
Eastern Europe	100
Middle East/Asia/Far East	719
Central and South America/Caribbean	136
Africa	64
USA and Canada	5612
Total	9462

which recognises printed characters (most type faces) in any text. The characters are grouped into words which are then analysed for pronunciation. The pronunciation is achieved through the use of over 1000 linguistic rules, plus a table of 1500 exceptions. Additionally, a stress contour over each sentence is calculated by a set of syntactical rules which provide appropriate inflections in the pronunciation. The KRM can read 200 different type-faces at up to 225 words per minute.

The performance of the KRM is highest when the print quality is good and the page layout is simple, as in a novel. A quantitative assessment made by Goodrich and others (1979) of the character recognition rate of an early system shows that rates varied between less than one per cent error and more than 20 per cent. Three different type styles (Elite, Pica, and Dual Gothic), and five different means of producing material (carbon film ribbon, cloth ribbon, carbon copy, a 'good' and a 'poor' quality photocopy) were used to represent common means of producing material. Errors introduced by 'poor' photocopying included the interpretation of small black specks as punctuation. The authors suggest that an error rate of about 3 per cent would be acceptable for general reading, but a reduction to about half a per cent would be necessary for reading when high accuracy was essential.

As a table top device the KRM is being used successfully in libraries, so that a blind person can gain access to most of the material that a sighted person would use. Not least among the advantages of this method are that it gives independence, and allows the reading of personal documents in privacy.

As access to library material is important in education, a reading machine has obvious potential. Already, a large number have been located in libraries for general use. As a personal device, the cost is a limiting factor, but there has been an increase in the use of reading machines in schools. One example is at the Beethoven School for the Blind in Boston, where a child summed up its use: 'What it does, it takes a picture and comes out in a voice. It's like a radio: you're like the radio announcer — you decide what you want to hear.' This was an interesting comment in relation to independent access to text.

Diagrams

Although braille transcription and OCR methods have been successful with text, there are limitations when diagrams have to be

Figure 10.1: The Stages of Character Recognition, Analysis and Speech Output of the Kurzweil Reading Machine (KRM)

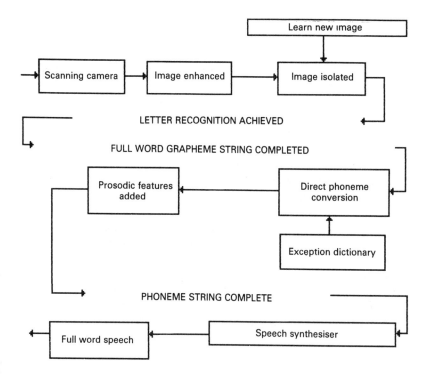

presented non-visually. The tactile diagram has already been referred to as an invaluable aid as a replacement for both graphical additions to text and a blackboard. A great deal of skill and time is required, however, in making metal masters from which plastic sheet copies can be vacuum thermoformed. A new development in this area has been a stereo copying system (Minolta) for the blind. The great attraction of this method is that the master copy is a black and white drawing or print. A process, no more complex than conventional photo-copying, produces an embossed version of the original. Central to this technique is a special paper on to which hundreds of millions of thermally-formed microcapsules have been uniformly coated. Upon absorbing the energy of light or heat, these capsules expand to hundreds of times their original volume. It is the black areas or lines representing a diagram that absorb the energy and expand. Diagrams can either be drawn or photocopied onto the special paper before processing. Hence, the method is appropriate for producing either single or multiple copies for a variety of teaching situations.

Using Residual Vision

The magnification of text enables many partially-sighted people to read it more easily. The development of Closed Circuit Television (CCTV) for this purpose offers a considerable advance because of the versatility associated with this technique: variable magnification, black and white reversal, colour, and movable viewing tables are some of the options. A common feature of these systems is a camera mounted above the text, a TV monitor and a control panel. With the text placed on a movable XY (horizontal and vertical) table, any text can be scanned and displayed with variable magnification.

Hand-held cameras are available which give more freedom of movement than an XY-table, but which demand greater control by the user. The introduction of a miniature fibre optic camera, and a flat, neon matrix, low resolution display screen provides a portable device that can give local access to printed material in the classroom or library. An example of this is the Viewscan, which was developed in New Zealand.

Writing

Recording information for personal use, or producing text for others to read, are two very important activities in education. For sighted students it is the 'pen and paper' which normally performs this function; in the case of visually-handicapped students, a variety of alternative techniques has evolved.

Braille

One of the advantages of braille is that the same code is used for reading and writing. Braille embossing devices, such as the American Perkins Brailler, are widely used in education, as they represent simple ways of recording text in a tactile form. A disadvantage is that it cannot be 'read' by sighted persons without knowledge of braille — that is, almost everyone. Thus there can be a communication problem. Two alternatives are then open to help resolve the problem: firstly, an intermediary who understands braille can transcribe the braille into text; secondly, the use of braille can be discarded in favour of a medium which a sighted person can readily read: for example, typewriting. The latter places blind people at a distinct disadvantage because they can no longer check directly what has been produced.

Two examples in education illustrate this point, and show how technology has overcome the communication problem.

Distance Teaching

At the Open University, students studying at home prepare assignments for their tutors, often in the form of an essay. Typically, sighted students handwrite or type their assignments before sending them to their tutors. Blind students generally adopt the method of brailling an essay for their own retention, and typing out the same essay on a conventional typewriter to send to their tutors: this duplication of effort is tedious and has little educational value. The identification of this problem in 1979 led to a research project aimed at using low-cost microcomputers to overcome the communication problem that blind students were experiencing.

At the start of the project, an attempt was made to combine the previously independent braille and text print methods used by a blind student. Smith and Vincent (1983) achieved this by adding microswitches and an electronic circuit to a Perkins Brailler which could detect keys being pressed and send encoded information to a microcomputer. Software was then developed to translate the encoded braille into text, and features were added to provide a disk filing system, and a print-out of the text, page by page, as it was embossed by the Perkins Brailler. A simple command system was developed for the microcomputer (Vincent, 1983) with synthetic speech as the output medium to confirm the action of the commands. For example, the pressing of the 'space-bar' on the microcomputer signifies the ending of the input of braille; pressing the letter 'P' produces a print-out of the transcribed braille. The simplicity of this action is very important for students working at home.

Examinations

In order that public examinations can be done in braille, special arrangements have to be made with examination boards, so that braille answers can be transcribed into text for the examiners. This is a very laborious task. It can take two teachers up to three and a half hours to produce a hand written script from a three-hour examination paper.

For this reason, a project 'Examinations and the visually-handicapped: an automated transcription system using a micro-computer-linked Perkins Brailler' was sponsored in the United Kingdom by the Department of Trade and Industry at Chorley-wood College in 1983. In summary, the objectives were that any information technology system should:

1. Retain the policy of students answering examination questions in braille.
2. Preserve existing examination practice for students.
3. Exist in parallel with the current method of examinations, thus avoiding problems that might arise should hardware fail.
4. Provide an automated transcription system for braille-to-text translation and printing, thus releasing teachers from this time-consuming task.

The problem was similar to that of the blind student in distance education preparing an essay for a tutor except that there had to be more dependence on the computer to take decisions during the examinations if there was to be no modification to existing practice. For example, there could be no requirement for a student to type anything on the microcomputer keyboard during the examination, therefore a filing system had to be maintained by the computer to safeguard the collection of answers for periods up to three hours. In order to develop the project, an examination room was equipped with 16 Perkins Braillers, which were linked in pairs to data collection units, based on a microcomputer with a disk-drive for data storage. The software on the disc was designed to commence collecting braille from the Perkins Brailler as soon as the first character was brailled, and to continue to keep a filing system of the braille throughout the examination. At the end of the examination, the discs were removed and the transcribed text printed out using the Spragg transcription software.

From the earlier experience (Vincent, 1983) of using a Perkins Brailler with a microcomputer, it was known at the start of the project that a high quality of braille would present few problems. However, the standard of braille declines, in most cases, during an examination (as does the writing of a sighted person), and it was this problem that needed investigation. A teacher who manually transcribes an examination paper is able to indicate to the examiner the seriousness of an error. This is important, because a single mistake in braille can destroy the meaning of a word, yet a similar mistake in handwriting might have little effect. For example, dots 1 and 3 in an isolated braille cell mean 'knowledge', whereas the addition of a dot (an easy slip to be made in examination conditions) to produce a cell with dots 1, 2, and 3 would mean 'like': this is not an obvious relationship to the uninitiated. As such a mistake can only be identified by the context of the word, it does impose limitations as far as a completely automated system is concerned. Hence, it appears that a combination of computer transcriptions, with teacher intervention to provide additional notation to the examiner, is likely to emerge. At present, the bulk of transcription, in a form for the teachers to add comments and markers, can be achieved within a few minutes of the end of an examination. It remains to see how far the technology can be used to help the teacher create a final version that is acceptable to the examiners.

Information Storage and Retrieval

Storage of notes in braille is widely used with such devices as the Perkins Brailler. It provides a personal filing system with random, manual access to the information, if the pages are indexed. A disadvantage is the bulk of material that is produced; embossed braille is bulky even in contracted form, therefore recent developments involving 'paperless' braille devices have been an important 'breakthrough'. Several are now commercially available: for example, Versabraille, Micro Brailler, Digicassette, and Braillex. A common feature of these devices is an electronic keyboard for entering braille characters, a cassette system for storage of the braille, and an electromechanical braille display. The units are small and portable, providing a compact information storage and retrieval system using braille.

The Versabraille system, for example, which is American, has been organised to store material in book format. Cassette tapes have a table of contents, chapters, pages, and paragraphs. Text can be skimmed quickly and random information located automatically. The equivalent of 400 pages of braille information can be stored on one C-60 cassette tape. Audio information can also

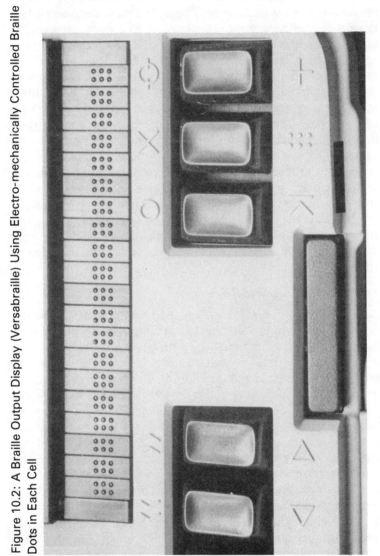

Figure 10.2: A Braille Output Display (Versabraille) Using Electro-mechanically Controlled Braille Dots in Each Cell

(Photograph courtesy Sensory Information Systems, London)

be recorded on the same tape. When braille information is retrieved it is displayed on a 20-cell display.

Because more than 400 pages of braille can be stored on a single cassette, the bulk associated with paper braille can be greatly reduced. For example, 500 pages in print of a conventional book might occupy four braille volumes about two inches thick. The same book recorded on audio cassettes would require over twelve hours of recording. Little more than a single cassette would be needed to store the book as braille.

Paperless braille devices are a very significant development for blind people in education. As portable notebooks with search and retrieval facilities, these devices overcome many problems experienced by students not able to use pen and paper. Further developments making these devices compatible with printers, embossers and other computers, will increase their potential even more.

Evaluation

An evaluation of cassette braille devices was carried out in America by the National Library Service for the Blind and Physically Handicapped (Evenson, 1981). The primary objective was to determine braille-reader acceptance of the concept of paperless braille. A number of magazines were prepared on cassette-braille and distributed to eighty volunteer readers. Digicassette, Versabraille, and Braillocord were used. Although the evaluation was incomplete, initial reactions indicated that single line displays shorter than a normal line of braille were a limitation, and that it would be preferable to display more than one line at a time. There was some evidence to suggest that the system was preferred by the slower braille readers.

In the San Diego Unified School District, an evaluation of the Versabraille (Doorlag and Doorlag, 1983) indicated that students using cassette-braille were able to read and write at a faster rate compared to paper braille. Positive advantages in the school environment were found to be that the device could be operated quietly and easily, and facilitated the storage, editing, retrieval, and interpretation of information. Reading and writing rates with cassette-braille were compared with paper braille. Reading rates with cassette-braille were slightly faster, but no difference in comprehension was detected. In searching for any word, page or chapter the cassette system functioned more efficiently. For writing, the editing features proved outstanding; insertion or deletion of letters, words and paragraphs enabled students to produce an 'error-free' product. Students found they could braille for longer periods without fatigue, and the machine's quiet operation avoided distracting or disturbing other students.

Text Without Braille

A major problem in the past of using devices with QWERTY keyboards to produce printed text, has been the lack of feedback to a blind typist, to ensure that the text is correct and to provide editing facilities. The IBM Audio Typing Unit overcomes this problem by adding a device to a typewriter which can monitor keyboard actions and provide an electronic speech feedback. The audio responses can take the form of characters, words or sentences. Students can revise what they have typed and have complete independence to produce high quality final copy.

Although typewriters with speech output are now used widely by blind adults in employment, the penetration into schools (particularly the United Kingdom) has been low. This situation may well change as the cost of these devices is reduced. Meantime, computers have been exploited to provide a variety of ways of creating, editing and printing text.

Access to Computers

During the past few years there has been a dramatic increase in the use of computers in education. In particular, it has been the increase in the number of low-cost microcomputers that has been the most significant trend. With a far wider range of software becoming available, the growth in computer-assisted learning is likely to continue. What are the implications for blind people?

As we have shown, computers and other microprocessor devices are making important contributions where problems associated with writing and reading exist. The conventional computer is not accessible to a blind person, however, because of the visual displays. This problem is being attacked through developments that seek to replace visual features by tactile or auditory devices.

Tactile Output

The visual display unit (VDU) is a common device used with a computer; text, instructions and keyboard entries may all appear on the VDU. For a blind person, it presents a similar problem to reading printed text, but there is one significant difference. The eye receives direct light from a VDU as compared to reflected light from printed text. In practice, this can be helpful to those with partial sight. For those who cannot satisfactorily see the VDU, or who cannot see it at all, an adapted Optacon could be used. The addition of a special camera to the Optacon allows text to be read from the screen in the same way as it is used with printed material.

A braille display of what appears on the VDU may be more appropriate. A braille embosser can be attached which replaces both the VDU and the printer, or a refreshable braille strip (20 to 40 cells) can be used. The latter is a feature of 'paperless' braille devices, many of which can be used as a computer terminal, or as a soft braille output device. One British 'paperless' braille device which was primarily intended as a braille terminal is the Brailink. It has a standard QWERTY keyboard (but six keys are switchable to provide braille entry), a display strip of 48 braille cells and a mini-cassette system for information storage and retrieval.

Speech Output

The publication in America of a double issue of an *Aids and Appliances Review* by the Carroll Centre for the Blind (1983) is indicative of the numerous and rapid developments in this field. A key feature has been the availability of low-cost modules that can decompose words into groups of sounds (phonemes or allophones) which can be reconstituted into synthetic speech. This means that text that would appear on a VDU can be redirected to the module which produces a spoken output, in effect, acting in the same way as a serial printer but producing a serial speech 'window'.

The addition of a speech module that only provides a serial record of what appears on the VDU does not give students full interaction with a computer. For example, a video display is two-dimensional and static, a format which allows a sighted user to scan and to select the appropriate information and to review it repeatedly for analysis and comprehension. By comparison, once a word is spoken, it is lost, and the scanning and selection process available with sight is not possible. Hence, spoken output alone does not enable a blind student to interact fully with a computer.

The development of software to provide facilities equivalent to using a VDU has attracted a great deal of attention. Through the software it has been possible to provide a wide variety of facilities to meet individual needs, and to give access to software packages that could not possibly be used with only a serial speech window. When blind students are word processing, they need to work interactively with text that may appear anywhere on the screen. They may need to know whether letters are upper or lower case, although too much information output as speech can slow down the interaction. In these circumstances, it is important for them to be able to select the level of speech output which may or may not, for example, include enunciation of punctuation.

Synthetic Speech

Good quality synthetic speech is difficult to achieve because of the dynamic properties of the human speech mechanism that have to be simulated. It is well known which essential components are required to generate human speech (Flanagan and others, 1970); research continues into the development of hardware and software to exploit this knowledge. Current developments with microcomputer speech synthesisers are described by Poulton (1983).

The term 'phoneme' has been introduced as the basic unit of the spoken language. It is the smallest segment of sound such that if one phoneme in a word is substituted by a different phoneme, the meaning may be changed. For example, 'c' and 't' in 'cold' and 'told'. The term 'allophone' describes a variant of a phoneme due to differences in context. There are slight differences, for example, in the way that the phoneme 'b' is produced in the words 'bat', 'able' and 'rub'.

The 'unnatural' quality of some speech synthesisers results from sequences of phonemes being spoken with these individual sound units remaining unchanged by the presence of other phonemes making up the complete utterance (word or phrase). This quality is improved by using allophones which do take into account contextual variations.

Of particular importance to the education sector is the emergence of low-cost, commercially available speech synthesisers which can be readily interfaced to a computer. Three types of speech synthesiser are being used:

1. With unlimited vocabulary, with codes input for the individual sound units (phonemes or allophones). They can be used for predetermined speech output, such as commands

but not with unlimited text unless additional software is used.

2. With unlimited vocabulary, with direct text input. This type includes a text-to-phoneme or -allophone translation program, and will attempt to synthesise any text sent to it. A speech-by-rule algorithm will not provide correct pronunciation for every word, therefore exception tables are included for these words.

3. With limited vocabulary resulting from human speech which is digitised, compressed and stored. Words and sentences are regenerated by simple codes.

Although limited vocabulary speech synthesisers generally produce a higher quality of speech, they do not offer the same versatility as those with an unlimited vocabulary.

Is the quality of speech significant for a blind person using a computer? Of course it would be desirable to produce speech as near natural as possible, but there may be more important factors determining the success of this technique, such as speed of response and reproducibility. The experiences of two blind students in the Open University make clear that even the simplest device available in 1979 provided adequate feedback for a number of computer-based applications (Vincent, 1983a). One student, who was Welsh, commented: 'It pronounces my home area of Penrhyndeudraeth as well as any tourist!'

Comprehension of synthetic speech by blind children has been studied in America by Rhyne (1982). Four blind students, aged 11 to 13, were tested to establish their listening grade levels, then they listened to tape recordings of the Kurzweil Reading Machine reading stories that were one level below their reading level. After each story (40, in total, over ten days), the children answered multiple-choice questions. The scores suggested that as exposure to synthetic speech increases, so does comprehension of synthetic speech. This research followed that of Goodrich and others (1980), and Scadden (1978), who developed a method of evaluating the intelligibility of synthetic speech reading machine outputs. Results from these studies indicated that blind adults can learn to comprehend synthetic speech after a short period of practice, with comprehension comparable to that of tape-recorded material, and that intelligence plays a role in comprehension of synthetic speech.

Input Devices

We mentioned earlier that a braille device such as the Perkins Brailler can be used satisfactorily to input braille into a computer for subsequent transcription into text. The same arrangement could be used to enter and execute programs. This is not desirable in many cases because of the complications of defining control and command keys as braille characters which would normally have another meaning. A standard keyboard is much better, with the key entries producing a suitable audio or tactile response for verification.

Computer Applications

The increased availability of microcomputers in schools, colleges and universities is likely to change curricula and teaching methods. If visually-handicapped students are not to be denied these changes then access to all computer applications will be required. As audio and tactile methods of representing the visual output from a computer have developed, blind students' chances of gaining access to all computer applications have increased. Some examples are described below.

Word Processing

Although word processing has its roots in business and commerce, there is new, widespread use of this technique in schools following the availability of software packages for microcomputers. Not only are there benefits to be gained for future employment through the development of word processing and keyboard skills, but this type of software has found many applications in language development. In addition, for visually-handicapped students, this is potentially an excellent technique for communicating with sighted people.

The 'Computing and the Blind' project at the Open University has produced a set of word processing programs for the BBC microcomputer with synthetic speech as the output medium. From a simple version for young children where text can be typed, edited and printed, more advanced features (search facilities, file-handling and formatting) have been added to give versions that are more appropriate for undergraduates and adults. In each case, text can be scanned by letter, word or sentence, and edited by insertion, deletion or over-writing. Simple menus (for example, 'P' for printing out current text) give immediate and uncomplicated means of using the programs. This simplicity of use is important for all age groups.

Other British projects include the OXTED (Oxford Text Writer) software written for the Apple II microcomputer and Braid text-to-speech synthesiser, which has been used on a trial basis by the Royal National College for the Blind, Hereford, and Worcester College for the Blind. Croft and Chaplin (1984), in a progress report, indicate some of the problems of introducing a new technique into a school where potential advantages of a system can be hidden by the need for students to change existing practice. It was thought, for example, that these students did not need a word-processor because 'touch-typing, even with mistakes, was sufficient for letters home, and possibly school work and assignments'. The report clearly confirmed the importance of 'user-friendly' software where synthetic speech is adopted for the output medium.

Programming

Computer programming is one of the professions that offers potential opportunities for the blind. At the Arkansas Enterprises for the Blind (AEB) a vocational course was first presented in 1975. It is reported (AEB, 1980) that there are now 17 blind and visually-impaired graduates of the course employed in programming positions. The students used a Honeywell 6/36 computer with braille terminals and speech synthesisers.

Programming in BASIC has been available to blind students at the Open University since 1981 (Vincent, 1983). This is achieved with a microcomputer (TRS-80 or BBC) that has a BASIC interpreter which provides for a synthetic speech output.

This type of interpreter is important because it gives visually-handicapped students an opportunity to write computer programs. It also allows computer programs written for screen output to run without modification and provide speech output automatically. The only limitation is that graphical features in the output are not converted, an inherent problem that does not have a ready solution. With the programming facility, all BASIC commands are available. Trapping and reporting of errors is enhanced, making for easy identification and correction. Subsequent editing is achieved through spoken cursor movement responses in the editing mode.

In order to accommodate both novice and experienced users, the speech response is modified according to criteria within the software. For example, a slow typing speed results in each character being spoken as a program is entered. If the typing speed is fast, the speech is suppressed (to avoid slowing down the typing), unless there is a pause, in which case the last few words are spoken. Thus, validation of typing can be achieved at any time by simply changing typing speed. This is analogous to a sighted person looking at the screen when it is necessary to check an entry.

The transformation of BASIC statements to a spoken format is an important function of the 'talking' interpreter. For example:

5PRINTCHR$(5)

transforms to

five print karacter string five

Keywords are extracted and are replaced by text that will give a spoken equivalent. The 'incorrect' spelling is used to achieve improved pronunciation.

Listing of programs and multiple line outputs are 'paused' after each line. Options are then available to speak the line again, or to speak the line character by character. The latter option is important when checking for errors in a program where incorrect syntax may not be detectable when spoken in words.

With many of the problems of non-visual output overcome, programming can proceed with the normal facilities available in BASIC language. A similar facility can be provided on a microcomputer when it is used as a terminal to a mainframe computer, the techniques described are more appropriate if the output from the mainframe is line by line, that is teletype access, rather than page by page (complete screen presentations).

Computer-assisted Learning (CAL)

There is little doubt that CAL will play an increasingly important part in education with the widespread availability of microcomputers. Providing means of access to a computer other than a VDU will increase the opportunities for visually-handicapped students to use the CAL materials developed for mainstream schools. In addition to this material, CAL can be used for topics that are specific to visually-handicapped people, for example, the learning of braille.

In England, at Shawgrove School, Manchester, the prospect of young children learning braille with the aid of a microcomputer was first considered in 1981. Initially, it involved having a Perkins Brailler interfaced to a microcomputer with synthetic speech as the output medium (Smith and Vincent, 1983). An introductory CAL package was designed to provide a spoken response for the alphabet, numbers, and simple words and sentences (no contractions or abbreviations). Thus a child who had not mastered the reading of the embossed braille could receive audible help. A screen or printer record was maintained for the teacher in order that the child could be left alone for short periods. Further packages were developed to test a pupil's knowledge of grade 2 braille. In this case, the teacher prepared in advance a vocabulary of words which could subsequently be spoken (synthetic speech) by the computer and the brailled response checked. Help was given for incorrectly brailled words. This technique was subsequently supplemented by using the same packages with a concept keyboard (A4 size and with 128 pressure-sensitive squares, see Chapter 9) that had embossed overlays for either the letters of the alphabet or all of the braille characters. In this case, the characters could be found by touch, and selected by pressing an adjacent area, that is, avoiding pressing on the braille character. Both methods have been successfully introduced into the teaching of braille, and the audible interaction with the pupil has proved to be enjoyable as well as educational. An important feature of this CAL material is that the teacher is provided with a simple means of creating relevant vocabularies thus removing constraints that could be present with pre-programmed software.

The technique of having a tactile overlay on a touch-sensitive keyboard was extended to having words, sentences and simple diagrams embossed. Selected areas were assigned to synthetic speech responses. An authoring program was used to create the individual touch/speech responses for the overlays. By touching the concept keyboard the teacher could assign areas, and then type in the text to be spoken. The touch pattern appeared on the screen to give visual assistance. An example of the screen presentation is shown in Figure 10.3 for 33 individual words. The black squares indicate which areas have been assigned a spoken response; the squares to the left of each marked square have no spoken response and indi-

Figure 10.3: Visual Aid (on VDU) to Assist in Configuring the Concept Keyboard for Speech Output

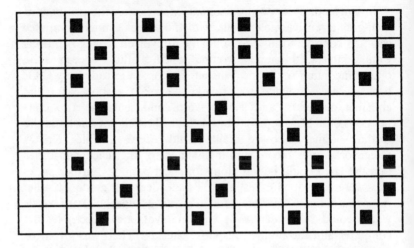

cate where the braille-embossed words would appear on the overlay. This example has been used by students learning to read braille.

A number of programs have emerged from the Logo language that provide a graphical output from a sub-set of the commands. The graphics may appear on the screen, or result from an external device (for example, a turtle) whose movements can be controlled, including the ability to raise and lower a pen.

As graphics, geometric shape and movement are areas that have special problems for visually-handicapped students, it is possible that this language could be of value. At the RNIB Rehabilitation Centre, Torquay, experimentation with a 'talking' version of a turtle graphics program has commenced. In addition to all the commands and messages being spoken, the turtle is controlled. It is possible for partially-sighted students to see the graphical output as the turtle draws with a thick pen. It is hoped that blind students may also benefit by feeling the movement of the turtle, thus experiencing how it is controlled. It may be possible to adopt the pen arrangement to give a tactile representation.

Workstations for Visually-handicapped Students

A microcomputer with the range of peripheral devices that might be used in education can present numerous difficulties for both teacher and student. These may relate to the hardware (making appropriate connections) or to the software (modification for various input and output devices). As the number of pieces of equipment are likely to be greater for visually-handicapped students, ease of using hardware and software must be of prime importance. In this context, workstations have much to offer.

At Concordia University in Canada, a workstation has been developed for student programmers taking an introductory course on computers and computing for the physically handicapped. It uses standard hardware, except for a purpose-built braille display unit (Grossner and others, 1983). The workstation includes a standard ASCII keyboard with programmable function and cursor-control keys, a VDU that assists interaction between blind and sighted users, a synthetic speech output that reads the contents of a file, a 20-character braille display, a printing device for hardcopy output in character or braille formats, a modem for communication with a remote computer, plus the software to make use of all these devices.

Fundamental to the work at Concordia has been the philosophy that 'a workstation intended for a blind programmer should enable him to use any program written for or by a sighted programmer'. This has led to the development of two categories of software: utilities specifically developed for visually-handicapped students (for example, a talking text-editor), and utilities that use the VDU but are provided with parallel speech and braille outputs.

In the United Kingdom, a workstation approach was adopted by the 'Computing and the Blind' project at the Open University when the first information technology collaborative scheme for schools for the visually-handicapped was supported by the Department of Trade and Industry in 1982. Initially, eight schools were equipped with a workstation based on a BBC microcomputer with the Perkins Brailler and concept keyboard as alternative input devices, and with synthetic speech, VDU and printer as output devices. All of the hardware was relatively low-cost and commercially available. This scheme was concerned with development and evaluation of software for children or students aged 5 to 16. The software included teaching of braille, braille transcription, programming and word processing. Subsequently, the same workstation has been used in higher and distance education, and with adults in employment.

In the Federal Republic of Germany, at the University of Stuttgart, a computer-based Learning and Working Environment for the Blind (LWEB) has been developed for blind students (Schweikhardt, 1980). The central unit is an IBM microcomputer. Output can be displayed as a single braille line. Drawings are plotted on a printer, and are copied off-line by an optical-to-tactile converter (OTAC). Particular attention has been given to a software system (KOTEXA) for constructive geometry, an important area with many problems in mathematical education. Drawings are constructed according to instructions in natural German language, and are generated immediately on a printer. KOTEXA has many helpful features for checking input statements for consistency and ambiguity. A tactile copy is made with the OTAC. For example, 'Faelle das Lot von A auf G' (draw the perpendicular line from A on G) is translated into 'lot AG'.

Some Other Experiences

In Israel, the Technological Institute for the Blind is developing aids for the blind, including a braille terminal, and a television system to enlarge pictures for the partially-sighted (Centre for Educational Technology, 1981). Teaching methods and instrumentation designed specially for blind students are also being examined.

Hinds (1983), an education advisor for the Royal National Institute for the Blind in England, concentrates on the use of microcomputers for young and less able children who are partially-sighted. He reports that the aim of software developed in conjunction with Nene College, Northampton and the University of Birmingham is to stimulate 'looking' in children who have a variety of visual difficulties, and to introduce very young children to the computer as a natural tool of learning.

Lunney and Morrison (1981) at East Carolina University in America write about the problems of adapting chemistry instruction to the needs of visually-handicapped students. They found that there was little help for students at college level. Because of the trend in the natural sciences towards instrumental measurements, and away from direct visual methods, they decided to develop a portable talking laboratory microcomputer with interface facilities for a variety of scientific instruments. A talking calculator program was used for a variety of chemistry experiments in conjunction with data-collection software.

Summary

Information technology has already made many contributions to the education of visually-handicapped students. Many devices now exist which give access to printed material and help to overcome the enormous task of producing braille in sufficient quantity to meet the demand for reading material. Problems associated with communication with sighted people are being eased through braille-to-text conversion and by adding speech output to devices that produce text in a printed form.

Fortunately, the inherent problem of using computers that are designed to produce visual output is being overcome by alternative tactile or audio outputs. In many cases, design of supporting software has been an important factor in ensuring access for blind students to software used by sighted people. With increasing use of CAL in education, this must be a prime requirement. The workstation approach integrates hardware and software into a convenient and accessible environment for each student.

11 EXPERIENCE AMONG DEAF PEOPLE

Uses of new information technology in education with deaf and hearing-impaired students fall into three categories: for general communication, thus facilitating instruction; as a means of teaching language skills; and as a means of teaching other skills (in which case the mode of operation may not vary from that used with the normally-hearing).

It is reasonably self-evident that individuals with poor communication abilities have considerable difficulties in educational contexts. Traditionally, a great deal of education has been based on the spoken word. Even teaching of the non-vocal skill of reading actually begins by linking visual symbols with sounds of words, and continues by using verbal reinforcement.

Oral Communication vs. Manual Signs

There has been much controversy, however, concerning method(s) of communication which might appropriately be taught to hearing-impaired children (see Chapter 4). The deepest differences have been between those who think that oral methods, using speech-reading and residual hearing, are essential, and those who think that these skills are largely inappropriate to many deaf children, the use of sign systems being more suitable. The discussion, in the case of children, actually encompasses two separate (though inter-linked) considerations. First, there is the need to provide the child with a means of communicating, in the educational context and as part of his socialisation into the world. Second, that communication ability must be used in obtaining an education, across the complete curriculum.

The need to consider both these aspects decreases as students become older, and at post-secondary level it may well be wholly inappropriate. For the adult or mature student, the most efficient means of learning is through the system he or she uses best, whether or not it relates to a particular philosophy of communication. Yet this raises a problem for those hearing-impaired people who have little residual hearing, find speech-reading very difficult and are unable to use manual methods with any degree of suitable efficiency (or at all). For this group, the argument about methodologies is irrelevant. The only method of communication which is sufficiently reliable and easy of use is reading.

Captioning Systems

Some research and development has been aimed at presenting the hearing-impaired student with a visual display of what is being said, in real time, using a computer terminal to generate characters and television screens as the medium of display (television captions are an example). Two philosophies pervade work to provide the most adequate display. The first tries to provide high quality accurate syntactical English, but in a reduced number of words, while the other gives a verbatim transcription of what is being said.

A major contribution to British development of the non-verbatim system has been made by the Open University. The system utilises a microcomputer with a conventional keyboard operated by a competent high-speed audio typist. Such a typist cannot, of course, type at the speed of speech, and so it is necessary to reduce the number of words. This is done by including in the system an 'interpreter' who listens to the original and dictates to the typist through a sensitive microphone link. The whole task can be accomplished by one person, but while this does not appear to affect accuracy, it does increase the rate of fatigue (Carver and Hales, 1974; Hales, 1976, 1978).

This system was originally developed to provide a service for mature hearing-impaired students of the Open University, studying in their own homes. It has been of great help to many, particularly those who cannot use the alternative modes of communication commonly adopted by the deaf. Roger is one of the students who has found this method of communication to be of great value.

Roger's native tongue is not English, and he suffered a total hearing loss later in life but before coming to England. This meant that he was unable to learn English aurally, and the quality of his use of the language was affected by this. Thus, in addition to the communication problems engendered by his deafness, and his lack of aural familiarity with English, he had the additional difficulty of studying in a language he had never heard. This constellation of problems meant that Roger's lip-reading ability at the commencement of his degree was quite inadequate for the purposes of study, and he knew no sign language at all. Thus the only mode of communication in which accuracy could be guaranteed for him was the written word, and he found the visual display system invaluable. Indeed, he would not have been able to study without it, as he admitted himself: on one occasion, when asked to choose between two optional summer school lectures, he said: 'I have no choice. Where the machine goes, I go.' He found the visual display system worked well, although it did mean that his attention was often diverted from the lecturer. The fact that the quantity of words was reduced also meant that each sentence remained on the screen for some time, and he was able to look away and still catch up with items that had appeared earlier. He sometimes found this an advantage rather than a handicap, as it meant that he could take short breaks from the continuous concentration.

Fatigue is not merely a potential problem for the handicapped individual using the system, but also for the interpreters and equipment operators producing the text. Open University research shows that the problems of fatigue are greatly alleviated by using two operators, one dictating a précis to the other, but if they are required to continue for a long period, their performance is bound to be affected. In almost all cases, however, it has been found that it is quantity of information, rather than accuracy, that begins to diminish.

This system has been used for lectures, tutorials, interviews and examinations. It has also been applied to real-time captioning of some live television programmes, in combination with teletext (Independent Television's Oracle system), where it is effective as a communication medium and appealing and useful to the audience. The fact that some of the material is missing is seen by some as a drawback to the system, either because they believe that a significant amount of the information is lacking, or because they are worried, as a point of principle, that decisions are being made for the hearing-impaired persons which they should, ideally, be in a position to make themselves. As for information loss, various investigations have shown not only that there is no significant reduction in the performance of groups under reduced presentation modes, but actually that 'edited' captions to lectures presented on videotape produce better results than either a verbatim script or a live interpreter (Stuckless and Loutrel, 1972).

Sargent and Nyerges (1979) suggest that in the teaching context, a system which could accurately synchronise a speech signal with its corresponding printed text would probably solve many of the language difficulties suffered by the hearing-impaired, especially the pre-lingually deaf. They have developed a speech/text synchronisation system designed to do just this, and the system is sufficiently flexible to allow the teacher to modify its performance in order to teach particular aspects of language training. The researchers give the example of being able to present the speech first and the print later if the student needs to practise auditory skills. This order can be reversed, or the two can be synchronised on a syllable-by-syllable basis. The whole system combines audio tape and disc storage, with the audio tape storing the speech signal and synchronisation pulses on two tracks, and the floppy disc containing the printed text and any additional control signals needed. One disadvantage of this system, and of many like it, is the large amount of time needed to prepare and correct the materials. Sargent and Nyerges estimate that it takes about 15 times real time (15 minutes of preparation for every minute of program) to prepare and correct the material fully, and consider that the minimum that will ever be achieved is 10 times real time.

There is a fairly long history of research to find a way of presenting all the information to the hearing-impaired individual in a way comparable with the reception of spoken material. The aim has been to produce complete verbatim text in real time, by using a computer to convert the output of shorthand machines ('Palantype' in Great Britain, 'Stenotype' in the United States) into normal orthographic English. The biggest problem has been the conversion program, because the shorthand machines, like manual shorthand, are based upon a phonetic methodology, which is not easily compatible with the requirements of a display in normal English. The techniques continue to improve, however, and such verbatim displays are now used as a normal means of communication for hearing-impaired students in classes at the National Technical Institute for the Deaf in the United States, as well as the captioning of television programmes in that country and in Britain (on the BBC's teletext, Ceefax).

There are now a number of students who have taken courses using these translation systems as their means of communication. In America, manual communication ('sign language') is much more widely used than in England, and direct comparisons can be made there between these two 'visual' means. The experiences show that deaf students are fairly evenly divided among those who prefer the visual display, those who prefer traditional interpreting and those who believe they are equally useful (Stuckless, 1984). The individual variation is great, however, and it has been reported that one student, an experienced 38-year-old deaf man who had taken over 80 courses at various colleges, attributed to use of the verbatim visual system the fact that he recently received his first 'A' grade!

The contribution of the operator of the system is crucial, of course. The pressure of the task is high, and it is necessary for the operator to know in some detail about the structure, content and likely pitfalls of the classes covered. This job can be carried out in such a way that it enhances the course work. A professor of history (Stuckless, 1984) wrote to an operator of a verbatim system for a deaf student in his class, saying,

> I want to commend you on the outstanding work you did in my History class. Both the deaf and hearing students profited from your skills. You did a superb job in a difficult course, prepared yourself before class by meeting with me and I was satisfied with the results. My most brilliant deaf student couldn't stop praising your work. I wish you success in your profession and I hope we can work together again in the near future.

Two problems still remain with verbatim systems. First, errors are displayed, either through translation errors or operator fault. Second, not all students find the systems easy to use. Print appearing at verbatim speed on a television screen is difficult to use effectively, and the more so for a deaf person who may well have significantly retarded language skills. Despite these problems, the system can be very valuable to the competent user in situations where it is vital that the presentation is as near as possible to the original in every way. Jack Ashley, a British member of Parliament, uses an earlier version of the system, designed to be portable, and with its help has been able to participate fully in the functioning of the House of Commons, despite a total hearing loss.

There is evidence of a need for more captioned television. In 1980, the Caption Center of the television station WGBH in Boston, Massachusetts, carried out a survey among its hearing-impaired audience. A 59 per cent response rate came from a sample which was largely deaf (rather than partially-hearing), with hearing loss relatively early in life, and of reasonably well-educated and informed people. Among this audience daily television watching was high (although not quite as high as the overall national average), with a considerable time spent watching such captioned programmes as were available. Action/adventure, news and comedy programmes were most popular, and while newspaper reading and general television watching behaviour was found to be linked to level of education, watching of the specially-captioned news programme was not. Indeed, the survey team reports that 'the appetite for news coverage, both television and print, is particularly marked' (Blatt and Sulzer, 1981).

One researcher in this area, however, has considered the question of what effect this sort of provision would have on the deaf child regularly presented with print which had the same transient, rapid 'real-time' quality as the spoken language (Stuckless, 1982). He speculates that it would affect quite profoundly the development of language in the individual, and suggests that real-time graphic display could lead, eventually, to an altered language curriculum which would focus more on enriching, rather than establishing, language.

Teaching Language Skills

Problems arising from the inadequate language skills of the deaf are a continual source of investigation, as they affect profoundly the potential of the deaf person for full integration into the community. It has been a consistent finding of research on education of the deaf that the primary deprivation is one of language. Poor linguistic competence and allied poor reading skills have been frequently reported, with suggestions as to the degree of the handicap which are remarkably unanimous. The majority of researchers in this field suggest a reading retardation of around seven years (for example, Myklebust, 1964; Conrad, 1977a).

Assessing the language skills of hearing-impaired students is very important, as well as the teaching and remediation that follow. It is often necessary to obtain an estimate of the level at which an individual is working, so that appropriate teaching may be provided. Some attention is being given to the use of new technology in assessment procedures. The Test of Syntactic Abilities, which is designed to assess syntactic skills in English of deaf students, is widely used but Jones and Grygar (1982), at San Diego State University, report that the amount of time needed to administer, score and interpret accurately the manual version of this test makes it unwieldy. They have developed a computerised version which reduces the time required and provides interpretations. Thus new information technology can be used in both assessment and teaching, and this raises the possibility of an overall approach, combining the two applications.

Remediation for language deficits can be provided at many levels. Project Video Language, in San Diego, California, addressed itself to the need to 'accelerate language acquisition in hearing-impaired children' and was designed to make classroom drills more exciting for the participants. In recognising that words or concepts often have to be presented to hearing-impaired students many hundreds of times, the project staff also realised that this process is sufficiently slow to exacerbate the learning deficit, leaving hearing-impaired children further and further behind in many aspects of their educational development. The system uses a series of fundamental syntactical patterns, with sentences which illustrate each pattern in every possible transformation. The patterns are 'brought to life' by the videotapes and other material, yet the whole programme remains under the direct control of the teacher, a factor seen by the authors as giving the system an advantage over more automatic 'mechanical' teaching. The materials were originally designed for the 'Apple Tree' language curriculum, but are not limited to that context, and teachers are reported as having found a high pupil interest level (Kreis, 1979).

Another approach is taken in the British research at Hull University (Sewell and others, 1980). Here an interactive computer-aided instruction system presents deaf children with material based on their own everyday experiences. Slides of their own work in or outside the classroom are the starting point for the preparation of sentences based on those activities. These sentences are manipulated by a computer program known as JUMBLE so as to be presented to the child with the words in an inappropriate order. The child's task is to rearrange the words so that a sensible sentence transpires. Words can be manipulated around the display screen, and the program is designed so that this can be achieved with a single keystroke. Visual reinforcement of the correctness (or otherwise) of a response is given on the screen, and as in so many such programs, a printout is finally generated which gives the teacher feedback on the performance of the child. To ensure further flexibility, the program is also able to accommodate the moving of whole phrases as units, and it is reported that it is easy to vary the difficulty of sentences. This work has shown that computers can intensify and clarify language teaching for profoundly deaf children, making the learning enjoyable and relating the whole to the child's experience and understanding. Gormley and Franzen (1978) have stressed the importance of relating reading tasks to a deaf child's experience and expectations.

The Hull University team (Sewell and others, 1980) is also working on a voice synthesiser to assist those deaf people who have inadequate speech and would appreciate a computer to do their talking for them.

The Hull system and others like it require deaf children to read and assume that they know what a 'proper sentence that makes sense' actually looks like. Other research addresses itself to the requirements of teaching earlier language skills. One project at Bristol University set out to 'offer deaf children a means of communicating in a purely visual way which utilised as many as possible of the rules of English' (Chapman and Wilby, 1982). This system uses a keyboard cover or overlay which provides the child with the ability to respond to symbols, not the alphabet, and thus construct sentences in Rebus characters. It is effectively a concept keyboard. There are various levels of complexity available, from simple matching tasks (where the child must press the symbol corresponding to the one displayed on the screen) to the generation of sentences. One element of flexibility in the program is the possibility for the teacher to generate his own covers and sentences. The response of teachers and children is reported as 'most encouraging', and the system has been used with children down to three-and-a-half years old. The project uses a Midas computer, which is relatively expensive, but the authors report that they adopted this in the full knowledge 'that programs can very easily be moved to any Z80 based machine or one like Apple or the BBC Acorn, both of which can carry a Z80 piggyback card'. It is hoped that this system will allow deaf children an opportunity of developing the necessary internal linguistic models, and that therefore they will reach a point where they no longer need the support of the system but can function independently.

Galbraith and others (1979) report American work using graphic displays to support sentences in sign language, where graphic representations of both the sign and the object are included. One major problem reported here is that of capacity, for under the system used each digitised word requires 16,000 bytes of storage. From this it will be seen that a vocabulary of 100 words, which although reasonable is quite modest, requires 1.6 million bytes, and creates problems for even the largest system.

One criticism which has been levelled at many programs designed to assist deaf children with language is that they are too static, only allowing children to insert words in sentence completion tasks, or limiting them to multiple-choice situations. At Thorn Park School for the Deaf in Bradford, a program called Wordplay is used that allows children to experiment with language by generating their own phrases and sentences from a predefined word list. The system makes extensive use of graphics, and gives immediate feedback, providing the pupil with clues to the source of his error in the case of incorrect responses while still not simply providing the correct solution. This is an experiential, experimentation system, and no scores are kept.

Some companies are now turning their attention to problems inherent in designing software for uses in language education. In America, the Spinnaker company is marketing the Story Machine, which provides stimulation through colour pictures, from which the child can build up a sentence. When the sentence is complete, the child is rewarded by action on the screen. The same company has a program called Facemaker which uses a similar structure for vocabulary development, teaching pupils to distinguish between emotions expressed facially. Despite developments like these, a common complaint from educators at all levels is that the quantity and quality of available software is not yet good enough.

As in many areas of language education, much effort is directed at primary learning situations and young children. Dolman (1980), at William Rainey Harper College in Palatine, Illinois, reported great difficulty in motivation and concentration among older deaf students in language classes. He followed some of the ideas of Goldberg (1973), who noted that most deaf students in English do not really appreciate what is expected of them, and do not fully understand the standards by which their work is to be assessed. Goldberg suggests that a great deal of practice should be given to such students, and very little formal explanation by the teacher.

Dolman introduced computer-based English work, each lesson aimed at providing the student with experience in a particular aspect of English (for example, irregular verbs, verb tenses, negative transformations, etc.), including much practice. His programs are available at two levels: Level 1 consists of differing exercises, ranging from filling in blanks to transformations, while Level 2 consists of incorrect sentences for correction or paragraphs with key words or phrases missing. Dolman admits that the introduction of computer work among these students has not changed 'the students' attitudes toward English from hostility to delight', but says that 'there is less frustration, both from their standpoint and mine, and they are improving'. He reports that because the work is done at computer terminals, students feel they are doing an adult task and do not lose interest. They are less likely to be discouraged by the enormity of the task because they make frequent concrete gains. The programs are written in BASIC, used on Hewlett-Packard Access 2000 equipment.

Ward (1981), at Hull University, has attempted to develop the JUMBLE approach (referred to above) to a level of more sophisticated linguistic processing, so that the computer will analyse and give feedback about sentences composed by the student. In the same way as the Wordplay system previously described, the vocabulary and syntactic possibilities are necessarily limited, but the possibilities are exciting and important. The level of understanding and written English of deaf children is known to be different from that of their hearing peers (Arnold, 1978) and a more flexible system would be a major step along the path of trying to make new provision in that field.

The Problem of Linking Symbol and Reality

One recent step which has exercised the minds of those involved is already implied in the work reported above. This is the need to link the work on the computer with the child's real experience. Attempts to forge bridges between the computer programs and real life offer much of the motivation to design interactive video systems. The object in such systems is to develop a package which uses the ability of the computer to ask questions, monitor responses, give feedback and store and score responses, and the capacity of the video medium to provide sound and pictures upon which the work could be based. Until recently, one substantial drawback of such systems has been the very slow access times of videotape machines, which led to long pauses and loss of attention and motivation in the student. The videodisc offers much faster access time and it is possible to select specific frames, and match them with specific points in the computer program. One relatively sophisticated attempt to build a teaching programme along these lines is taking place at the California School for the Deaf in Riverside. Here a videodisc is linked with an Apple computer in such a way that the child is presented with visual film sequences from the disc, and then asked questions about what he or she has seen, with multiple-choice responses. The programming includes repetition sequences and explanations of incorrect solutions. One advantage of this system is its great flexibility: it can be used for other teaching functions, the microcomputer and the videodisc player remain autonomous and can still be used separately, and the pupil's response can be through the Apple keyboard or by use of a lightpen touching spots on the television screen. The system has been used for job training, and can also be used to train in social and interpersonal skills. At the time of writing, one major obstacle is cost, for even with material preprepared and assembled on videotape, the cost of conversion to videodisc is high, running to thousands of dollars per master disc (see Chapter 8).

Experimentation with the combination of microcomputer and videodisc has been slowly expanding during the last few years, despite this cost. The Media Production Project for the Hearing Impaired at the University of Nebraska-Lincoln has produced interactive videodiscs designed to 'help develop independent thinking skills in intermediate-age hearing-impaired students'. This was an attempt to encourage positive and logical problem-solving behaviour by 'leading the student through a structured and guided exploration of the decision-making process' (Nugent and Stone, 1982).

The Nebraska researchers say their students responded positively, and that as well as encouraging involvement, the system enabled students to work towards correct solutions of the problems, using decision-making strategies. The students did find, however, that some of the linguistic structures in the computer-generated text were difficult to understand, and that some parts of the branching network were too complex. It is possible, though, to rewrite the text and the branching logic while leaving the visual material intact, a substantial advantage in system flexibility, and this was done (Nugent and Stone, 1982).

Computers and video have also been used in the Moore-Norman Area Vocational-Technical School in Oklahoma to support and facilitate vocational-technical education of hearing-impaired students. These students are in normal classes, with instructors who are usually skilled craftsmen with little knowledge of the particular needs of deaf students; this, coupled with the expected low language and reading ability of the students, can lead to substantial difficulties in ensuring that the students learn the concepts required.

Fox (1979), of the Learning Technology Institute in America, reported development of an Interactive Visual Image Controlled system (Vis-I-Con) that might be suitable for, among other things, the creation of material for videodisc masters. He used super-8 film cassettes and addressable audio tape to develop programmes for deaf and hearing-impaired students. He saw his system as very portable and flexible.

It is also possible, and cheaper, to use computer and videodisc in parallel, but not interfaced, with the computer giving instructions and the individual finding the relevant sections on the disc himself, as directed by the computer program. The United States Department of Education has sponsored a demonstration of this technique in the Washington DC metropolitan area (Withrow, 1982).

The DAVID system, developed at the National Technical Institute for the Deaf, Rochester, uses a videotape in place of the videodisc. One tape contains a simulation, the 'Job Interview Game', aimed at improving the hearing-impaired individual's performance in a demanding situation which is especially difficult for him, and where he needs to make a good impression on the other person. The tape provides much practice of difficult sentences. Students who have used it show enhanced performance (Cronin, 1979; Sims and others, 1979).

Other Experience with the Technology

The technology is also being used in other subjects besides language. In St Louis, Hight (1982) has developed a system which converts sentences typed on a microcomputer into animated mouth movements or high-resolution graphic images, which are displayed on a screen as an aid to the teaching of lip-reading.

Hight admits that the system will not replace face-to-face teaching or practice, but feels it will add to the range of techniques available to the teacher. The program also includes sequences in which the student has to make choices or supply corrections.

Teachers face an additional burden when they turn to the technology, in that they must be somewhat familiar with the technology in order to use it efficiently. This problem has been tackled at the California School for the Deaf in Fremont, where Irwin (1983) has developed an authoring system for teachers, with which they create computer assisted instruction, without any knowledge of programming. The authoring system, known as Blocks 82 (its predecessor was Blocks 80), allows teachers to use simple English commands and peripherals such as a graphics tablet to develop computerised lessons, with much visualisation built in, through which students can work at their own pace. The system also enables teachers to keep track of progress and make lesson plans, using an inbuilt management system.

The idea of involving computers in management of the education of deaf students has become more attractive as software has expanded and become more user-friendly. The Kendall Demonstration Elementary School for the Deaf, in Washington DC, is implementing a computer managed education system which will provide access to a variety of descriptive, psychological, medical, audiological, educational and socio-emotional student data. The system will provide both standardised reports and user-defined reports, from a student database and an objectives database, with other databases to be developed to provide management information about staff and material resources. It is designed to perform administrative functions, curriculum management, computer-assisted instruction and special services. The hardware consists of seven Apples and two IBM personal computers, interconnected with a Corvus Systems hard disc and Omninet networking hardware and software.

The Kendall School will probably provide software systems and technical support to other schools for the deaf which want to replicate portions or functions of the system. To plan sensibly for this service, a national feasibility survey was conducted in 1982, covering more than 500 teaching projects serving the deaf. Of those schools using microcomputers, it was found that they were used for instruction 62 per cent of the time, teaching computer languages 16 per cent of the time, clerical tasks 4 per cent and management tasks only 2 per cent. The most common problems reported (Deninger, 1983) were lack of finance, lack of software, lack of training for teachers and inadequate numbers of computers.

The Kendall scheme will be taken up elsewhere in the United States by schools for the deaf which will in turn become demonstrations for other schools in their regions. Between six and ten such schools are being set up, to start with, using the Kendall curriculum. In time, such approaches could well expand the concept of how computers may broadly improve the education of deaf and hearing-impaired people, rather than concentrating on single programs to solve specific difficulties.

In England, a wide-ranging look at these problems is being taken by the Microelectronics Education Programme (see Chapter 13), which has identified five major areas: teacher training, information and advice, software production, software distribution and hardware (Hope, 1983a). The Programme has set up regional centres to disseminate information.

Jones (1983), of Donaldson's School for the Deaf in Edinburgh, argues that information technology must be incorporated in the curriculum for deaf children. He thinks they should learn the basic skills that will give them access to information, and bring them into contact with a much larger group of people than was previously possible. This in turn will help them with their cognitive and linguistic development.

New information technology was brought into Donaldson's School, which already had a policy of Total Communication, using signed English. This policy has specifically enabled pre-lingually and profoundly deaf children to start reading at a much higher level and at a much earlier age than orally-trained children. Conversely, the school also has some children who have entered the school at a later age and with less adequate reading and language skills. The school chose deliberately to use programs which foster interaction between the child and the computer, not simply 'drill and practice' routines. By using programs such as JUMBLE, LUCALD, MODEL VILLAGE and Logo, deaf children at the school are being directly involved in using information technology for their own education.

Technology and Employment of Deaf People

The new technology is available as a tool in teaching hearing-impaired students. It could easily be argued that use of computers has had some considerable impact on the lives of this group of handicapped people, because much of the technology employs a visually-based interactive system, in which the ability to hear plays no part. Perhaps hearing-impaired people stand an equal chance with hearing people of becoming proficient with computers and related technology, and perhaps their employment aspirations should rise. The barriers in communication experienced by deaf people, however, make it generally more difficult for them to achieve qualifications and acquire jobs commensurate with their intellectual and practical abilities. Increased unemployment over the last few years has exacerbated this problem. Many old jobs are being fully or partly automated, and new jobs sometimes have communications requirements which place the deaf individual once more at a disadvantage.

McLeod (1981) has argued that there are not many deaf people in systems and programming work partly because there are relatively few deaf graduates in the market, and partly because there is a lack of a 'computer-oriented culture' among deaf people. He reports that there is no record of efforts to teach computer programming to deaf students prior to high school, and to ascertain whether such training was possible, a three-week experimental course was conducted for five deaf children, aged between 14 and 16. Class time was limited to an hour a day (so as not to lose students' interest) and the language selected for teaching was COBOL. Teaching was accomplished with the aid of an experienced interpreter and liberal use of visual aids, and overall the students appeared to perform on this course at much the same level as would have been expected from their hearing peers. Special care was taken to ensure that concepts likely to cause difficulty were presented clearly, students had a great deal of visual support (including a specially-written textbook) and the teaching took place in a stimulating learning environment. McLeod concludes that special thought should be given to attracting young deaf people to careers in computing.

Summary

Thus the experience of deaf students with the technology is already quite broad. Their major need is to communicate and to interact with their world. They need competent language, and this is especially crucial in the educational environment. Much of the work described in this chapter is aimed at making it easier for deaf children to acquire a higher degree of language, and of course this will permit greater access to all other areas of the broad educational curriculum, which are denied the person with poor language. The aim of many of the applications of new information technology is to broaden the horizons of handicapped people and to increase opportunity, particularly educational opportunity, by trying to make easier those activities which, for them, are especially difficult.

12 EXPERIENCE AMONG SPEECH-IMPAIRED PEOPLE

Development of workable and reliable techniques of speech analysis, which could lead to a sound-to-vision device, could lead in turn to a substantial reduction of problems for deaf people, and would ease many of the difficulties we outlined in previous chapters. Unfortunately, although research is progressing well, the issues are complex and it will still be some time before a useful tool is available. By contrast, speech synthesis has developed quickly, making possible vision-to-speech communication. This is useful for the blind when handling written material (see Chapter 10) and for the speech-impaired as a prosthesis to aid active communication in an 'oral' mode.

Voice Output Communication Aids

Voice output communication aids are of two main kinds. One can be programmed with a limited number of words or phrases, each of which is accessed easily and quickly, perhaps by a single keystroke. The other, more elaborate, version uses a microcomputer to generate speech from input via an alphanumeric keyboard. It has a much larger vocabulary, to which words may be added, usually by typing them in.

Devices of the first kind are particualry useful for people who have short-term needs, including especially those who have had operations which affect vocal performance: laryngectomies, tracheotomies, etc. Such aids are portable, cheap and easy to use. Experiences with the Vocaid in Michigan are reported by Eulenberg and Rosenfeld (1982). This device is a development of the 'Touch and Tell' educational toy manufactured by Texas Instruments, using similar circuitry and keyboard (see also Chapter 9). The keyboard contains 36 keys, each of which is programmed to a specific word or phrase. Several sets of phrases may be used, however, by replacing the plastic overlay which indicates the meaning of each key. The overlays automatically identify themselves to the machine, so that the operator is relieved of the necessity of switching from set to set. Preproduction tests took place at the Jackson County Medical Care Facility and the Torrant Center, Jackson County, and those carrying out the evaluations stated that they could see 'significant benefit', and that 'many persons who have lost the ability to speak because of a stroke will also be able to use the Vocaid, both for practical communication and as an aid to therapy'. This last point is particularly important, for in many cases the person for whom the communication was intended could read the message from the keyboard, without the machine saying anything!

Although some of the early problems of intelligibility of cheaper forms of synthetic speech are now being overcome, there is still some resistance to using it. At King's College, London, work has been progressing to program a speech synthesis device that will provide control of inflection and emphasis, and to deal with phonetic problems. In this work, each phoneme can be modified to suit the taste of the individual user, and it is hoped that this will encourage more speech-impaired people to use speech synthesis techniques. Another aspect of the same project is looking at intelligibility, in the hope of making synthetic speech more intelligible (Tollyfield, 1984).

'Intelligibility' of synthetic speech is more than simply a matter of the degree to which it duplicates tones and patterns of human speech. The question also arises of *whose* human speech, and whether it is appropriate for people who will be using the device. This point is demonstrated in the work progressing at the Cheyne Walk Centre for Special Children, Chelsea, London. Here, very young children learn to use hand-movements to choose Bliss symbols from an array of four presented on a screen; they make their choice by shining a light on the array. The light detectors are also able to control movement of the display of four symbols, giving access to 14 pages of four symbols each, and, as well as the chosen symbols being displayed on the screen, the relevant sentence which is thus built up is printed onto paper. The project is developing, however, a speech synthesis system to 'say' the symbols as they are chosen, based on a BBC microcomputer. It is here that appropriateness of the synthetic speech has been proved to be important. Sanderson (1983) has found that the 'adult' sounding speech from the BBC computer is unsuitable for children, and they are producing their own child-voice chip for the BBC computer.

The same group is also working on a link between a BBC

microcomputer and a stereo audio-cassette recorder to develop a device for use by nurses, which will tell stories to the children. One audio track is used for the story, recorded by the nurse, while the other track records the data for synchronised pictures; these are chosen from predefined sets, and include some interactive parts.

Non-manual Control

The input method used for most speech synthesis devices is normally manual, but the ability latent in any residual muscular movement capability can be utilised. In the Department of Computer Science at Michigan State University, Rahimi and Eulenberg (1983) have investigated the use of myoelectric (EMG) signals produced by one muscle or a group of muscles as the input function. They used a two-dimensional representation of phonetic symbols, with the user directing a cursor about a screen, stopping it at will by the momentary flexing of a muscle. Output has been by synthetic speech.

This work has also investigated the use of the voice as the controlling medium, which may be especially valuable to those people who can produce sounds, but not in the conventional patterns which comprise language. Rahimi and Eulenberg report, 'individuals were able to learn to use sequences of sound patterns to encode phonetic strings'. The words were then spoken by the speech synthesis system.

They suggest that for people with severe motor problems which interfere with using switches or keyboards, such avenues could give 'much higher rates of information transmission, adding to their fluency and articulateness'.

As voice recognition becomes increasingly feasible, so the use of 'voice' input becomes potentially more sophisticated. In 1982, the Artificial Language Laboratory at Michigan State University reported (Alpert, 1982) that a student was using a 128-word Heuristics voice recognition system to speak his commands to his computer. He is reported as 'able to program in standard computer languages such as Fortran, to draw graphs and diagrams, and to do high-quality word-processing — all by voice command'.

The problems of those with minimal movement and no speech have been investigated, too, by researchers interested in eye-movement patterns. Several centres have developed devices which are attached to a special pair of spectacles (see Chapter 9). A computer monitors eye movements, enables the user to select a symbol and initiates the speech synthesiser to speak the word associated with the symbol. To date, there are two main problems: one is the difficulty of working with the very young, which makes it somewhat hard to teach operating skills and how to control the technology. The other problem is the time and effort involved in training the nurses in the most basic of computer-handling techniques (for example, loading programs), which the nurses find tedious and time-consuming (Sanderson, 1983).

More thought is being given to developing systems that do not need manual input, but are controlled by gaze. The SPA-SYN-COM system, developed by Polhemus Navigation Sciences Inc. in America, and described in *Communication Outlook*, vol. 2, no. 3, places a sighting device and electromagnetic sensor on a spectacle frame and gives the individual a target board containing the symbols to be selected. By use of a tracking device, the system can measure the position and orientation of the user's head-mounted sensor and interprets this information to make the selection.

Loss of any function, or indeed part of the body, whether it be temporary or permanent, is traumatic. The psychological sense of loss is substantial, and in the case of those who have lost the power of speech, the provision of a 'voice', however artificial or limited, may reduce the level of anxiety experienced by the patient.

Portable Communication Aids

Hermes is a typical portable communication aid, developed by the Data Processing Department of Wayne County Intermediate School District in Michigan, but designed with a multiple output choice in mind. It uses similar hardware, with touch-panels which are adjustable to different overlays, although expanded in concept by the ability to combine selected squares together into larger blocks, to provide larger panels and less choice for those for whom this would be an advantage (for example, someone with poor motor control, or someone with impaired vision). As items are selected they are stored in an output buffer, although they may also be fed directly to a synthetic voice or display. The device may be attached to a printer, and the vocabulary can be divided into more than one level. It can contain a 'permanent sentence stack', with sentences that are not accessed directly by activation of particular touch-panel squares but by a set of stack command keys. There may be several stacks, and one suggestion (Turner, 1983) is that sentences could be grouped thematically.

Such is the rapid development of this particular aspect of technology, however, that it is easy to forget the very considerable impact it has on people's lives in real, human terms. In March 1982, Michael Williams, a professional writer, gave a speech to the Stanford University Rehabilitation Engineering Conference. Michael is speech-impaired, and made the speech with a voice output communication aid. In it, he said (Williams, 1982):

> Two years ago I was introduced to the most exciting technological development for disabled people I've ever seen: synthetic speech. If, when I was a little boy, someone had told me that I would grow up and make speeches to large groups, I would have called him either a fool or a madman. Yet, here I am ... I can only say this: modern technology has allowed me to release my creative spirit where it can soar, free, high above the clouds. Without the fruits of modern technology, I would probably be stuck in a room counting the hours until my death.
>
> To some people, this synthesiser may be an ugly box with cables. To me, however, it is an analogue for freedom. Let freedom ring.

Independence and freedom created by using a communication device is an oft-repeated theme in many of the reports by or on individuals. Patty Thomas has cerebral palsy, which has affected her ability to talk as well as her motor control. It is difficult for her to use a conventional keyboard, yet she has learned to communicate through a Zygo 16, a communication system she borrowed from Stanford University, which provides the user with a screen divided into 16 panels, each carrying a communication message. Patty operates the system with a pedal fixed under her chin.

That was not the end of the story, however, because other pupils also made use of the machine (located in their school) to develop other language skills, and many who were considered noncommunicative are able to practise and develop their language skills, and learn new material, new words. The children experienced, for the first time, communication as a rewarding experience, rather than the frustration so often evident among verbally-handicapped children in lessons. Patty's teacher, Rona Gertzulin, is reported as saying (*Santa Cruz Sentinel*, 15 March 1981) that in a two-year period 'non-oral communication devices have achieved a thirty percent increase on average in the language, intelligence and social-emotional growth of the communicatively handicapped'.

Stanford University has also been involved in the development of the Versatile Portable Speech Prosthesis (VPSP), designed to assist severely handicapped people who are speech-handicapped but linguistically capable. The system includes a Canon Communicator which is added to a wheelchair, thus retaining the handicapped individual's mobility, by not requiring a link to a static piece of equipment. First a prototype system was designed that allowed for unlimited new word creation by the user, using syntactically structured menu page layouts and page hierarchical organisation, which could be operated with a single switch, although later work added a joystick interface and a keyboard input interface as well, making the whole package very versatile (*Communication Outlook*, vol. 2, no. 3, August 1980).

Attempts to reduce the complexity of the information at input are quite critical, and have led to developments where the input is in terms of signs rather than words. Minspeak (see also Chapter 18) is such a system, and basically recalls phrases already stored in response to input which relates to symbols. The symbols represent general communication ideas, and the user can either adopt those supplied, or make his own. Thus the system is capable of vast expansion, for the meaning of the symbols is determined by the user, and the meaning of each key can change according to the context. Although in some circumstances accuracy may not be complete, the advantages to the user of this sort of semantic coding system are great, and appear to have great potential (Baker, 1983).

The idea of 'linguistic capability' already referred to leads many people to suppose that non-vocal children must have acquired reading skills before they can use many of the alternative systems available. At the Tufts-New England Medical Centre a communication aid has been constructed which has a phoneme and syllable menu of 300 items. These are represented by symbols, colours and phonetic spelling, with output through digitised speech, and the system has been used with non-vocal children who do not yet read, and it seems that they are able to use this language representation system (Goodenough-Trepagnier and others, 1983).

It is very easy to assume that people who need voice synthesisers require them because they have no speech ability of their own. This is not always entirely true, for some have abilities to make sounds which are sometimes of use. Often such people are able to communicate with those who know them well, although the noises they make are rarely intelligible to others. If a computer can recognise the sounds made, and translate them into the appropriate words (produced by a voice synthesiser), this enables the individual to use the equipment to talk intelligibly.

Wallace (1983) reports developments which have tried to follow this path, with various degrees of success. Using an Apple and a Speechlab circuit board he attempted to give his subjects a 32-word vocabulary, and rapidly discovered that this was too large a first step. His users could not all produce 32 sufficiently distinct noises. His system improved by a Mountain Hardware Supertalker mated with Speechlab, Wallace developed what he calls his 'Grunt Converter'. Among his technical problems was providing a large enough vocabulary with an acceptable short delay between inputting the 'grunts' and hearing the compiled words synthetically produced.

Wallace's system has been tested at all stages with people with speech problems, at a holiday centre and a special school. He sees the system as becoming a speech training aid for children, and this idea has progressed to a fairly complicated training program which not only teaches but also keeps the child interested by presenting words according to his or her success in pronouncing them. This tale demonstrates that there is a wider future in this whole area, and for those who have some ability to make consistent and recognisable sounds, developments in synthetic speech are valuable and useful.

Of course, the ability to utilise systems and equipment to 'say' individual words, or even build up sentences, is of little use if the skill cannot really be used to participate in interactions with others. This ability relates to the speed with which the system can be used, ultimately determining the rate at which synthetic speech is spoken. It has been established that this is important, as non-vocal people with production rates below four words a minute are rarely able to participate in conversations, whereas those who are able to achieve a higher level (even if it is not much higher, only five or six words a minute) are able to participate genuinely in conversational interaction (Goodenough-Trepagnier and others, 1982).

The very slow rate at which most people using synthetic speech devices operate is a cause of concern to many workers in the field, and has been tackled in a number of ways. Beukelman (1983), at the University of Washington, has developed a morse code project, choosing this particular code because it can be learned quite quickly, and while using it through one or two single-switch devices, the students can still use their eyes to acquire additional information. Using morse, students select letters, words and portions of sentences, and some are engaged in word processing and computer programming. Beukelman reports that speed of input is good when compared with other methods.

As we have already mentioned, the speed problem arises with visual communication devices intended to communicate with the deaf. Here, one avenue of investigation is the use of shorthand machines ('Palantype' or 'Stenotype'), to produce faster speeds for those using synthetic speech prosthesis. At the Veteran's Administration Hospital in Palo Alto, California, a modified stenotype keyboard is in use, to 'allow manually dextrous speech-impaired people to communicate in a personal style at near normal conversation rates'. The researchers are aiming at around 120 words per minute (Wood and others, 1982)! Design of the input function is crucial. But research and experience show that use of phoneme sequences rather than alphabetic input increases the overall level of efficiency. One study reports an improvement in communication rate by 30 per cent (Goodenough-Trepagnier and others, 1982a).

Programs containing vocalised output in synthetic speech are not only of value in communication devices for those with no speech. They can also be used in training speech-handicapped children. As mentioned in Chapter 9, in some cases the workers see the computer support as 'scaffolding', which will be removed later as personal ability improves. This is the point of view taken by Meyers (1983), at the Speech and Communication Research Laboratory in Los Angeles, where very young children use a synthetic voice to name a picture when the picture is touched on a touch-panel. Working with pre-school children, Meyers documented some remarkable improvements, with children rapidly learning to indicate preferences and vocalise in cases where this is possible. Children are led to use the keyboard and then expand on their newly-acquired interest.

Individual Differences and the Technology

Underlying much of the previous discussion is the relationship between the technology and the handicapped individual, already referred to in previous chapters. In a report concerning artificial voice production at the University of Bristol, Duncan (1983) wrote:

> [Our group members] have, moreover, different expectations of an artificial voice. One is happy to take his machine to the shop around the corner; he doesn't care what it sounds like as long as it is understood. Another will come to terms, reluctantly, with the machine only when it produces a voice as clear and euphonious and feminine as the voice she has lost and when it is small enough to be concealed.

This same report relates a number of case-histories of how individuals came to terms with using the equipment provided for them, reiterating the point that individual variation is extremely high. This arises because of differences in the abilities of specific people to learn to handle the equipment and because of the vastly different handicaps of people using this micro-controlled voice synthesis system. Even among those with the common factor of impaired speech, very different aetiologies giving rise to the dysfunction mean that some have motor problems, others have perceptual difficulties, and some are coping with the results of wider-ranging brain damage.

Some of the 'coping' strategies required by users of synthetic voices do not relate to the equipment, or even themselves, but the reaction of others. Many people find it a novel and not immediately simple process to communicate with someone using an artificial voice system. Williams (1981) reports how he was side-tracked from a meal with his wife in a restaurant by a head waiter who wanted to play what Williams called 'a little game of "can you say this on that machine?" ' Williams goes on to say that this is a 'major preoccupation of novice voice output communication aid listeners'.

The interface between the individual and the technology is perhaps more crucial in speech handicap and speech prosthesis than in many other contexts. On the face of it, many of the devices being developed are largely similar: they take some sort of coded input, and compile this into information strings which permit the speaking of a synthetically-produced word. Some will combine to produce sentences.

However, this similarity is only at the production end of the process; the vast and detailed variation comes at the input end. The ways in which people are able to conceptualise and input the required coded information are almost as many as the number of people who require the equipment. Some can use keyboards, some have only minimal residual movement, some can use only muscle tone, while others have no effective motor control, and must learn to utilise sounds they can utter, or direction of vision.

Some, too, are handicapped not by (or not only by) their physical difficulties, but problems they have with conceptualising language. Some have benefited greatly from increasing facility in the technology to handle such codes as Bliss symbols, particularly the young, who have not yet learned the whole range of language skills. Those with an expressive language handicap have limited ability to learn and improve their language skills. Systems which can be applied in an educational context unlock the real potential of those who are unable easily to communicate their understandings to the rest of the world.

Perhaps the experience of speech-handicapped people themselves, and those researching the systems and working with the individuals, shows above all that here is a field in which it is crucial to match the system to the individual.

Summary

Throughout the reported experiences of people with speech-handicaps and synthetic speech devices, one thing stands out: that most of these people feel they are brought a step closer to interacting with other people and the environment, like everyone else. People who lose their speech through an accident are able to regain something of their old way of living. For those who have never spoken, the technology brings them into a new community, based on speech. Thus it is able to bring them a step closer to full rehabilitation, which is the final goal of all research and development in this field.

PART FOUR
Issues

13 EDUCATIONAL ISSUES

There are many educational issues relating to new information technology in education generally. These have been discussed extensively elsewhere (see, for example, Hawkridge, 1983; O'Shea and Self, 1983). This chapter focuses on more specific issues, divided into four broad categories: those concerning the introduction of new information technology into education of disabled students, and those concerning the hardware, the software and the teachers.

Introducing Students to New Information Technology

Two aspects of the use by disabled students of the technology must be taken into account when they are introduced to it. First, some devices and systems, hardware and software, simply enable them to use the same technology as everyone else, and in much the same ways. For instance, bigger keyboards or special keyguards are in this category for students who do not have sufficient motor control to use a conventional one. Synthetic speech enables blind students to 'read', after a fashion, the screen display of a microcomputer. Here the students' major requirement is for supplementary technology that will enable them to use the main technology, perhaps for learning computing or for computer-assisted learning in any of a range of subjects. They must therefore learn to operate the main technology, through the supplementary one. Second, other devices and systems based on new information technology enable students to do what they could not do without it. Into this category fall speech synthesisers for those with little or no speech. Such students want a substitute, and they only need to know how to operate the equipment to supply the missing human function.

It is by no means easy to bring new information technology into a school, or to introduce students to it. Take, for example, the experience of the California School for the Blind, in Fremont near San Francisco. The School caters for blind children who cannot follow a normal school curriculum: the others are 'mainstreamed' into local schools. A microcomputer arrived in the school office in

1981; it had no graphics or colour, and has stayed in the school office ever since, being used mainly for word processing, but not by students. Next, three terminals arrived, for use with a central processing unit, but they have never been used in a network as originally intended because the telephone lines could not carry the required rate of messages. A windfall of funds at about the same time brought to the school a Kurzweil Reading Machine, a Versabraille, an Optacon and an Echo Speech Synthesiser (see Chapter 10 for details of these devices). These, and audiotape cassettes, have all been used regularly by the students, with some consequent decline in braille usage. But two years after the first computer arrived, not a single student had learned on one. More computers were expected, probably under the 'Kids can't wait' scheme run by the State of California and a local computer manufacturer, and policy in the school district is for teachers to take the computers home for the first year, to learn all about them before 'letting the students loose' on them. Teachers can take computer education courses at local institutions (Jenkins, 1983).

What should the new technology be used for in educating disabled children and adults? Teachers and parents alike have to consider what the new technology should be used for in educating disabled children, and disabled adults should consider the same question, for themselves. There are two aspects to the question: first, the technology can be used to compensate for a disability, such as speech-impairment; second, it can be used to teach across the curriculum, given appropriate software. It is essential to start from a careful assessment of needs, which fall into three related categories: the nature of students' disability, the stage of their intellectual, social and physical development, and their educational level.

How can the technology be matched to the needs of individual disabled students? Goldenberg (1979) stresses the need to explore this question very fully. As a rule, the nature of children's disability is first diagnosed medically. Here the new technology can assist. Barker and others (1983) describe a kit, developed at the Children's Hospital at Stanford, for systematic quantitative assessment, essential before a suitable device can be selected for a disabled individual. The kit tests that individual's ability to control devices used for mobility, communication and environmental control. For education, communication is particularly vital. Barker and her colleagues point out that first it is necessary to identify what the disabled person can actually do, anatomically speaking, when positioned properly. Next, she discovers what input devices the person can operate at all: these devices include single switches, joysticks, small keyboards, etc. Some of these are in the kit and others can be attached with appropriate adaptors. Finally, the person tries out the devices and his or her performance is measured, so that the best device can be chosen, taking into account the user's preferences. The measurements monitored by the kit include duration, frequency, reaction time and number of errors. Thus data are collected on speed, accuracy, fatigue and repeatability. Where such sophisticated test equipment is not available, rougher assessment must be attempted while students try out several different devices.

Goodrich and others (1977) report measures of reading speed and duration for adults who were learning to use a variety of low vision aids, including closed-circuit television. They conclude that 'since the data showed large intrasubject variability and large increases in reading performance, the clinician should be cautious in rejecting low-vision aids on the basis of a single-day trial'. Further, 'for the same reasons, the final prescription of a low-vision aid should be made only after a trial period in which performance can be carefully examined'. As the introduction of new technology will require adjustment by students to new hardware and software, perhaps including acquisition of added skills, it seems likely that assessing individual needs of disabled students will become more extensive and sophisticated. Software-based versatility offers, in many cases, a higher degree of individualisation than used to be possible.

The stage of intellectual, social and physical development reached by a disabled child is usually established by professional observers, with help from the parents. A ten-year-old disabled child who has developed normally, intellectually speaking, may well be ready to begin using a microcomputer for school, and his or her social development will probably have proceeded more or less in parallel. If, however, physical development has been arrested, this may cause practical problems, which Rostron and Sewell (1984) discuss in some detail.

The educational level reached by a disabled child or adult clearly also determines whether he or she can benefit from using hardware and software currently available, including that produced to meet the needs of particular kinds of disability.

An example from a Californian school shows how important it is to match the technology to the student. Spychala (1983) reports that Ted, a spastic teenager, was provided with an Autocom, a concept keyboard costing several thousand dollars. Ted was able, with difficulty, to press the appropriate square to make a letter or numeral appear on the display, which carries about 30 symbols at a time. The trouble was that Ted could hardly spell. His use of the keyboard was very limited, yet it can be programmed for no less than 60 levels (that is, each square can stand for up to 60 symbols, words or even sentences). Ted simply could not memorise more than one or two levels.

At Hereward College of Further Education near Coventry, an assessment scheme operates to serve physically-disabled further education students in England and Wales who may be helped by using the technology, as Firminger (1983) reports. Students come into the College and have opportunities to use the technology under supervision and observation, so that their individual needs are carefully judged.

How should disabled students be taught to use the technology? Not very much has been written on this topic. Behrmann and Lahm (1983) propose a standard five-stage plan for teaching infants and young children to use computer-based technology. First, the child is assessed and, if necessary, taught the cause-and-effect relationship between using a switch and getting a visual or auditory response (say, a smiling face or the spoken words, 'Good, Jim') from the equipment. Second, the child is taught how to select one picture from two on the computer's screen, by using a switch or key at the moment when a flying cursor is on or next to the picture he or she wants. To motivate the child, the computer can be programmed to activate an electrical toy, animate a picture on its screen or name the object and speak words of praise when the choice is made. Third, the child uses his or her new skills to select more abstract pictures in response to both visual and computer-spoken stimuli, learning the words in the process. Fourth, the array is increased from two to four pictures and the teaching repeated. Fifth, the pictures are used to present categories rather than single objects, thus teaching the child many more words.

What should be the content of teaching using the technology? As Richards (1983) says, hardware and software should be selected not only to suit the special needs of disabled individuals but also to serve teaching aims that are the same as for able-bodied students in the class. He places stress on making correct decisions about the curriculum for the students before looking for the technology.

Richards suggests, for example, using new information technology to: facilitate communication, promote language and speech in deaf students, encourage reading across the curriculum, reinforce learning, compensate for disabled students' difficulties with abstractions, teach learning strategies, stimulate questions, promote hand-eye co-ordination and fine motor control, increase attention span, foster co-operative behaviour, and give access to parts of the curriculum closed to disabled students. These are all laudable proposals. The fact is, however, that there is little agreement on curricula for disabled children in either the United States or the United Kingdom (Green and others, 1982; Swann, 1983) other than that they should pursue a curriculum suited to their stage of development. Many intelligent but disabled children and adults show that they can pursue an academic curriculum possibly leading on to university courses. The technology often helps them to work faster and with less physical effort.

How do disabled students learn by using the technology? Whether children or adults, they learn by using the technology to read, write, speak, compute and draw: in short, for all the kinds of activities that able-bodied students engage in while studying. They may also use it for computer-assisted learning in several subjects, just like other students. But should the technology be only temporary scaffolding? For some disabled students, it provides what Bruner (1978, referred to by Meyers, 1983) calls 'scaffolding'. That is to say, it is a means to an end, to be dispensed with where possible when that end is achieved. For some disabled students, the technology should be a temporary aid, rather than a permanent communication prothesis.

For example, in Meyers' (1983a) development of methods of teaching American non-communicative pre-school children to speak or otherwise communicate, she uses a number of simple toys, some clockwork, or common objects in a purse. Pictures of these also appear on a touchpanel (membrane keyboard). Input by the child is either through the touchpanel, or the keyboard, to a standard microcomputer, into which Meyers has put her own programs (PEAL: Programs for Early Acquisition of Language). Output is through the computer screen, a speech synthesiser or a printer. She talks to the child about the toys and other 'props' to arouse interest, encouraging and provoking activity; her technique is detailed in Meyers (1983). The child can easily recognise a picture of a toy or prop on the touchpanel; touching that picture causes the microcomputer, through the voice synthesiser, to name the object and/or display it on the screen. Children do not seem to mind the robot-like accent, but become excited and press the panel repeatedly, to make the computer talk.

Roberts (1983) reports that in a videotape made by Meyers of her work, one 26-month-old child quickly improved, catching the vowel sound of the words in isolation first, then the labialisation and finally the nasal consonants. Another child of the same age almost immediately and perfectly captured and vocalised the name of the toy, a helicopter. The videocamera caught the obvious amazement on the face of an adult watching.

Later, the child learns to name the action associated with the object, like 'move' or 'wind'. Requests come from the child, through the computer or in other ways, for moving or winding up toys. Very quickly the child learns to indicate what he or she does or does not want, and vocalises requests, which is more direct than using the touchpanel. Sooner or later, the child dispenses with the computer's power to vocalise, being able to vocalise now for him or herself. Meyers (1983) states that the young children she works with employ synthesised speech for only a few months. Her achievements are also reported by Trachtman (1984), and Meyers (1984) gives further case studies of young disabled children acquiring language through using the technology.

The Hardware

What hardware is needed for educating disabled children and adults and on what educational grounds should it be selected? Teachers want devices and systems that match individual students' needs. A system should provide choice between single or multiple switches, whether based on gross arm movements, eyelash flick, tongue movements, or suck and blow. As Hope and Odor (1982) say, the ideal way of working will vary from student to student: some go faster than others, for instance. They point out that because of this need for flexibility, many inventors have chosen to 'base their systems on the lowest common denominator, the single or multiple switch controlled menu system, even where the user has other remaining abilities which could be exploited'.

Many involved in research and development in this field hope that a relatively small range of microelectronic hardware plus a wider range of software will be the ultimate answer to problems of meeting the individual needs of disabled students (Pickering, 1983). Even then, specialised software developed for disabled people, including students, can be very expensive and because needs are so individual, modifications are often necessary. Therefore some say it may be best to find the software to meet particular needs and then buy the hardware to implement it. For example, if a program for Bliss symbols (see Chapter 9) is marketed for only one make of microcomputer, it may be best to purchase that make (Hope and Odor, 1982). Apart from microcomputers, some devices are programmable and can employ increasingly sophisticated software, including educational software, as their disabled owners learn how to use them.

There are good reasons to use, where possible, hardware available in mainstream schools. Economic benefits stem from buying equipment in a general rather than a specialised market, and software is more likely to be compatible with the hardware. Devices can be added to standard equipment to improve disabled students' access to it, of course. This approach was taken by Vincent (1983b) in developing a workstation for visually handicapped students: standard items for the workstation include a microcomputer, disc drive, monitor, printer and concept keyboard, plus a speech synthesiser and a Perkins Brailler, the latter requiring a non-standard interface. Specialised use of such a workstation is provided through software. For example, Vincent reports use of packages for braille to text transcription, a BASIC interpreter (with speech as the principal output medium), and a talking word processor. Without this software, the workstation could be used for software development by a sighted teacher. The programs could then be made available to a blind student without further modification by running them with the alternative talking BASIC interpreter.

In both the United Kingdom and the United States, local educational authorities and agencies have tended to commit themselves to one or two manufacturers, in the hope of reaping benefits of standardisation and interchangeability. This policy is not easy to sustain in the face of a rapidly changing technology marketed with vigour by many different companies. In the United Kingdom, the government has backed and funded British products much more strongly than foreign ones.

There is a general problem of many small and almost parallel hardware and software developments proceeding at the same time. Standards have not yet been established, and a strong user network is slow in coming about, in both the United Kingdom and the United States. Competition between developers contributes to the main problem, which is poor communication between inadequately funded projects. Slowly these problems are being overcome through journals like *Communication Outlook* (from Wisconsin) and newsletters like *The Catalyst* (from California) and through exhibitions, conferences and networks of special centres. Computerised databases are being built up in America and the United Kingdom, but these are not devoted specifically to educational applications of new information technology. Instead, they are more general and concerned with all kinds of aids for disabled people, as in the case of the British Database on Research into Aids for the Disabled (Sandhu, 1984). In America, Goldenberg and others (1984) list electronic resources for special education. There are several electronic networks and bulletin boards that link scattered projects, some educational. From Washington DC, the National Association of State Directors of Special Education operates SpecialNet, which provides electronic mail, access to major databases of many kinds and electronic bulletin boards on computer applications, employment opportunities, legislative activities, etc.

The Software

Is there good quality educational software and on what educational grounds should it be selected? All working in this field agree that there is still a chronic shortage for students generally and not least disabled students. Computerised databases listing commercially available and other software contain many titles, but few programs that command teachers' respect. However elegant the graphics and programming, and however user-friendly the approach, the educational content is often trivial or irrelevant to the curriculum.

Yet who should write these programs? Teachers know the problems faced by students and understand the curricular issues, but very few of them have the time, training or skills to become good programmers. First-class programmers rarely know enough about teaching, and are seldom paid to work with teachers, to produce good educational software. All this is true for educational software in general, but particularly so for software designed specifically for disabled students. Engineers, teachers, medical scientists, mathematicians and computer programmers have separately written programs, but not to great effect.

Attempts are being made to overcome this problem in the United Kingdom and the United States. The Lancasterian special school in Manchester, for example, worked with staff and students from a nearby college to produce programs for one particular physically-disabled student at the school (Rees and Bates, 1982). Elsewhere, the problem is being tackled by bringing together top-class multidisciplinary teams, as in the Learning Company in Menlo Park, California. These teams of teachers, programmers and others tend to be costly, however, if costed realistically.

The question of how much centralisation of production is desirable remains unanswered. Programs are in fact being written for disabled students in perhaps a thousand localities, as local enterprises, often without sufficient resources. Piestrup (1983) of The Learning Company suggests an electronic conference network linking children, teachers, designers, scientists, programmers and engineers, for the purpose of developing new programs.

The Scottish Microelectronics Development Programme (SMDP), with the aid of funding from the Department of Trade and Industry, is producing a software package (the Microspecial Starter Pack) for children aged 14-16 who have learning difficulties. This is an important initiative, although not specifically designed for disabled students. If it is successful it could be a model for production of software for specific groups on a national basis. A feature of the scheme has been its consultative approach, involving all parties interested in or affected by such a development. These include teachers, local authority advisors, Her Majesty's inspectors, other educational computing centres, researchers and developers. Workshops and seminars have been held to identify areas of software development needed by this particular group of children and to provide guidelines to the programming team at the SMDP. Issues raised at early meetings (SMDP, 1983), with implications far beyond the scheme, included software standards, documentation of programs, hardware specification, alternative input devices, interfacing standards, copyright and teacher training. Each of these has to be resolved if progress is to be made in providing the necessary designs for programmers to work on.

Teachers who cannot write their own programs in a programming language can use an authoring system to prepare teaching programs. For example, at the California School for the Deaf in Fremont near San Francisco, Irwin (1983) has developed Blocks 82, a very versatile system which has been used by some 50 teachers in the school and is sold to many other school districts. Teachers using the system, which provides for heavy use of graphics, have many opportunities to teach deaf children in visual terms and can tailor lessons to the needs of their own students. The system gives them full control over content and style, within a 'branching programmed learning' format based on statements followed by a multiple-choice question. It demands no knowledge of programming, although some simple skills in operating a microcomputer are necessary. A 'management system' is built into each lesson: students name themselves and their teachers at the start, and any teacher can easily check the computerised record of progress for his or her students.

Does the software help with areas of the curriculum that cause learning difficulties? Software now available does include some that is valuable in these difficult areas, ranging from teaching reading, writing and arithmetic to young children, right up to calculus for adults.

For example, at Theurkauf School in Mountain View, California, speech-impaired children use a word-processing program, the Bank Street Writer (from the Bank Street College of Education in New York). They lack words to communicate and the program provides talking points and labels that they can use to begin building up a vocabulary. The logic programs produced by The Learning Company, in nearby Menlo Park (see Rheingold, 1983), are said by teachers to reinforce these children's capacity to remember 'chunks' of information (Neu, 1983).

Some of the software can overcome that most difficult problem in dealing with many disabled children: poor motivation. Miriam is working with Justin on one of the educational game programs from The Learning Company. In fact, she entirely controls use of the keyboard, although she allows Justin to hit a key occasionally. Despite this, Justin is the one who knows the answers and tells her what key to press. Both of these disabled children are deeply involved with the words on the screen. Again and again, they reward themselves for 'winning' against the machine, exclaiming 'I did it!' or 'I keep on winning!' or 'I won!' Sometimes they even applaud their own achievements.

Beukelman (1983) points out that congenitally dumb children tend to learn by rote how to spell words, but have difficulty in using them in context. They also find that their thought processes and their progress through the school curriculum outstrip their spelling skills. Software can provide spelling, and even syntax and grammar, far beyond the level they have acquired. Do these programs then enable the students to cope with learning problems at a higher level than their language development?

But who evaluates educational software and is it good enough? Although computer manufacturers and software companies have many educational programs for sale, selecting those of high quality is far from easy. Program reviews in magazines and journals tend to be uncritical descriptions of content. Many programs have not been written to fit into the normal school curriculum. Those that fit tend to cover only a fragment, at no small expense.

The Teachers

Are teachers willing to change role when disabled students use the technology? Classroom teachers have to change role when able-bodied students begin to use microcomputers (see Hawkridge, 1983), because the students become increasingly self-motivated and independent of their teachers. Disabled students may still require help in operating the equipment, but for their teachers the role change is even greater as the students find a degree of independence in their learning, far beyond what they have previously experienced. Some teachers may share Griffin's (1982) view that the technology may be 'dangerously intoxicating' for them.

In many special schools, one or two teachers become the 'computer experts'. These teachers very radically change role, but the rest leave the computing to them and thus avoid changing their own roles. In general, it would be better if many more teachers gained at least some understanding of the technology, because the experts become increasingly separated from the rest as they master new developments and do less and less ordinary teaching. A 'community of users' among teachers and students is well worth establishing, with a full range of novices and experts. This has been done successfully in many conventional schools. Not all teachers need become experts, by any means; novices learn more when they need to, within such a community, and are helped over any 'computerphobia'.

Beyond such informal and collegial arrangements, how should teachers be given formal initial and in-service training in using the technology for teaching disabled students? Although initial training in the United States and the United Kingdom is beginning to include training in using the technology, the majority of teachers are already in the schools. A programme of in-service training is required, along the lines of the Microelectronics in Education Programme in England and Wales, or the Scottish Microelectronics Development Programme. The former consists mainly of local workshops backed up by packages of training materials produced by the Open University and with the support of the Special Education Microelectronic Resource Centres (see below). In the United States, several states have set up in-service training consortia and networks of centres, such as the Teacher Education Computer Centers (TECC) in California and the Minnesota Educational Computing Consortium (MECC) in St Paul.

Raising Awareness

What resource centres and means of information exchange exist to foster use of the technology in educating disabled students? The CALL (Communication Aids for Learners in Lothian) project at the University of Edinburgh is an interesting British example of a resource centre plus action research in applying new information technology to communication needs of disabled learners. In the centre is a range of hardware and software for loan to groups or individuals willing to collaborate in evaluation. Staff of the centre are studying use of the technology by five particular students with communication handicaps, as well as trying to develop additional devices and systems. The centre also distributes American publications from the Trace Center (see below).

In the United Kingdom, four Special Education Microelectronic Resource Centres were established in 1982 with Department of Education and Science funding in Bristol, Manchester, Newcastle-upon-Tyne and Redbridge (near London). These centres provide information and advice about the use of microcomputers and other microelectronic devices in special education and foster software development; enable schools to try hardware and software before any purchasing decisions are taken; promote and contribute to in-service training of teachers by running courses, offer 'hands-on' experience and stimulate discussion of good classroom practice. Their work is aimed at teachers of children with mental handicaps as well as of those with physical or sensory disabilities.

A British centre with educational interests is the Handicapped Persons Research Unit at Newcastle-upon-Tyne Polytechnic, which among other activities organises exhibitions, maintains an important and comprehensive database of research and fosters manufacture of educational aid prototypes invented in the Unit (Sandhu, 1984).

In the United States, the Federal Department of Education funds the National Institute of Handicapped Research, which in turn funds projects such as ABLEDATA, a database produced by the National Rehabilitation Information Center in Washington DC and covering over 6,000 products for use in rehabilitation programmes, not all of them educational. Government-supported databases on teaching materials in special education include NARIC, from the National Rehabilitation Information Center, from the same Washington DC centre, and NICSEM, produced by the National Information Center for Special Education Materials in Los Angeles. The electronic bulletin board (SpecialNet) of the National Association of State Directors of Special Education raises awareness, too, but mainly among those already quite aware.

The Trace Research and Development Center for the Severely Communicatively Handicapped, at the University of Wisconsin, maintains a register of programs written or adapted for use by individuals with physical handicaps, including students, and sponsors workshops and conferences. Its staff are in touch with most American and British researchers in this field.

How can awareness of what is available to disabled students be raised? For example, initial training for teachers seldom includes study of what new information technology has to offer to disabled children, although there is some in-service training in this field. Few medical students are taught a basic understanding of the technology and its applications, and the same is still true in training of professionals who help disabled children and adults. As training changes to include these topics, awareness of professionals will increase, and this will have a major impact on sales to institutions and individuals. Doctors and teachers occupy powerful positions, as they frequently decide (and at least advise) whether devices and systems should be purchased for or by a disabled child or adult.

What role does the technology itself have in raising awareness? Raising awareness of what is available occurs in many ways, but not very effectively yet through new information technology itself. For example, a sampling of Prestel (the British videotex system) in 1983 showed very little specifically for disabled viewers: an out-of-date schedule of BBC broadcasts, sketchy details from the National Bureau for Handicapped Students, and facts about services available to disabled telephone users. These might be of some slight use to people interested in informal education, but not formal.

Similarly, in California there is an electronic bulletin board, Wellnet, set up and contributed to by several colleges and available night and day. All disabled students at the colleges receive training in how to use it, including how to leave their own messages on it, but they can do so only if they have access to it through a modem and microcomputer. They must also pay the telephone charges, at local rates.

A project in Scotland is exploring use of a private videotex system, run by the Scottish Microelectronics Development Programme, as a medium for exchange of information and computer programs among special education professionals (Daly, 1983). This project has interesting potential in a country where some schools are rather isolated geographically. Over 40 centres are being provided with equipment that will enable them to receive information and programs over telephone lines. Funding is from the Department of Trade and Industry.

Summary

This chapter has discussed educational issues that arise when new information technology is introduced into the education of disabled children and adults. These issues are by no means resolved to the satisfaction of teachers in the field. Teachers hold the key to some of them, but government departments, specialised agencies, manufacturers and other professional groups must play their part.

14 SOCIAL ISSUES

This chapter separates three specific social issues regarding disabled students from the many social issues concerning education on the one hand and disability on the other. First, whether or not disabled students should use the technology; second, how the technology helps or hinders integration, and, third, the issue of access for disabled students to benefits brought by the technology to able-bodied students.

Should Disabled Students Use New Information Technology?

Prejudices do exist against the technology, among people who work with disabled students. For example, some expect the students to damage or break it. Disabled children, in particular, are often seen as even more likely to break the equipment than their able-bodied agemates. To some extent, this view is based on misunderstanding the durability of electronic machines. It is true, however, that many physically-disabled children cannot cope with workstations crowded with components connected by trailing wires: their difficulties must be taken into account in designing the equipment. Other students need help in getting started: somebody else must load those relatively delicate floppy discs in cardboard covers.

There is also a fear that the technology isolates disabled students or prevents them from communicating with others, disabled and able-bodied, because they are 'tied to a computer screen'. Some school speech therapists, for example, think that electronic communication aids will remove children's motivation to learn to speak. Here too there may be misunderstanding about what the technology can do and how children enjoy working together with it. There is perhaps a fear that they will progress well without as much help as usual from teachers.

Humphrey and Kleiman (1982) describe an American project in which two teachers found that their disabled students had few problems learning to operate the microcomputers being used, did not break anything and learned a good deal in a very happy and collaborative atmosphere. In particular, the teachers reported that their children enjoyed being able to erase mistakes 'without leaving a smudge on the screen' and that they gained self-esteem through being able to control and interact with the computer in the process of producing neat schoolwork.

Some fear that the technology has a dehumanising effect and leads to over-reliance on mediated learning. Hawkridge (1983) discusses this point in some detail. It seems that children use the technology as a complement to other ways of learning, never as the sole or dominant way. Of course, disabled children gain many more communication benefits from the technology than their able-bodied classmates.

Some educators say that the technology can constrain or change the nature of communication so much that it undesirably emphasises the condition of the disabled user. Thus slow conversation or dialogue with a very limited vocabulary on one side soon ceases to be real and the non-impaired speaker can seem to be condescending (Pickering, 1983). Unfortunately, this can be true with or without the technology, which may actually alleviate the problem. One of the greatest social problems for physically-disabled and speech-impaired people is the slowness of their communication. This hinders considerably their social development, particularly their relationships with able-bodied people, who can scarcely avoid dominating any social interchange. Unaided, a physically-disabled or speech-impaired person may take ten to twenty times as long as an able-bodied person to speak or write a sentence or to do an arithmetic exercise. New information technology can help them considerably, although they may still take four or five times as long. For a physically-disabled student, for example, the technology may make the difference between being totally unable to complete classwork or homework and being able to finish at least the essentials. Abbreviation programs can be useful: a single keystroke may produce a commonly used word or sentence. More elaborate 'codes' of keystrokes can express complete ideas (see Minspeak, Chapter 18).

Joanna, a physically-disabled student at Essex University, started in 1973 to use a Lightwriter, a portable typewriter with visual display. Eight years later, she decided that she would benefit greatly from using a computer, and she now has an Apple II, which she uses chiefly for word processing. Joanna says that even with her Lightwriter working she cannot easily enter into casual conversation. Other people see the device as a clever toy rather than a communication aid. When she asks a serious question through it, the person reading it may respond 'Oh, isn't that clever', sadly failing to see that it is her, not the device, that is 'talking' (Mahon, 1983).

Finally, on the negative side, are ignorance and apathy. For example, large numbers of personnel working in special education are simply not yet aware of the technology and its potential, nor is there much evidence that they wish to be informed.

Prejudices in favour of the technology also abound. From disabled people themselves comes the view that information technology is desirable because its use confers greater dignity and independence on them: as Glen (1982) points out, this was the goal of designers of one of the first systems, Possum (Patient-Operated Selector Mechanism; 'possum' is also a Latin word meaning 'I can'), which has been imitated in many forms. Instead of helpers doing things *for* the deaf to enable them to 'take part', as in years gone by, now the work is aimed at enabling decisions *by* deaf students about how they will take part. If a deaf student wants to participate in classwork by using a technological aid, he or she frequently can, being no longer excluded by a disability.

Strong claims are made that the technology gives disabled students greater control over their learning, and that this motivates them more than almost anything else. Given the technology, they are dealing with a finite system, in which they can make mistakes but recover from them. This is important for able-bodied people, but doubly so for disabled users.

Disabled students, except perhaps the very young, must often be involved in decisions about provision, use, modification and replacement of the technology. Firminger (1983) emphasises that in the Hereward College project (see Chapter 9) it is the students who become the true experts in using the technology to overcome their own handicaps, and who know the benefits and pitfalls. She warns that their views must be heeded and reminds us that many aids based on earlier technology were received with enthusiasm by professionals and then discarded at the first available opportunity by users.

Bob, a blind student at the Open University, started in 1980 to use a microcomputer and speech synthesiser for scientific calculations. His choice, that year, of a technology foundation course, was significant because his earlier courses were from the social sciences, where he did not need computing facilities, although his preference was for a degree in technology and computing. By 1984, Bob had progressed to higher level computing courses with the continuing assistance of his 'talking microcomputer'. His programming skills had developed to the extent that he is now producing software for use by mentally-handicapped children.

Does the Technology Assist Classroom Integration of Disabled Students?

Beliefs and attitudes about disabled children and adults have had a very substantial impact on the manner in which education has been provided for them. Disability has been judged for many years in clinical terms rather than social, resulting in separation of disabled children into special schools, along with children who are educationally subnormal. 'Treatment' of these children has been carried out, with the best of intentions, in such a way as to increase their dependence on others and to stress their differences rather than their similarities with other children. Disabled adults have been placed at a similar disadvantage. Yet what separates the physically-disabled student from the able-bodied is only a physical dimension, as Foulds (1982) says. The latter may be able to run faster, reach further or talk quicker. The former may possess all the intelligence needed for academic achievement, but may not be able to write. If they have sensory disabilities, at present they often move from school into further or higher education, within a supportive setting that consists largely of students with similar disabilities. Blind students associate with blind, deaf with deaf and so on, to their advantage but also to their disadvantage. Signing among deaf people increases this separation and isolation. They are obliged to keep each other's company (Booth, 1983). Information technology is able to break down these barriers to some extent, as British students have found at Hereward College (for physically-disabled students), but integration, some say, will do more.

In the United Kingdom, integration of disabled children into ordinary schools is proceeding, following the Warnock Report (Department of Education and Science, 1978). In the United States, a similar process is taking place, under a different name, 'mainstreaming'. The general goal is the same in both countries: to secure maximum participation in ordinary school life for disabled students.

Integration and mainstreaming require some accommodation in ordinary schools to the needs of disabled students, whether they are physically-disabled or have sensory disabilities. Some students may be able to work in ordinary classes, with or without special help. Others may leave ordinary classes to receive extra individual attention elsewhere for part of the day. Still others may belong to classes in specialised schools, but visit ordinary schools for certain subjects. Provision of new information technology is affected by these patterns.

Daren, a partially-sighted student at Castlecroft Primary School, Wolverhampton, is in a class of sighted students. He uses a Perkins Brailler for his classwork: this creates a communication problem for most of his teachers and fellow-students, who cannot read braille. The problem has been overcome by linking the Brailler to a microcomputer with software that translates his braille into text (Vincent, 1983). The text is displayed on a screen and can be printed out at any time. Daren has simple commands available on the computer to control printing of the text, and these commands are 'confirmed' by a voice synthesiser. This simple facility to produce simultaneously braille and text has proved to be invaluable. Daren produces work for teachers which would otherwise have required manual transcription by a braille-reading person using the embossed braille sheets. Continuous display of text on the screen enables Daren's teachers to see his work in much the same way as they look at other students' written work, during lessons. Although it is not necessarily desirable for other children to see Daren's work, the screen provides a new and interesting dimension. They see what he is writing and Daren and his computer have become a central feature of the class rather than being on the periphery. Before, he was working in a language other students could not understand: it was Greek to them, and he was isolated by it.

In the United Kingdom, as Chapman (1982) points out, new information technology has arrived since the Warnock Report. The Committee did not foresee that microcomputers might solve certain problems for disabled students, that individuals without speech and with only minimal motor control would be able to write and speak through the computer, admittedly slowly, or that a severely spastic student would do arithmetic and play games with classmates. They did not foresee computer interaction which stimulates children 'whose motor capabilities are otherwise unrewarding to themselves' and overcomes problems of distractability. In fact, awareness of the new technology is still not high: Booth and Potts (1983) do not mention computers or new information technology in their extensive discussion of integration in British schools.

Chapman says that teachers in special education are reporting that children with access to computer games are showing improved motor control, fewer behavioural problems and a positive attitude. Voice synthesisers and braille writers help blind students, and Chapman's own computer-based rebus reading scheme for deaf children permits profoundly-deaf children to use a graphic form of language with English syntax from the age of two. Chapman notes that in society and in schools, ability and achievement are assessed in terms of quality of communication. He thinks technology can and should be used to bridge the gap for disabled students, although Beukelman (1983) is more doubtful because it is not really fast enough. Perhaps its promise will be realised fully only when personal and portable systems, one for each student, become available.

Teachers in ordinary schools, faced with dealing with disabled children, will want support and advice, if only because they have never been trained for this kind for work. Warnock (1983) says that trainee teachers asked by questionnaire about integration of disabled children into ordinary schools were in favour of it, in principle, but most said they did not expect to be personally responsible for these students in their own teaching. She suggests that legislation that followed the report of her Committee requires us to think

> not in terms of what is wrong with a child, what he suffers from, but in terms of what he needs. We are not to think where he can be put, out of the way, but of what positive help he can have so that he can be educated alongside his contemporaries. We ought not to underestimate the change that is demanded ... The whole ethos of the secondary school is against the (Warnock Report's view) of special needs.

She points out that if parents have a choice, they still tend to send their disabled children to schools that take pride in serving these children well, and these schools may or may not be for high flyers too. Doubtless these are the schools that are more likely to provide new information technology to their disabled students.

Do Disabled Students Gain Proper Access to the Technology's Benefits?

While overcoming their disabilities by using information technology, disabled people also want to use the same computer programs as anyone else, to learn how to accomplish the same tasks. Vanderheiden (1982b) gives the example of a blind person who wants, through a text-to-braille program, to learn to use standard word processing, spreadsheet and database programs. A physically-disabled person who, through a single switch, can word process may also want to learn to use accounting and business management programs. Thus the technology must compensate for disability and also provide the same access that able-bodied people enjoy to the new world of information technology. In general, this is only beginning to happen, mainly for technical reasons (see Chapter 17). A text-to-braille translator is not very satisfactory for a programmer who cannot see the screen; for physically-disabled programmers, alternatives to using the keyboard are again rather unsatisfactory.

Summary

This chapter has discussed whether disabled students should use the new technology. Clearly this book would not have been written had we not believed that they should do so, but we think there should be debate on the matter and opinions ought to be expressed. We also think the technology can assist classroom integration to some extent. Finally, there is some doubt about whether disabled people can get full access to the technology's benefit, although the situation may improve (see Chapters 18 and 19).

15 POLITICAL ISSUES

This chapter looks at several political issues concerning promotion and provision of new information technology by disabled students, access to it and how it affects their vocational prospects. Again, the chapter does not attempt to cover broader political matters relating to disability, although these are receiving much attention from government: for instance, in the United States, Hofmann (1983, 1984) reports on Senate and House of Representatives Bills intended to amend American law so that subsidies for the purchase of technologically advanced sensory and communication aids are more widely available to disabled Americans, and, in the United Kingdom, Sandhu (1983) says that the Department of Health and Social Security needs a policy on research and development of microelectronic aids for disabled children and adults and should help to fund this work.

What is Government Doing to Promote and Provide the Technology?

The question does not ask why government is not doing more. That is a separate issue. Governments are not, of course, society as a whole and it is society that has a general duty to look after its disabled members, in many ways. It is a fact, however, that governments have wide roles in encouraging and facilitating provision of the technology and in developing relationships between various interested parties. Government can influence education authorities and teachers. Some of these need to be convinced that disabled children and adults can succeed academically, just as some employers need to be convinced that many disabled people are efficient employees (in the United Kingdom, working days lost due to illness are less for disabled employees than for the able-bodied). Difficult as it may be to believe, some authorities and numerous teachers do not yet know what new information technology can do to help disabled students: here too government has a role to influence and educate.

During the International Year of the Disabled Person, an exhibition of computer-based aids for disabled people was held in London at the House of Commons. A Minister from the Department of Health and Social Security, Sir George Young, in a speech to open the exhibition, drew attention to the importance of microelectronic technology for many disabled people. He went on to say:

> It would be unwise, given the present constraints on public expenditure, to expect progress with microcomputer aids to be anything but modest. There is an enormous amount of goodwill in this country towards disabled people, and help can, and I am sure it will, come from voluntary sources.

His statement must have been disappointing news for many of the exhibitors who had been working in relative isolation in research groups, small companies and schools, and who were hoping for a central initiative to promote the technology.

It was fortunate that the British government designated 1982 as Information Technology Year ('IT82'), as this gave an opportunity to re-examine, in a new context, technological initiatives that might be taken for the ultimate benefit of disabled people. Various microcomputer-based aids could be considered as possible products of small companies. Subsidies could be provided to these companies as part of a general plan to promote industry in the United Kingdom. In fact, numerous projects involving information technology and disabled people have been funded since 1982 through the Department of Trade and Industry. Some projects have focused on adults at home and at work, others on students in schools, colleges and universities. For example, the Department has funded Remote Work Units, which enable disabled people to work at home. It has paid for the establishment of exhibitions and databases concerning aids for disabled people (for example, at the Disabled Living Foundation in London and the Handicapped Persons Research Unit in Newcastle-upon-Tyne), and for a system to assess the needs of physically-disabled students at Hereward College, Coventry. In other cases, the Department purchases devices such as concept keyboards, Edinburgh Turtles and Sound Bubbles (see Chapter 9) from British companies and distributes them to special schools. Through its IT Awareness Programme, the Department has raised awareness of new technology and what it can do. 'The Concerned Technology' is a travelling exhibition which has toured the country and even been abroad. Among the devices displayed in the exhibition were several that are products of initiatives taken during the International Year of the Disabled Person.

Another government scheme has had a significant impact on English and Welsh schools, including special schools. The Microelectronics Education Programme was funded with £9 million, of which £1 million was set aside for special education. This £1 million has been used mainly to establish the Special Education Microelectronic Resource Centres (see Chapter 13) and to pay for software development. The Scottish Microelectronics Development Programme linked up with the Department of Trade and Industry to introduce information technology into more Scottish special schools (Walker, 1983). Three regional development centres, based in three special schools, operate under this arrangement and are equipped with the technology, including microcomputers for individual students, concept keyboads, Edinburgh Turtles and BBC Buggies, video cameras and recorders and interactive videodisc. The teachers have large screens, five feet square, on which they can display the work of individual students, direct from the students' own computer screens. New devices are being added each year on the advice of the teachers.

The use of microelectronics to help children with learning difficulties is now a recognised part of the British educational map, as Hope (1983) says, and government has succeeded in fostering teachers' awareness and enthusiasm. What Hope questions is how, in the longer term, local government will be able to take over what has been started. She argues for central government funding of careful evaluation of present use of the technology in special schools, plus more research on how computers can enhance learning for children in these schools.

In the United States, national schemes are more difficult to mount in this field, because education is chiefly a state and local matter, not a federal one. The Division of Educational Technology in the US Department of Education has conducted several studies (for example, McLaughlin and others, 1983) that have touched upon special education only incidentally. To date, there has been no Federal initiative to parallel the schemes backed by the British government. Some states are extremely progressive in their general provision for disabled people: California, for example, under recent legislation provides all registered deaf adults with a free device that enables them to use the telephone. With the device, which is similar to the British Vistel, the 'speaker' can type a message, which appears on the screen of a similar device attached to the 'listener's' telephone. California also has a very good system of special schools in which much state-funded microelectronic technology is now being used, particularly communication aids. Local school districts are often equally generous in providing funds for technology for use by disabled students.

What Can Parents Do to Ensure That a Disabled Child Has Access to the Technology for Education?

In the United Kingdom, Newell (1983) says that under the 1981 Education Act, which came into force in 1983, parents of a disabled child can ask for a formal assessment of their child's educational needs and a statement on how the local authority plans to meet these needs, including any professional advice the authority has received. If the parents are dissatisfied with the assessment and statement, they can insist on meeting officials and professionals. If they remain dissatisfied, they can use appeal procedures, right up to the Minister responsible for special education.

Thus officials, professionals and parents may all come to consider what information technology can possibly do to meet the educational needs of a particular disabled student.

Similarly, in the United States many state agencies for disabled students now require schools to prepare Individualised Educational Programs (IEPs) for each student. Computers are reducing paperwork needed in setting up and using these detailed sets of objectives based on each student's needs (Enell, 1983). Technology may be provided or recommended for students who can benefit from it.

What Are the Employment Prospects for Disabled Students?

The ultimate question for many disabled students is what kind of job they will be able to get when they have finished studying. For instance, Goodyear (1982), says that most deaf children leave school at 16 with a reading age of only seven. Are they prepared for life after school? How does information technology affect their vocational prospects?

Preparatory courses for students about to leave school sometimes help, but there is a lack of purpose in the planning of these courses. When they leave school, disabled children encounter prejudice among employers. At school, their dependence is accepted and even understood: immediately on leaving, and for many years thereafter, independence becomes a vital factor in obtaining employment. It is a fact, in the United States and the United Kingdom, that a very high percentage of disabled teenagers face the prospect of not being fully employed, or not being employed at all, for the rest of their lives. The employment future looks gloomy for able-bodied youth, but it is much worse for disabled youth, who usually go from school to some sort of sheltered environment in which employment is episodic, infrequent and incidental to their existence. If they get a job, it is often poorly-paid and in a dirty and noisy place (Walker, 1982). In both countries, legislation that obliges employers to give special consideration to disabled applicants has been inadequate to change significantly this situation. Provision for disabled school-leavers is split between different government departments, with poor liaison. The best that can be said is that some schools teach their disabled students how to seek a job (Dickson, 1979).

If new information technology brings with it some hope of greater employment in adult life, it will be doubly welcomed by disabled students. There is no doubt that learning to use the technology to overcome or compensate for their own disabilities puts these students in quite a strong position to exploit it for employment. For them, microcomputers and other microelectronic devices and systems do hold vocational potential, far beyond the work of, say, a blind audiotypist. They can acquire programming, software design and systems analysis skills, in particular, and can use them to earn a living.

Consider the Spastics Society's Neath Hill Workshop at Milton Keynes in the United Kingdom. The centre is a commercial company, marketing computer hardware and sofware and providing a professional service of systems analysis, programming and implementation for business and industry. About half the staff are disabled, some being spastic, others blind, deaf, paralysed by stroke or multiple sclerosis. All of these have degrees and a deep interest in computing. The centre is run much like other companies and has a long-term efficiency target for its spastic staff of 85 per cent of able-bodied output. Staff with speech problems use keyboards and screens to communicate, rather than voice synthesis, which some of them tried and found slow and disruptive. Disabled staff use standard hardware, with software modifications, but originally with some interesting variations. For example, spastic staff had difficulties in handling training and other manuals, therefore they used two- and three-screen workstations, one screen carrying the manual, another their programming and a third for notes, subroutines and general communication. All three screens were under the control of a single microcomputer and keyboard. Several disabled staff have left the workshop since it started and have moved into open employment, one as a computer consultant. One member of staff runs training courses in computer programming for other disabled people in the community.

Stevenson and Sutton (1982) report on a study of employment opportunities for physically-disabled people in computing. This study was initiated by members of the British computing industry and funded by the Social Science Research Council. They point out that jobs in the computing industry are not merely programming and systems analysis, and that many physically-disabled people can train for jobs such as data preparation, administrative and office functions, technical or engineering work, and hardware design and construction. They see 'sheltered workshops' or 'working at home' as possible long-term options for physically-disabled people. For the immediate future, companies will want their staff to be at the office.

Steward (1983) describes a project that examined the relationship between vocational classes in high school and attainment of competitive (open) employment by visually-handicapped students. It involved 35 such students who had graduated between 1970 and 1982. The 26 who had been available for work (the others were still studying) had been employed 59 per cent of the time since leaving school, in an area of generally high employment over that period. In the survey, vocational classes were rated as helpful in obtaining employment, but there was no correlation between the number of vocational classes taken and success in obtaining employment.

The range of employment options goes well outside computing industry skills, however, because by using information technology many disabled adults can train for jobs that were previously closed to them. These information-handling jobs include setting up, maintaining and searching computerised databases for commercial firms; operating booking, accounting and banking systems; undertaking computer-aided design; using computers for stock and purchasing control; managing library stocks; and word processing. A particularly interesting British example is CAD/CAM (Computer-Assisted Design/Computer-Assisted Modelling) at Queen Elizabeth's Training College for the Disabled at Leatherhead. Students at the College are trained to use a CAD/CAM system (see Chapter 9) and go to jobs in companies that have similar equipment (Rochester, 1984).

As disabled teenagers and adults with these new skills seek jobs, attitudes towards employing them will change and opportunities for them should increase.

Beverly is 22 and has a rare disease that stunts her growth. She uses a wheelchair. On completing a university degree she started work at home using a microcomputer, telephone and specially adapted furniture, all provided through a special government grant of about £10,000. Her job is to arrange sessions for candidates wishing to take the examinations of a professional society.

Christo is a blind physiotherapist working in a London hospital. New information technology is helping him to overcome two problems that arise in his work: written communication with sighted colleagues, and record keeping. Christo uses braille extensively to keep notes about patients but they cannot be read by other people in the department who are sighted. The linking of a Perkins Brailler to a microcomputer has provided a means of producing printed text simultaneously with braille (thus overcoming a common problem experienced by blind people in employment). Patients' notes are stored in a filing system on magnetic discs. The operation of the system is made possible by synthetic speech output which is used also to 'read-back' patients' notes for checking and up-dating. In the United Kingdom there are over 300 blind physiotherapists which makes it a significant area for professional employment. It is important that new information technology maintains this opportunity.

Jenkin (1982) says that computer-based training for disabled employees is not yet well-developed, but he gives three British examples: secretarial training, particularly in word processing, using a computer that measures performance and sets exercises accordingly; training in fault-tracing in the chemical industry, using a program that combines tutorial self-instruction with simulations; and training in using data entry and interrogation systems, such as airline reservation systems, using a computer-based package. He suggests disabled trainees can benefit from the self-instructional nature of computer-based training, which they can take up at their own pace, and often where and when they want to.

In the United States, the training picture for disabled people is similar. After IBM gave a lead some years ago in sponsoring computer programming training, disabled trainees can obtain help through banks, insurance companies, government departments, universities and many other channels. The Maryland Project, which started in 1973, is a model: it has involved Johns Hopkins University, state government and private business, and after eight years had enabled more than 400 people to become independent financially in the data-processing field. In Madison, Wisconsin, Computers to Help People Inc. trains disabled people to use computers in their work. Its founder is John Boyer, a programmer who is deaf and blind (reported in *Wall Street Journal*, 7 Feb. 1984).

Disabled students clearly need advice on the technology. Are some right in spending their government disability allowances on holidays rather than on technology that is expensive to buy and maintain? If user and helpers have to learn to use the technology, and the technology does not bring enough benefit, in their eyes, why should it be adopted? If high technology is unreliable and must be backed up by low technology (pencil and paper, say) plus helpers, is it worth buying? Will a job come with it, or as a result of using it?

Summary

Providing for disability is said in some quarters to be something politicians do to catch votes. If this is true, it may account to some extent for government provision of the new technology, although it is clear that governments in the United Kingdom and the United States are at present doing more to promote the technology than to provide it. Government can do much to increase disabled students' access to new information technology, and, through regulation, can improve the chances of disabled people obtaining jobs involving use of the technology. These are all political issues that require political solutions.

16 ECONOMIC ISSUES

This chapter looks at several difficult economic issues surrounding new information technology for disabled students. To a large extent, these issues cannot be separated from general ones of disability and technological aid, but they are particularly problematic in educating disabled children and adults.

How is the Technology for Disabled Students Developed?

New information technology for disabled students is developed through stages that do not differ very much from those for many other inventions. Somebody, whether a disabled person or a professional dealing with disabled people, has an idea. That person, or somebody else, undertakes the designing of a prototype, which then has to be made. Next, the prototype is tested and the results of its evaluation may be quite widely discussed, in attempts to find risk capital and a manufacturer. Once a manufacturer takes it on, proper marketing and servicing arrangements must be made.

Unfortunately, developing the technology through all these stages is usually costly, and the price of any device or system produced specifically for disabled students is likely to be rather high. A wheelchair costs much more than a bicycle, and devices for disabled students may well cost more than standard microcomputer accessories. This is because disabilities vary so much from individual to individual, and any single device may meet the needs of only a comparatively small number, perhaps not enough for mass production (see below).

What are the Problems of Funding This Research and Development?

Financial support for the stages up to testing a prototype may be found fairly easily, but it is difficult to obtain risk capital and persuade a manufacturer to go into production engineering, to mass-produce copies for sale. Reynolds (1980) says that production engineering involves conversion of a prototype into a product designed to be manufactured in large quantities, according to regular production schedules, with extremely high product consistency and quality control. A prototype may provide proof that a concept is worthwhile, but it tells a potential manufacturer very little about whether it can be manufactured and marketed successfully. Market surveys in this field are notoriously unreliable, as a British bank found when it introduced a pilot project that offered laser-generated large-print bank statements for people with poor sight and was inundated with thousands of requests. The diversity in, say, speech-impairment also makes for no single large market for a particular device. In general, the volume of sales for any single device will be low.

One way to overcome the problem of manufacturing cost and risk is to find a commercial use for the new technology which will recover the investment, but leave the device or system available for use at marginal cost to disabled people. An example might be a speech device invented for deep-sea divers, who have trouble speaking in their pressurised suits. The cost of developing, testing and making the device is negligible to a deep-sea diving consortium in relation to benefits obtained. Afterwards the device can become available cheaply to speech-impaired students and others. Occasionally, it is possible to develop a device that suits many disabled *and* able-bodied customers. The push-button telephone is an example.

Eulenberg and Rosenfeld (1982) describe how an American company, Texas Instruments, developed the Vocaid, a communication device for speech-impaired people, from an educational aid, Touch and Tell. They note, however, that a complete product development cycle was needed for the Vocaid, involving extensive retooling in the factory, more circuitry in the device and a doubling of the speed at which the circuits operate (to improve voice quality). To recover the costs of this work and because the market for the Vocaid is considerably smaller than for Touch and Tell, the company set the Vocaid price (about $150) two or three times above that for Touch and Tell.

Occasionally, part of a device or system invented and marketed for another purpose turns out to be very valuable to disabled people. For example, the circuits from the Polaroid sonic focusing camera are now used to provide blind people with a cheap device that tells them how far away they are from solid objects.

What Role Should Government Play in Funding Development?

As we mentioned in Chapter 15, public funds are being used in several ways to support development, manufacture and purchase of new information technology for educating disabled children and adults.

Because government at all levels, in the US and the UK, wishes to foster development and manufacture of information technology, quite large sums are being made available. In the United Kingdom, the Department of Trade and Industry has provided several million pounds to boost research and development in universities and commercial companies, and has paid for British manufacture and supply of specialised equipment to schools and hospitals (see Chapter 15).

In addition, subsidies go to registered disabled people through the Department of Health and Social Security for aids to day-to-day living and from the Manpower Services Commission (MSC) for aids to employment. Both sources, after careful consideration of individuals' cases, may pay for communication aids that have education or training applications. Bennett (1983) says that the MSC believes that 'disability does not mean inability'. For example, funding priority may be given to blind computer programmers who need an Optacon or Versabraille (Chapter 10) for more advanced training as well as to carry out their jobs more efficiently. The MSC will provide several kinds of hardware, including Versabraille, Brailink, Optacon and Microwriter devices for blind trainees, Possum for those who are physically-disabled and Vistels for deaf trainees. The list is added to from time to time as new devices come on the market.

Similarly, the United States Department of Education is subsidising many development projects through its National Institute of Handicapped Research (Beukelman, 1983). For example, it supports work in research laboratories, such as the Department of Speech Pathology at Washington State University in Seattle, the Smith-Kettlewell Institute of Visual Sciences in San Francisco, the Carroll Center for the Blind near Boston, the National Rehabilitation Information Center in Washington DC, and the Trace Research and Development Center for the Severely Communicatively Handicapped, at the University of Wisconsin. More specifically, it recently paid for sophisticated measuring equipment used by blind chemistry students at Eastern Carolina University.

The equipment translates visual displays into synthesised speech, enabling the students to do experiments without relying on a sighted person to take readings for them.

The Optacon Dissemination Project in America received funding from the United States Office of Education/Bureau of Education for the Handicapped. In the first two years (1976/7) of the project, over 400 teachers of visually-handicapped students attended special university seminars on the use of the Optacon, and nearly 800 blind students were given training. By 1978, nearly 200 of the blind students had reached print reading independence and received the loan of an Optacon for their educational and personal use. The statistics illustrate the advantages of a concerted national effort that integrated the provision of hardware and the training of teachers and students. No subsequent single new information technology development has received such a concentrated support. The extent of the project in America influenced other countries. Two examples, in Japan and Italy, were described in Chapter 10. By 1983 there were a significant number of Optacons world-wide. Figure 16.1 shows how they were distributed between 15 countries.

Figure 16.1: Distribution of Optacons in 15 Major Countries

Major Countries	Total Number of Optacons	State and local governments	National governments	Rehabilitation	Service groups	Individuals	Private foundations	Schools	Employers	Others
Italy	617	487		68	12	19		19	12	
United Kingdom	289	6	43		145	29	37		29	
Sweden	284	114	43	14	48	39	9	6	11	
W. Germany	255	64	153			13	25			
Japan	205	22	22		65	55	2	36	3	
Netherlands	186	18	138		18	4	4		4	
France	139			68	17	13	5	4	32	
Australia	118		14	24	7	39	4	26	4	
Spain	92			87		5				
Switzerland	68		33	2	7	5	13	7		1
Austria	60	8		48	2	1				1
Belgium	47		42			4	1			
Brazil	45	4		6		28		1	6	
Israel	45					1	43		1	
Finland	45		40			1		4		

Source: Telesensory Systems, Inc., California, 1983

There is some evidence to support the view that new information technology for disabled students, expensive though it still is, can save governments money. The Rehabilitation Institute of Chicago estimates that one particular electronic communication aid, provided to one child at school for eight hours a day, pays for itself in 148 days (*US Congressional Record*, 17 November 1983). Such figures are mainly based on notional savings in time of teachers and other helpers, but could also be based on faster studying by students supported by government grants. A disabled student who graduates from a publicly-funded university in four years instead of five is costing the government less.

Who are the Developers, Makers and Suppliers?

On both sides of the Atlantic, development of information technology (hardware and software) for use in educating disabled children and adults is largely in the hands of the non-profit sector: universities, hospitals and research institutes. The commercial sector is represented mainly by a few companies producing communication aids. In America, perhaps the most notable are Prentke-Romich of Shreve, Ohio; Telesensory Systems of Mountain View and Phonic Ear of Mill Valley, California; Kurzweil in Cambridge, Massachusetts; Triformation Systems in Stuart, Florida, and Sensory Aids Corporation in Illinois. In the United Kingdom, the best-known firms are Possum Controls of Slough, Buckinghamshire; Clarke and Smith, Wallington, Surrey, and Erleybridge Communications, London. Texas Instruments, in the United States, developed the Vocaid (see Chapter 9) specifically for speech-impaired people. It was the first of the big electronics manufacturers to enter the market with a purpose-built device. IBM developed a talking terminal for blind people.

Notable among the companies working on adaptations, for disabled people, of standard office equipment is Microwriter Ltd, in London. The Microwriter (see also Chapter 9) was developed for able-bodied workers, but it was soon evaluated by physically-disabled people. They liked it because without any modification its keypad requires only a vertical movement of the fingers without any movement of the hand. They found it small and light, and could place it in a variety of positions as needed. The company responded to requests by producing a left-handed version, and then a scanning keyboard that required the use of only one key instead of 'chords' of keys.

The Microwriter was and is sold at a substantial discount to disabled people, and it is worth noting that a similar device developed specifically for physically-disabled people would have been far more expensive. Now, the addition of a speech synthesiser has made the Microwriter accessible to visually-disabled people, but this application has been less successful because the synthesiser can only act in the same way as a printer, in that continuous text can be spoken but the interactive features involved in editing a text (deleting words, moving them around the page, etc.) cannot be associated with spoken responses. To provide this, a major software modification would be needed and this would probably add considerably to the price.

Sandhu (1983) comments that in organising a recent major non-profit exhibition of electronic technology for disabled people he found small companies more likely to want to exhibit.

What is the Nature of the Market?

Marketing a device for disabled people is unusually complicated, as LeBlanc (1978) points out. It is seldom sold off the shelf, but requires the intervention of doctors, psychologists, teachers and other professionals, all of whom must become more or less knowledgeable about it. A disabled student's needs must be assessed properly before any device or system is purchased, whether the purchaser is an agency, a parent or the student. Health or social welfare administrators, or medical insurance assessors, must be satisfied that the cost is justified. Even where the price of the device is low, costly modifications may be necessary to make it suit individual needs. In other words, the consumer seldom comes to the product, the product (along with supporting personnel) has to come to the consumer. Consumers are scattered, too, adding still further to the cost of marketing the product.

Hazen (1982), estimates that if only 2 per cent of American disabled people bought a microcomputer, 400,000 would be sold, a large enough market. This hardware market is divided into many segments, however, because the disabilities vary widely, and the information technology must be modified to suit individual needs. No major computer manufacturer has yet ventured into the business of making hardware specifically for disabled people, still less specifically for the education of disabled children and adults, although Apple Computers (1981) prepared a short resource guide on personal computers for disabled people, as a public service.

The same pattern prevails for software. An American study of over 700 educational programs supplied by 35 companies showed that software for disabled students was one of the lowest priorities (Shotwell Associates, 1981). Here too the market is highly segmented. Commercial suppliers are in no hurry to meet the needs of small segments. Manufacturers will not slow down their computer games to make them suitable for disabled players.

It has to be recognised, however, that many disabled people lack the motivation to learn to use devices and systems at present on the market, and many may never want to purchase them. For example, older disabled people, including those who are partly deaf, blind, physically-disabled or speech-impaired, may feel that they cannot learn or that there is little point in doing so. Certainly they will not trouble to learn to use complicated systems that are not rather user-friendly. As user-friendliness increases, however, and as older people include more who have used information technology a good deal during their working lives or for leisure, before becoming disabled, these attitudes will change, and the market will expand quickly. Manufacturers therefore have to take a very long-term view of investment in this field, looking a generation ahead.

Summary

New information technology is developed for disabled people in much the same stages as other technology, but there are problems in obtaining risk capital for mass-production of specialised hardware for relatively small numbers of consumers. It may be best to market a product suited to able-bodied people too. Governments have an important role in promoting and funding research and development, either directly (say, in universities and hospitals) or by subsidising hardware and software when it is purchased by disabled people. Developers and suppliers are mainly in the non-profit sector at present, with the exception of a few companies making communication aids. The market is peculiar in that purchase usually requires decisions from many besides the disabled consumer, and all these people need to become better informed about new information technology.

17 TECHNICAL ISSUES

A large number of technical issues surround information technology, but this chapter deals with only a few that are particularly relevant to disabled users in education. It looks first at how far technology can compensate for disabilities, then goes on to examine general technical factors that must be taken into account in selecting appropriate hardware and software, and, for that matter, in modifying it. Finally, it takes up some technical problems for users and the question of hazards.

To What Extent Can Technology Compensate For Disabilities?

Even in the Utopian climate created by governments, manufacturers and suppliers, we are bound to ask the question whether technology really can compensate for disabilities. Can disabled people use technology to function at anything like the same level as able-bodied people?

As Baker (1983) says, the central problem for speech-impaired people is the time required to translate their thoughts into words, whether written, printed or computer-spoken. New information technology helps them, but they still have to press keys or use a switch many times to produce the words they want, with the result that their 'speech' is very much slower than that of voice-spoken speech. A system based on letters (like a typewriter) is the most flexible, but needs far more key-presses than one based on words or phrases. Unfortunately, a large vocabulary or 'phrase-bank' poses problems of finding the right word or phrase quickly. A computer can be programmed so that when a speech-impaired person 'types' the first few letters of a word, several possible endings are flashed onto the screen, and only one more key-press selects the right one. Or, at a more advanced level, whole sentences can be built up in the same way. Vanderheiden (1983) points out, however, that a conversation is very difficult if one person is communicating at two to eight words a minute and the other at 180. The usual rules of conversation have to be set aside, and interactions are 'short, dominated by one party and highly frustrating'.

A synthetic speech output added to a word processor enables a blind person to enter, edit and format text with all of the features available to a sighted person. This provides opportunities for employment. But speech output is a relatively slow output medium and may not provide the same efficiency as a screen. If, for example, all help messages and commands are spoken each time they are displayed, the operation of the word processor would be considerably slower. One way of reducing this time difference would be to have information that appears repeatedly, listed as paper braille with a short spoken prompt to enter a command or request help. This may enable the same function to be completed within a similar time-scale, an important factor in employment.

What General Technical Factors Should Be Considered in Selecting Hardware and Software?

Many involved in research and development in this field hope that a relatively small range of microelectronic hardware plus a wider range of software will be the ultimate answer to problems of meeting the individual needs of disabled students (Pickering, 1983). Even then, specialised software developed for disabled people, including students, can be very expensive and because needs are so individual, modifications are often necessary. Therefore some say it may be best to find the software to meet particular needs and then buy the hardware to implement it. For example, if a program for Bliss symbols (see Chapter 9) is marketed for only one make of microcomputer, it may be best to purchase that make (Hope and Odor, 1982). Apart from microcomputers, some devices are programmable and can employ increasingly sophisticated software, including educational software, as their disabled owners learn how to use them.

Hardware need not necessarily be visible to the user, any more than telephone exchanges are visible to users of the telephone. Jaffe (1983) suggests that devices for disabled people may contain 'embedded microcomputers' and gives the example of a voice-activated robotic arm. A student using the arm, perhaps to carry out a scientific experiment, would speak commands into a microphone and the microcomputer, not necessarily near at hand, would convert these commands into signals to the robot.

What Kinds of Modifications Can Be Made to Suit Individual Needs?

Ideally, each disabled student requires information technology, probably including a microcomputer, modified to suit his or her needs. There is a sharp debate, however, over whether special devices should be developed for specific disabilities or whether it would not be better to concentrate effort on modifying standard, commercially-available hardware and software to the needs of disabled users. Among modifications that can be made are those that are transparent and semi-transparent (Vanderheiden, 1982b).

A transparent modification is one that cannot be detected or interfered with by standard software being used in the system, although it may be completely visible or otherwise obvious to the student. Vanderheiden's simplest example is a weight on a hinge that can be tipped over to hold down the shift key, thus permitting a one-fingered or headstick typist to input shift characters from the keyboard. An emulator that electrically imitates the keyboard is also transparent: for example, an infrared system for detecting eye movement may tell the computer which letter on the screen a person is looking at, but the signal the computer gets will be the same as if that letter on the keyboard had been pressed. Another transparent modification is a 'screen' that speaks to a blind student, who moves a cursor round a tablet beside the keyboard. As the cursor crosses words or letters from the computer's programs and 'written' electronically on the tablet, it speaks them, thus permitting the student to scan and 'feel' the information, rather slowly, a word or letter at a time. Yet the computer works as if the usual visual display were in use.

Transparent modifications are particularly valuable to disabled students in enabling them to use information technology systems normally used by able-bodied people. All the usual programs can remain in these systems.

There are disadvantages, however, in adopting this approach of transparent modification to software that has been designed for a specific input or output medium. For example, many computer programs include menu selection, which is ideal for visual presentation because it is fast and users can select an item by a single keypress. Menu selection is very slow for a blind student who must either scan all the items on the screen with the help of spoken output, or simply use on spoken output by itself. In either case it takes a long time to make a choice, much longer than it takes visually. More efficient ways of handling menu selection will almost certainly require modification of the original computer program.

Semi-transparent modifications are cheaper, because they usually involve more software and less hardware, but they interact with programs in use, and sometimes interfere with them. Vanderheiden says they are often programs stored in little-used sections of memory, or in read-only memory (ROM, see Chapter 6). An example of the latter is the Adaptive-Firmware Card (Schwejda and Vanderheiden, 1982), which is essentially a piece of elaborate programming stored on a low-cost card so that the main computer memory does not have to be used. This card provides a variety of input routines including scanning, Morse code and direct selection, and they can be used in conjunction with standard software. For example, a disabled student might use a microcomputer fitted with the card to control a program for working on a numerical 'spreadsheet' or a word processing program.

Software can also be available in ROM that intercepts output to a visual display and provides a parallel spoken output. In practice, this arrangement is seldom satisfactory unless the software interface in the ROM can change the form of the output to suit a different medium. For example, a statement in a BASIC program may appear on the visual display as: 1OFORI = 1TO1O, that is, without any spaces in the statement. Sending this directly to a speech synthesiser would produce an incomprehensible spoken output, unless it was in a mode where each character is spoken. Preferably, the reserved words, punctuation, numerals and variables are isolated by the software in ROM before outputting to the synthesiser. The example would then be spoken as: ten for I equals one to ten.

What Hardware Modifications Should Be Available?

Unfortunately, hardware is not always adapted to individual needs. Anna is a young child with spina bifida. She likes to work with the Edinburgh Logo turtle, with help from her teacher, who talks her through the sequence, which is usually for drawing shapes. First she tells her teacher what shape she would like to draw, then how many times forward she wants the turtle to move, and so on. She has some difficulty using the concept keyboard's touch-sensitive pad because sometimes she presses a box twice unintentionally, due to her poor motor co-ordination and control. It is also possible to press two keys simultaneously. Here are two instances of the child having to accommodate to the system, rather than the other way round, with negative effects. The fact that she has pressed a key twice, or pressed two at once, is often not apparent until the end of a sequence of commands when the turtle is expected to do something but does not. Then Anna and her teacher have to start afresh, which is very frustrating (McConnell, 1983).

The Special Technology expanded keyboard provides several features that help a physically-disabled student to overcome problems presented by a conventional electronic keyboard. In its initial format, it operates in parallel with the keyboard of the BBC microcomputer. Each key has a circular guide above it to help a student to press it 'cleanly'. The response time can be varied so that casual brushing of a key has no effect but pressing for a few seconds does, thus compensating somewhat for tremor. The keyboard also overcomes the problem of 'double key entry', that is, pressing two keys at once as in using shift and control with other keys. The length of pressing time required before a key begins 'auto-repeating' can also be changed. All these variations are available over quite a wide range, to meet individual needs.

The modification of an existing device to meet specific needs can be expensive if major physical changes are involved. It is preferable often to provide an additional component which extends the use of an existing device or an interface which links two existing devices together. The Special Technology expanded keyboard is an example of the former as it is added without any need to modify the microcomputer to which it is linked. In this case the keyboard is a specialist component but the cost can be relatively low because it only incorporates the keyboard function and not the remainder of the microcomputer facilities. In terms of a complete system (including disc drives and printer) it may represent only 10-20 per cent of the total cost to provide a hardware modification for a specific need, considerably less than a special microcomputer developed for physically-handicapped people. If two existing devices are linked together then costs can be even lower. For example, a Perkins Brailler can be used as an input device to a microcomputer. Although the brailler is a specialised device its versatility can be extended beyond its normal use by the addition of a simple interface (Smith and Vincent, 1983). The cost of interfacing is less than 10 per cent of the complete system.

Hardware interface may consist of components that ensure that data is transferred without loss (by adding a buffer) or to provide compatibility between devices (by changing codes that represent data). As low cost integrated circuits are readily available for these purposes, interfaces can be designed to meet many needs. Many devices now contain interfaces as standard. The serial interface (known as an RS232 or RS423) is probably the most popular for linking devices together as data can be received (R) or sent (S). The data is transmitted serially (single bits of information follow each other on a common wired link) between devices. Unfortunately this 'standard' interface has a number of variations which requires detailed knowledge of the arrangement for each device, however, when this is overcome it then provides very good two-way communication.

As more devices are linked together it may require that selection switches are added to enable more than one device to be connected to another. This is a feature of a microcomputer system used by David who is blind. His system consists of a microcomputer, disc drive, printer, speech synthesiser and Microwriter. Three of the devices link to the microcomputer via the serial interface. David has a rotary selection switch which gives him various combinations of the facilities that they provide so that, for example, he can send text output to the printer after it has been input from the Microwriter, and checked with the speech synthesiser. His system only required a single switch because each device had an adequate internal interface, a modification that cost less than one per cent of the system.

What Other Technical Problems Occur for Disabled Students in Using the Technology?

Substantial barriers stand in the way of standardisation in this field, as Vanderheiden (1978) points out. At the development stage, ideas must be given full rein and are likely to diverge from existing technical standards. Manufacturers, on the other hand, must consider retooling costs. In general, developers, manufacturers and users all show concern about compatibility between new and old devices and systems, yet great incompatibility exists and is likely to continue. Teachers, parents and students alike have real problems in keeping up with manufacturers' hardware and software changes;

information technology is evolving very quickly. School authorities have to make difficult decisions about purchasing devices and programs that suit well an individual or suit only fairly well several students. Without some standardisation, they cannot hope to economise by linking up different devices into systems appropriate to different needs. Vanderheiden, while acknowledging such problems, considers that standardisation will come through increased communication between developers of the technology.

Technical problems also arise when hardware items are linked even if the interfaces are standard. For example, adding a speech synthesiser to a microcomputer will require protocols (sending data in a form that can be 'read' by another device) so that text can be transferred correctly. Additional software will be needed within the microcomputer to direct output to the speech synthesiser when necessary, and in a form that will provide intelligible and intelligent speech. All of these stages present potential problems that can be crucial for a blind person if assistance is not to hand. Similar situations can arise from other combinations of devices to meet special needs. Fortunately, there is increasing evidence that suppliers of peripheral devices are giving more attention to information and software that overcome or avoid these problems.

Are There Any Technical Hazards in Using NIT?

It would be wrong to alarm disabled students by saying that there are great dangers in using the technology, but equally it would be wrong not to warn them about electrical hazards. There are some general guidelines for the comfort and safety of users (see Chapter 9). Smye (1983) gives examples of technical problems that crop up when physically-disabled students use MAC (again, see Chapter 9). Can a wheelchair user get close enough to the keyboard? Is he or she then at the right distance to read the screen? But these are problems, not hazards.

The research literature contains assessments of one or two particular hazards: for instance, Clarkson (1981) reviews in detail potential hazards in using infrared light for detecting eye movements and concludes that the levels used in prototype equipment developed in Britain are well below what might be hazardous. Occasionally, hazards are reported from the field, as Uslan (1983) reports. During a workshop he was conducting on new information technology for disabled students, one person was in great discomfort from high-frequency sound probably emanating from a television or computer screen. According to one source he quotes, users with inner ear damage may be particularly susceptible and prolonged ringing in the ears (tinnitus) may result.

Summary

It is clear that new information technology cannot completely compensate for disabilities of the kinds we discuss in this book. Finding exactly the right software is more difficult than obtaining the hardware to run it on. Many modifications of software and hardware are feasible, but often costly for individuals to implement. Standardisation in this field is slow, and to some extent not even desirable if individual needs are to be met with individual solutions. Other technical problems, such as those met in linking up hardware, also stand in the way of wider use of the technology by teachers and their disabled students. Despite these difficulties, the technology contains few technical hazards that would threaten disabled students.

PART FIVE

The Future

18 THE NEXT FIVE YEARS

Predicting, in general terms, what is likely to happen in this field up to 1990 is not very difficult, simply because social systems change comparatively slowly. For example, almost all the teachers who will be teaching disabled children in five years' time are already in the schools, most of the researchers are already in universities and laboratories, and even the politicians in power may be much the same people. More than 90 per cent of the buildings are already constructed and much of their equipment will still be in use five years from now. What kinds of noticeable change will occur, then, in this short time?

Forecasts are optimistic or pessimistic, depending on who is making them and for what purpose. For example, forecasts by manufacturers overestimate the spread of new information technology, while those by educational administrators underestimate it. By 1990, at least two-thirds of the 70 million families in the United States are expected to have a home computer and the market for software for home computers will be $3 billion or more (*American Family*, a newsletter quoted by *The Catalyst*, vol. 2, no. 5). These figures are eye-catching: to what extent will the computers be used for education? In 1983, only 14 per cent of American school districts did not 'use computers' and more schools began to use computers in that year than in any previous year (*The Catalyst*, same issue), but the same source mentions that in many schools few teachers know what to do with the machines and have the time to do it. Moreover, one computer per school, or even per class, is only a beginning, and for disabled students much greater provision is needed. By 1990, doubtless every class will have several computers, including some that are already obsolete.

The experience of disabled people, presented in Part Three, indicates that the potential of information technology to meet specific needs in education is high. Commercially available devices are available that help with or overcome difficulties associated with speaking, reading, writing and gaining access to computers. Despite this, we have found that the use of these devices by students is generally low. The main reason for this appears to be financial. As development costs of special equipment are high and the final market is relatively small, any specialised product is likely to have a high price. This factor has prevented many schools, colleges and individuals from purchasing devices that could meet the needs of students. Wider use of information technology devices among disabled adults in employment is related to provision of funding by employers and government agencies.

With costs of microelectronic components continuing to fall, prospects for the next five years are encouraging. For example, microcomputers are continuing to decline in cost but at the same time their capacity in terms of memory storage and processing time is increasing. If a special device for, say, a partially-sighted student had a microcomputer as a major component then the cost benefit would be passed on. For this reason there may be more attention given in the near future to adaptation (through the software or hardware) of existing devices rather than developing completely new devices.

Pickering (1983) reports three trends: first, decreasing costs of memory and processing power; second, decreasing physical size of main memory and processors and increasing program sophistication within microcomputers and, third, less rapid decrease in physical size of backup storage. The first two favour development of information technology to assist disabled students, the third less so. There is some evidence, however, that Pickering's assessment concerning backup storage is too conservative: recent changes in the technology include new forms of miniaturised storage, such as bubble memories and small tape and disc drives.

A few years ago, two American leaders in this field, Eulenberg and Vanderheiden (1978), noted that despite impressive advances in communication aids technology, its impact was yet to be felt in the lives of the majority of human beings it could serve. That is still true, and for new information technology in general, in the lives of disabled students. They saw the main challenge as transfer of the technology to those who need it, and suggested six strategies (summarised below) for speeding up this transfer:

1. Help concerned agencies to recognise the role they can play in introducing the technology.
2. Introduce the technology into training of professionals (including teachers) working with disabled people.
3. Encourage funding of research and development and enlist the

support of talented individuals to apply their energy and imagination in this field.

4. Increase incentives for manufacturers to produce and market appropriate devices, and ensure that cost does not prevent individuals obtaining what they need.

5. Spread news about the technology and encourage discussion of its social and political implications.

6. Take a holistic view of individuals' disabilities and in doing so avoid an approach based only on technology.

These strategies are needed just as much now as they were in 1978.

Cook (1983) notes that during his 1982 visit to the United Kingdom he saw many exciting approaches to using computers and other new technologies to enhance communication and that much of the work was going on in schools and resource centres, as part of routine educational activity rather than as a specific research effort.

The Next Five Years for Physically-disabled People

Chapter 9 brings together much evidence from the recent experience of physically-disabled people, and contains some suggestions about future trends. Here, we summarise changes that are likely to occur over the next five years.

Software and Artificial Intelligence

It seems certain that there will be substantial improvements in software for use by disabled students, both software available generally and that developed specially for them. The BITSTIK and its associated programs are an indication of the latest graphic capabilities, but more important for physically-disabled students will be developments in text-handling software. Already intelligent text-editing programs, being written for commercial publishers, are drawing on artificial intelligence techniques. For example, researchers at the Open University are looking into intelligent editing of such text items as tables, which are notoriously difficult and time-consuming to set up using ordinary typewriters or even ordinary word-processing equipment. 'Automatic' systems, which enable users to construct tables and modify them very easily indeed, would be particularly valuable to disabled students, saving them a great deal of time. More generally useful will be programs that anticipate, in an intelligent way, what a writer is trying to say, thus providing faster input for fewer keystrokes. Pickering and Stevens (1984) have something like this in mind for disabled people, but their efforts might well be overtaken by commercial software houses, which wish to sell such programs to many kinds of writers in business, industry, journalism and so on.

Hardware Developments

It seems certain that new information technology will be equipped with much larger memory and faster systems during the next five years. Disabled people, including students, will benefit from using more powerful machines, but probably not as much as their able-bodied colleagues. Faster processing will cut down the time required by the machines to respond to commands from disabled users, but these users will require much the same time to input commands and data, unless new and very different input methods are devised.

The most likely improvements on the input side involve voice, gaze and touch. Improved voice and sound recognition are certain over the next five years, and at a cheaper price. Equipment that cannot distinguish clearly between slightly different 'grunts' may well be able to do so with further development, and the range of words 'understood' by computers will certainly increase. Gaze-controlled systems such as Sutter's (1983) will probably become more widely available and experience gained with them may lead to cheaper and more portable versions. Gaze has the advantage of being very fast, faster than voice or touch. Some of the problems of using systems mounted on spectacles may be solved in the next five years, too. Touch-sensitive screens, already available, are likely to become very useful to physically-disabled people who possess fair precision of touch in one limb at least. The screens at present available with, say, microcomputing systems, provide rather small areas for touching, but they can be enlarged without encountering great technical problems. Some physically-disabled people will still perhaps have difficulty reaching the right part of the screen.

On the output side, the next five years will probably see development of printers that are more automatic and save disabled people the trouble of a great deal of paper-handling. Better voice output is already becoming available and is likely to improve further and become cheaper. Visual displays on flat screens that take up less space and weigh less will be more useful to physically-disabled students than the present 'tubes', which are heavy and make many microcomputers less portable.

In general, the next five years should see new information technology becoming more flexible, portable and interchangeable. All three of these changes will be of benefit to physically-disabled students.

The Next Five Years for Blind and Partially-sighted People

Access to Text and Information

What has information technology provided so far? A blind student can read text independently with a tactile representation of characters (Optacon) or synthetic speech that pronounces words as a book is scanned (Kurzweil Reading Machine). In both cases optical lenses 'see' the text and convert the images into representations that can be converted into tactile or audible forms. This has been a very significant step forward in giving independent access to existing printed material. The disadvantages are that the tactile method demands a high level of skill, and the equipment to 'read' a book and speak the text is expensive and not portable which restricts its use to libraries.

The next five years could see a device that combines features of these reading aids to produce one that is both portable and provides speech, braille and tactile representation of characters and words. An adaptation to the Optacon to provide a speech facility is described by Groner and Savoie (1979). They anticipated that it could become available by 1981 following the evaluation of a prototype. But this did not happen as reduced government funding prevented further research and development. This ambitious target in 1979 of a portable reading machine may be more readily achievable in the near future as the technologies associated with it have advanced significantly. The further miniaturisation of micro-electronic circuits, the increased memory capacity and processing power of microprocessors, improvements in camera technology and optical character recognition are important factors. These advances have taken place through the wider commercial interest in optical character recognition rather than specific developments for the visually handicapped. Despite these advances there are problems that remain to be solved. For example the hand tracking of a small camera over text will need to be aided if the camera is held rather than controlled by a scanning mechanism. This may involve a secondary output (tactile or audible) which indicates that a straight line is being scanned over the text. The ability to accommodate any character font or style is necessary. Fender (1983) describes the problems in producing a personal and portable reading machine following a survey of approximately 40 people knowledgeable about these devices. With the problems well defined and the advances being made in the technology, it is likely that such a reading machine will be available in the near future.

Optical character recognition is being used successfully to convert printed text into a computer readable form. This technique has found increasing applications in business and commerce. It is being used increasingly in braille production because once the text has been entered into a computer the translation of text to braille is possible, and the braille can be embossed on paper. This method is likely to contribute significantly to braille production as it overcomes the slow stage of entering the text (or braille equivalent) manually. Increases in the speed and efficiency of braille embossers that can be used with a mainframe computer will provide a higher capacity. It remains to be seen how far this will go in meeting the demand for brailled material. It could overcome some of the problems experienced by students in obtaining a large range of text books in braille, essential in providing for a wide curriculum at all levels.

What is desirable in the future is that access can be provided to all printed matter that is created on a computer. Ideally, any computer typeset material could be made available for translation into braille which would reduce even further the time and effort involved in this conversion. Achieving this objective will require the resolution of issues concerning compatibility and transferability of digital information.

Some sources of information are now available from a screen. These include teletext and viewdata. What are the implications for visually handicapped people? Teletext and viewdata differ from most printed information as colour and graphics are widely used. Colour may be beneficial for some people with low vision but could be detrimental for others. The text can be magnified easily with a larger screen but this is limited due to the low resolution of teletext and viewdata displays; characters appear as connected blocks when enlarged which does not improve their legibility. Despite these problems, teletext and viewdata offer exciting possibilities because it is possible to convert the transmitted information into another medium. For example, speech and tactile outputs have been studied as alternative outputs at Southampton University (King and Omotayo, 1982, and Cope and King, 1982). They concluded from an examination of typical page layouts of a viewdata system (Prestel) that there is a need to identify and reformat the following types of layout features: continuous text, list index, instruction index, tables and multiple columns. This was followed by the development of an automatic reformatter for each page of information to prepare it for a spoken or braille output, thus enabling a blind person to read each page; a keypad provides a facility to scan the information.

Low-cost adaptations to microcomputers to convert them to teletext receivers or viewdata terminals are becoming widely available. Adding a speech or tactile output together with reformatting software will be a means of giving blind people access to electronic information in the future. As access to information at present is a greater problem than for sighted people, this is an important development. Cope and King (1982) conclude that 'Dynamic braille displays are likely to come into increasing use, and their adoption in education for the blind would open up opportunities for specialised viewdata type systems to become a source of educational material.'

Closed-circuit television (CCTV) has been used successfully in schools and colleges for partially-sighted students. Quillman and Goodrich (1979-80) point to the need, however, for continuing research in low-vision. They estimate that of the 3 million registered legally blind people in America, approximatelly 2.5 million have some usable vision, and argue for a greater emphasis in the near future for the development of truly portable closed-circuit television systems, especially acceptable monitor displays. Severe performance deficits (for example, in reading speed) resulting from smaller monitors are indicated with some portable devices (Goodrich and Quillman, 1978). The availability in the near future of flat television screens to meet more general demands are likely to be important for portable closed-circuit television. This will allow the size of the screen to be maintained but at the same time reducing its bulk and enhancing the portability.

Recording Text and Information

Many blind students use a Perkins Brailler to record braille on paper. This mechanical device has been in use for 40 years with little change to the original design. As indicated earlier this method does present problems for communication with sighted people who do not read braille, a common occurrence in higher education and in integrated schools. Successful attempts have been made to adapt the Perkins Brailler as an input device to a microcomputer to provide a means of transcribing the braille to printed text. This is likely to be superseded in the next few years by an electronic brailler which provides improved features for brailling (as electronic typewriters have done for typing) and enhanced communication features to other devices that can produce a text version of the braille. In England, the Mountbatten Memorial Trust has funded research at the Royal National College for the Blind to achieve this objective.

At present, the embossing of braille as it is typed requires mechanical features which add to the size and weight of a brailler. The immediacy of the embossed copy may not be as important in education as portability and quietness of operation. For this reason portable electronic devices that combine an electronic keyboard with memory storage are likely to make important contributions. The present commercial devices that can achieve this offer many more advanced features which are not necessary always for recording notes during classes or lectures. A simpler and cheaper version could be achieved by the adaptation of a portable microcomputer. Research is now producing CMOS chips and storage media (bubble memories and battery-backed RAM packs) which will lead to small, powerful and high capacity microcomputers which could be adapted for this purpose. Overall, the prospects of achieving a small electronic notebook are very good within the next five years.

Handwriting is not used very often by blind students as checking and correcting is not possible, however, it does offer an immediacy in communication with sighted people. Handwriting is more a learned motor skill than a visual skill, but it is difficult to acquire writing skills without vision. An interesting computer-based system has been developed at Michigan State University's Artificial Language Laboratory (Macleod and Jackson, 1979) which provides handwriting training. Information about pen movements and letter shapes is provided through a wrist cuff containing eight small vibrators which stimulate the wrist to indicate the direction to follow. A classroom-portable version of the system is planned for the near future.

Access to Computers

Microcomputers are being used increasingly in education for programming and computer-assisted learning. This has raised problems for blind and partially-sighted students because they have normally a visual display. The experiences of students, described in Chapter 10, involved synthetic speech, embossed braille and refreshable braille as alternatives to a visual display. A survey (Blenkhorn and Tobin, 1983) of schools and units for visually-handicapped students in the United Kingdom shows a recent increase in the number of microcomputers available with an average of three per school or unit, a trend that suggests a growing awareness of the potential of information technology. Shortages of peripheral devices and software indicate that this development is at a very early stage for meeting the various needs of visually-handicapped students.

Synthetic speech is likely to continue as an important output medium for microcomputers in the near future. The cost of speech synthesisers is likely to fall further with the quality of speech improving further. It is well established (King and Omotayo, 1982; Vincent, 1983) that considerable reformatting of visual output is necessary before it can be spoken. A speech reformatting read-only memory (ROM) for a microcomputer has been developed at the Open University (Turnbull, 1984) which intercepts and reforms all information that would appear on the screen as well as keys that control cursor movement. It is independent of the computer language in use which gives maximum potential for accessing standard software. A different approach has been taken by Audiodata with a Tactile Acoustic Screen Orientation system for a microcomputer. This gives access to the screen information through horizontal and vertical sliders which move a second cursor to any position from which a spoken output can be produced. Different tones are emitted to indicate blocks of lines and characters as they are scanned, permitting direct access to standard software without modification.

Braille output has been used mainly for transcription systems because of the relatively high cost of braille embossers. The next five years may see an increased use of this medium as lower cost devices emerge. One development reported in America (Jampolsky and others, 1982) uses printing equipment already available to sighted people. Software converts text files into braille files which are printed with the period character only on sheets of plastic instead of paper. A simple thermopneumatic process converts the black dots into a raised braille pattern. A cost reduction factor of ten compared with current methods is anticipated.

A British, low-cost braille output device for microcomputers has been developed at Bristol University (Chapman, 1983). At any one time, 40 braille characters can be displayed on a narrow strip of plastic. This is achieved through a continuous loop of plastic, which is pre-embossed with six dots in all cell positions. When a new line of 40 characters is displayed, the plastic strip is rotated to a new position with appropriate dot positions being flexed upwards. The exposed part of the strip can then be read. When the next line appears as the tape rotates to a new position, the dots that have been flexed upwards are returned to a downward position. This flexing of the plastic dots is a unique feature in reducing the higher cost associated with electromechanical devices controlling each dot position.

Information Technology Awareness

As information technology applications increase in education they will place increasing demands on teachers as well as students. For teachers there will be a need to adjust to the potential of information technology in the education of visually handicapped students. The next five years will be an important period for in-service training as this period will see also continuing and rapid growth in the application of the new technology. It is very unlikely that any electronic device will exist for the same lifetime as the Perkins Brailler which has already reached 40 years.

Computer literacy among visually handicapped students is discussed by Ryan and Bedi (1978). They describe a Visual Impairment Project (VIP) at Baruch College, Manhattan, which introduced workshops in computer programming for visually handicapped students. The experiences of the workshops are analysed, and guidelines for training in computer related fields by educational institutions are presented. They conclude that computer literacy is attainable for visually handicapped students but it does require a substantial availability of equipment and software, and a high quality course with a broad academic growth perspective rather than a limited vocational goal.

The Next Five Years for Deaf People

The next five years will tend to see refinements of developments already in hand, rather than great new projects opening up new vistas. The aims are still the twofold ones of using the new technology to provide the deaf person with better communication, and to improve educational opportunities, particularly where these relate to language.

The development of real-time graphic display is progressing well, and the next five years should continue to see developments here. The two contexts in which this is being used are for the captioning of television, and the presentation of visual displays in lecture rooms for students. Both developments are progressing in England and the United States; in both countries a certain number of television programmes are now captioned as a matter of course.

The major technological achievement would be the possibility of displaying on the screen a verbatim text of what is being said, with a delay of only a few seconds. The biggest research project in this respect in the educational context is at the National Technical Institute for the Deaf in Rochester, NY. Work on accuracy of this system, which translates from a stenotype machine into a display in normal English, shows that accuracy is now at about 95 per cent. It may be, however, that the last 5 per cent is the most difficult, for the system still relies on the ability of the students to cope with the errors which occur. In some cases, this will involve the mistranslation of the input from the keyboard, and the display in these circumstances can bear little or no relation to the original intention of the speaker. Alternatively, the display can include a mistranslation that is actually wrong, but could possibly make sense. Stuckless (1983) reports an occasion when the system translated 'Kodak has just introduced a new disc camera' as 'Kodak has just introduced a nudist camera'.

This can raise particular problems for the deaf, because of the generally less sophisticated structure of English in their conceptual framework. They are less likely to spot such a situation as an error, and therefore pick up false information believing it to be correct. At least when the output is obviously wrong, even those with the least sophisticated language are likely to recognise it as an error.

The necessity of using the stenograph system arises because the computer is unable to analyse the speech directly. However, research into the problems of speech analysis continues, usually using programs that give a graphic display of various characteristics of the sound spoken into the microphone. Very little is known about how the deaf perceive speech (or indeed any sounds), and such knowledge is extremely hard to ascertain, because the hearing do not have the perceptual framework of the deaf, and cannot understand it, and the deaf do not have the perceptual framework of the hearing, and so cannot explain it. Whitehead (1983) is working on use of computers to analyse speech, in terms of trying to improve the speech of deaf people. He aims to use the graphic displays to give them feedback on their performance and improve their speech functions. One clear point that has arisen from this work is that to be able to analyse sufficient parameters to make the whole procedure useful, the technology has moved beyond microcomputers. Whitehead is using minicomputers and small mainframes, which are non-portable installations.

One development which has been particularly noticeable during the last ten years has been the reduction in size of many technological aids to hearing, in particular the hearing aid. Improvements in microphone technology, reductions in the size and higher capacity of batteries, have permitted hearing aids to be fitted which are precise in response and yet inconspicuous in use. Many handicapped people wish not to be conspicuous, or to be seen to be 'different', and this is a factor which will be no great problem in the next five years with the development of the Autocuer.

Cued Speech has been a very useful system for those deaf people relying largely on lip-reading for some years (see Chapter 4), but it relies on the non-deaf person knowing and utilising the system, so that the deaf person may see the signs. How much better if this could be facilitated automatically, so that cue signs would be available to the deaf person whoever was speaking, whether they knew the system or not.

This was the principle behind the development of the Autocuer, designed by a NASA applications group at the Research Triangle Institute in North Carolina, and specialists at Gallaudet College, Washington DC (Wadsley, 1983; Cornett, 1983). The central part of the technology is built into the frames of a pair of spectacles, which contain a microphone which picks up the speaker's voice. The sounds are then translated by a microprocessor, and the appropriate shape is projected by electron tubes so that to the wearer the signs appear in front of the speaker's mouth. The project has suffered some delay because of waiting to take advantage of new hardware developments, but subjects for field trials have been selected; training programmes were planned for early 1984, with first use of the wearer units in the middle of the year. It is expected that these devices will be operational and available within the next five years.

Some institutions have plans to use the possibilities now available to expand many areas of the educational environment for the deaf. At the Model Secondary School for the Deaf, Washington DC, thought has been given to paving the way for a richer educational experience (Dietz, 1983). Incoming students will in future have a keyboard familiarity course (which will not only be limited to computer keyboards), and it is hoped that this will be useful in the development of an Instructional Enrichment programme. It was discovered that some of the hearing-impaired students at the school were showing some of the same characteristics as the culturally deprived, probably because of the lack of communication and the lack of availability of information. It is hoped to use Logo to expand the cognitive skills of the students; one or two classes on an experimental basis were planned for 1984, with the possibility of doing more.

Ward and Arnold (1982) question whether information technology systems can handle the English language well enough for educating deaf people. Arnold (1978, 1981) states that research on deaf children's written English shows that their syntax is often different from that of hearing English writers and they do not grasp morphological rules such as production of plurals. Computers can certainly help at the lower levels, but Ward and others (1983) consider that it is too early to say whether computer-assisted learning leads to linguistic gains for deaf children, and many thousands of hours will be needed to prepare programs that are more complex, to serve more complex needs than those served by the rather elementary products in use now.

This progress may be assisted by refinements expected over a few years in the uses of interactive video. These are being developed in several places, and one use is to improve the teaching of language skills to deaf children (Brawley, 1983). Here the sophistication of the branching of the programs is the key to much further development, so that the system can respond more flexibly to the responses and needs of the child. Also, an increase in speed of operation would be advantageous, although developments are progressing well.

One development which is essential over the next five years is an expansion of the availability of suitable software. Many teachers complain of the lack of suitable software, but although they know the requirements they are largely unable to write the programs. Indeed, systematic knowledge of availability is lacking in many areas, and a beginning of an attempt to rectify this has been made in California, with the publication of a software catalogue compiled by a teacher at the California School for the Deaf, Riverside (Jost, 1983).

Attempts to broaden the horizons of deaf children in a wide educational context even extend to the area of music. At the Model Secondary School for the Deaf, Washington DC, Letterman (1983) provides a musical, tactile and visual experience for his students, trying to give them some concept of what music is. They sit on a free vibration platform, and watch a visual correlate of the sounds they cannot hear, using sound-to-vision converters and lasers to include as many dimensions of the sound as possible.

The next five years, then, are likely to produce improvements in the systems now being developed and used, both in the fields of communication and education, such as a faster, more accurate and efficient means of providing visual interpretation to those who need it, and the use of smaller, more portable and less conspicuous aids to communication, whether this be devices like the Autocuer, or improvements in hearing aids. During the last five years, many new and good ideas have been started; it will be in the next five years that many of them will bear fruit.

The Next Five Years For Speech-impaired People

New information technology for speech-impaired people may well improve over the next five years in these respects: speed of functioning, ease of inputting code, and portability and size. These three are inextricably bound up with each other.

Speed of reaction time of equipment is less important than the speed of the operator. It is possible to use a disabled person's residual ability which is reliable, even if it is minimal, to obtain greater precision, but not necessarily to increase speed.

The trend is away from individually entered letters, words and phrases, and towards systems which allow the users to decide on the concepts about which they want to talk, and what they want to say about them. The next few years may well see significant advances in semantic coding systems. Minspeak ('minimum speak') is an American semantic coding system developed by Baker (1982) and designed for disabled people who cannot express themselves through speech or hand signs. A person using a microcomputer attached to a Minspeak board with fewer than 50 keys can produce thousands of clear standard sentences with less than seven keypresses for each sentence. Users do not have to know how to spell and they can make up complete sentences without selecting letters, phonemes or even words. The sentences are spoken through a voice synthesiser.

Semantic coding does not use single letters or words on the keys. Instead, each key has symbols on it, varied according to the user. The sequence in which keys are pressed defines the exact meaning of each. Baker says that 'each key has a range of significance, including a function, several activities, a style and a mood'. In his system, pressing any one key twice designates that key's central image as the topic, then all keys pressed thereafter designate ideas associated with that topic, until the change of topic key is pressed. This is much more like natural speech than using a keyboard with letters or words. For example, pressing key 1 twice establishes the topic of eating. If key 2 is pressed next, the synthesiser says, 'Get that food out of my mouth', but if key 3 is pressed instead, it says, 'The position of my chair is not right for eating', and key 4 would produce, 'Look out! The food is getting on my clothes'. Thus the system, now marketed by Prentke Romich, is able to reduce drastically the number of keypresses required to speak or type complete standard sentences.

It is, of course, easy to consider speed of output as the only major goal, whereas there are others. Foulds (1980) pointed out that rate of communication is only one factor in the applicability of alternative modes for fluent communication. Chapanis and others (1972) measured the amount of information and found this quite different in a problem-solving task. Solution time using speech was only about half the solution time using written messages, despite the fact that speech is many times faster in use. Chapanis and others (1977) also found (by linguistic analysis) that spoken messages were high in redundancy, and written and typed modes had an extensively modified language structure. This leads to the supposition that the various ways in which the speech-impaired are forced to communicate are not so inadequate by comparison with speech, after all.

One of the developments which will undoubtedly be refined in the next five years concerns the parameters by which aids are related to the individual who will use them. Goodenough-Trepagnier and others (1982) put forward a framework to account for the various design factors which determine the final output rate by their interaction. They suggest there is an interaction between three factors: cost in language units per word; code length in motor acts per unit; and time per motor act. For use in the situation in which items are displayed before the handicapped person, for selection, they propose a technique which produces lists of units which include many words, or letter sequences which are parts of words, based upon frequency counts and elimination of ambiguities.

They suggest that trade-offs between the three factors take place, which determine rate of output, showing, for example, a speed advantage of coding words with five keys over direct selection from the alphabet. The more precise investigation and specification of these performance factors will have a significant effect on improvements in system design and system/individual interfacing.

Thibault and Foulds (1982) have begun to turn their thoughts towards the limitations of speech synthesis devices, saying that they have always been limited either by quality of sound, or size of vocabulary. They based their work on the concept of the diphone (Peterson and others, 1958) and added a group of the syllables which occurred most frequently in English. Thibault and Foulds located and extracted the diphones from continuous speech by converting a recording to a digital representation, and performing spectral analysis. They report successful attempts to synthesise words in this way, and further report that spectrograms of the words thus created and the same words spoken were identical, whereas that produced by a more 'traditional' voice synthesiser (Votrax 'Type 'n' Talk') was different.

Investigations such as this will improve the quality of the production of synthetic voices, and this can only lead to a better functioning for the handicapped person. The identity between the user and the equipment is a complex one, and as the voice from the synthesiser sounds more natural, and less artificial, so it will be easier for the individual to accept it and use it as part of the whole person. This point of view is supported by Jim Brooks, who is a speech-handicapped computer science and linguistics student at Michigan State University. He has written (Brooks, 1984):

> Previously, research in the area of artificial speech generation was based more in the qualitative understanding of the human speech mechanism without much consideration for the underlying principles of speech (I consider that to be absolutely necessary before we can make machines 'talk').

Increased Use of Microcomputers for Administration

There is little doubt that computers will be used much more widely for administration, particularly record-keeping, where disabled students are involved. Full records must be kept for their benefit to assist in assessment, and also for reporting planning statistics to various government departments.

Several systems are already available, in both the United Kingdom and the United States, for use by schools. For example, in California in 1983 at least two-thirds of the 100 special education planning agencies used some type of computerised management information system, according to Enell (1983), who also reports that in her own school district in Carmichael, California, a mainframe computer produces 30 different kinds of documents. For teachers, it produces registers, class lists, test reports, annual review lists, etc.; for administrators, it produces statistics for planning and draws up an assessment calendar for each student, and for drivers it produces bus lists. Her district was, at that time, the only one using computers to collate specific achievement data on its special education students.

There is a move away from mainframe computers, now widely employed, towards using mini- and microcomputers plus commercially-available programs for assessment reports (for example, the Unistar Report program from Microsoft), Visicalc, etc. Ferguson (1982) reports on his microcomputer programs for administrative analyses of children's records in special education in part of Wales.

What developing information technology devices and systems may be of use to disabled students? Videotex systems are potentially very useful to them. Even blind students may be able to use these systems, given speech synthesis of what appears on the screen. In Canada, the Ontario Federation for the Cerebral Palsied is conducting trials, although the main aim of these is to give disabled users a chance to test thoroughly the Telidon system, rather than to provide formal education. The sets will not be in private homes but in centres where disabled people gather. Users can obtain information on local services and communicate with users at other centres (Hicks, 1984). Similarly, there is no reason why teletext, broadcast to television sets, as in the British Ceefax and Oracle systems, should not be accompanied by speech synthesis.

Summary

Although there are some barriers against change, particularly a lack of funding, we take a fairly optimistic view over the next five years. It seems certain that the technology, hardware and software, will continue to improve, to the advantage of disabled children and adults. In particular, their education is likely to benefit, as their abilities to communicate increase.

19 TO AD 2000

We found this the most difficult chapter to write, simply because the technology is changing so rapidly that forecasts 15 years ahead are likely to be quite incorrect. Authors such as Martin (1977), who are well-equipped to prophesy technological futures, provide fascinating scenarios up to AD 2000. Martin himself suggests that Western society will have changed radically by then, with industry automated and commercial transactions and administration more or less completely electronic. Communication networks capable of carrying huge amounts of information are vital to this scenario, linking homes, workplaces, libraries, leisure centres, shops, banks, schools and universities. Computers and terminals will be as widespread as telephones are today, video systems will be commonplace. Most people under 30 will be able to operate computers and many will know how to program them. Martin also says that many authorities consider that advances in molecular biology (genetic engineering) will have merged with electronic technology. The wider implications of such a merger are not easy to predict, with the possibility of extremely fast computer components, including large memories, made of organic materials.

Stonier (1983), another technological prophet, suggests that there will be a massive expansion of education in the 1980s and 1990s. He raises many questions about the social and economic payback of such an expansion, and about the role of the State and use of mass media. Internationally, he suggests that 'the information gap could be closed by bringing into every Third World home electronic education devices designed to provide relevant information on a wide range of subjects'. He sees the emergence everywhere of an electronic home-based education system, with a television screen and computer terminal at its heart, linked via national and international telephone and cable networks to local education authorities and other agencies providing education. The 'human factor' in this system could be 'mature citizens' in society, whom he describes as the 'Western World's most under-used resource'.

His forecast is supported by significant changes in use of information technology by the Open University. In 1971, even radio broadcasts could not be received everywhere in the United

Kingdom, and some students had to visit study centres to listen to tape-recordings. Television broadcasts were also available in study centres, in film form, for students whose homes were out of range of the signals (as well as for those who missed the broadcasts because of the times at which they were transmitted). In 1984, the Open University is depending much more on electronic technology available in students' homes. Radio and television sets are nearly universal in United Kingdom homes. The University mails audio-tapes direct to students, who have their own players, and it sends out videocassettes on request, knowing that videocassette recorders are accessible to a high percentage of them. Most students are on the telephone, and the proportion having access to a micro-computer is rising very fast. Some students already have modems and use these with their microcomputers to communicate with the University's academic computing network. Already these appli-cations of information technology are paying off for disabled students, of whom there are some 2000 in the University. Research has recently begun on how blind students can access computer-assisted learning with the aid of a braille or speech ter-minal, and on how deaf students can communicate with a tutor using electronic mail. In both cases, students will work at home, not in a study centre. Within five years, some of Stonier's prophecy will be fact for these students.

Benefits to Disabled People

On a wider front, it seems reasonable to suppose that disabled children and adults will benefit from technological advances that benefit the general population. In some respects, they may benefit more. For example, there is no doubt that by AD 2000 many more disabled adults will be able to work at home, if they wish. Computer-based terminals will be so ubiquitous that a blind adult, say, will have little difficulty in carrying out a wide range of work activities at home. A deaf adult will converse quite freely about work by telephone, possibly with speech-impaired friends. And physically-disabled adults will be able to use computer-aided design equipment at home to prepare drawings as architects and engineers. Working at home is a great advantage for disabled people. It is also a disadvantage in that it may increase their physi-cal isolation from other human beings.

Videotex and teletext networks offer to disabled people less social isolation. Although these systems were not designed with disabled customers particularly in mind, they will provide increasing access to banking and shopping (already available in some areas), and their keyboard-and-visual displays are particularly suitable for people with certain disabilities, such as speech-impairment and deafness. Community services of other kinds, such as fire and burglar alarms, medical and social care, neighbourhood contacts for new or elderly people, are quickly being added to many of the systems. Physically-restricted people will surely benefit.

So far as education is concerned, disabled children and adults seem certain to benefit from further advances in new information technology, provided that it is not merely another bandwagon.

The Information Technology Bandwagon

Is information technology for education merely another bandwagon? Special education is susceptible to new hardware. Those who work in it know that special education contains many difficult problems, and has adopted gimmicks before. Education of disabled children and adults is historically based on medical categories. It is still very heavily skills-oriented, with an inherently unbalanced curriculum that favours the introduction of hardware for skills training, therefore professionals in this field have to make an extra effort to redress the balance. This effort is vitally needed because disabled users, particularly children, take to the technology very readily and it can become a principal focus of their lives.

The balance can only be redressed through sustained development of a good range of suitable educational and other software. We agree with Richards (1983), who stresses that technology must suit learning objectives, not the other way round and should serve a rounded curriculum for special education, such as that proposed by Wilson (1981). Disabled students can use much educational software produced for able-bodied learners, but also need specialist programs written for them. Without high quality programs, information technology *is* a bandwagon for education, even if disabled students can benefit from using communication devices. Teachers must avoid putting mere trivialities into their programs:

they must use them to teach what children find most difficult.

Only people like King Canute's courtiers will ignore what is happening in this field of new information technology (Cleveland, 1984). For example, opportunities will continue to develop in post-secondary education for deaf and hearing-impaired students, who were formerly deprived, largely because their language skills were poorly developed (Hamp, 1972; Department of Education and Science, 1972; Stuckless, 1973). Visual displays of voice characteristics have been used for some years by teachers of deaf children, and these displays will increase in sophistication and accuracy. Progress will be made towards a more efficient real-time visual communication system, as verbatim displays improve. More flexible systems with lower error rates will increase students' chances of developing language skills. Ultimately, a visual display direct from spoken speech will be available at low cost. The technological problems are already being solved, difficult as they are.

More use will be made of alternative physiological channels. Macleod and Jackson's (1979) work is but a prototype. They successfully taught blind people to write with a wrist cuff which provides tactile stimulation to indicate the direction in which the hand should be moved, on the assumption that writing is largely a motor skill, because sighted people can write with no real difficulty with their eyes shut. Voice, minor muscle movement, changes in skin potential and even in brain waves all offer possibilities that will be exploited much more fully than hitherto. Should speechless people become able to control their communication aids by thinking, the distinction between use of a natural larynx and a synthetic one will soon be blurred.

Artificial Intelligence

Based on a recent study, Pickering (1983) suggests that basic research on communication processes among both normal and disabled people may be needed before new information technology can be fully exploited for the benefit of the latter. He perceives work being needed to bring to bear the findings of artificial intelligence. He also sees hardware developments as favouring the disabled: for example, large touch-sensitive screens, suitable for computer-aided design, could be very useful to disabled students. He believes that development by commercial companies of sophisticated word processing programs that include intelligent text handling, with spelling checks, word prediction and even semantic-based text editing (see Chapters 12 and 18), will also benefit disabled students once prices fall. 'Office of the future' projects, incorporating electronic mail and other automated procedures, will have spin-offs for the education of disabled people. Electronic mail, for instance, provides for messages composed slowly to be transmitted quickly. Teletext technology offers substantial learning and employment opportunities for disabled adults.

Pickering is not alone in suggesting that artificial intelligence research may provide disabled people with what are termed 'intelligent knowledge-based systems', or 'expert systems'. By AD 2000, such systems will incorporate some degree of limited intelligence and a large computerised database, and will be able to anticipate to some extent students' wishes. They will be particularly useful to physically-handicapped and speech-impaired students, in producing or amplifying written or spoken language, and to deaf students in translating what is said to them into written or other visible language. Prototypes already exist, and the falling price, decreasing physical size and increasing capacities of micro-computers will favour incorporation of artificial intelligence into devices and systems for disabled students. It may be after AD 2000 that computer vision, as described by Mayhew and Frisby (1984), becomes technically and economically feasible for blind people to use, but this too will be a product of artificial intelligence research and development.

Along similar lines, Waters (1982) calls for increased efficiency in communication devices and systems for physically-disabled and speech-impaired people, having noted how inefficient many of these are at present. He suggests that what is required is increased output for the same or reduced input, to bring output rates at least to 50 per cent of those for able-bodied people. One way of achieving this is to take advantage of users' abilities to do more than simply operate a single switch: many can use more complex switches, which in turn provide for more complex codes. These complex codes enable users to produce more varied messages with only a few keypresses.

The Bionic Option

We draw distinctions between devices and systems designed to replace a human function that does not work at all, those intended to replace a function that does not work as well as it should and those intended to repair a function that has become unusable.

There are three main kinds of intervention and they represent a progression. Physical intervention includes medical and surgical work aimed at rehabilitation. Stitching of wounds, setting of broken bones, corneal grafts, stapedectomies, and drug regimes to control diabetes all come into this class. Technological intervention comes about through provision of a device or system to amplify or replace, in full or in part, a function. Spectacles, hearing aids, false teeth, environmental control systems, speech synthesisers, Microwriters and many others belong in this category. Reparation intervention consists of surgical and neurosurgical repairs, including brain surgery, bypassing of failed nerve pathways and, perhaps soon, direct access to sensory reception centres.

Within each of these kinds of intervention, development to AD 2000 will not run in parallel with the others, nor follow in sequence. Instead, progress will be at different rate at different times, and there is still far to go in all three. Early physical interventions, and technological ones too, now seem primitive but helped very much those who used them. Wooden legs were very much better than nothing. They were superseded by artificial limbs and prostheses as greater attempts were made to produce something that was a *direct substitute* for the missing function. Functions that were not working properly or not at all were rehabilitated, with some blind people seeing again, and some deaf hearing.

Where rehabilitation cannot be arranged, technology may be able to provide devices and systems that take over the missing functions. Speech synthesisers now speak for those who have no speech, environmental control devices perform physical functions for those who cannot move around, hearing and low vision aids help those who want to capitalise on the small amount of residual ability they may still have.

Many technological developments discussed in this book were impossible a decade ago, therefore it is not surprising that large numbers of disabled students are waiting to take advantage of such technological intervention. Yet full rehabilitation will only come about with full healing and restoration. Work in this new field is only now beginning. In time, but perhaps not by AD 2000, it will lead to technological intervention along present lines being superfluous. If damaged nerve pathways and brain tissues can be repaired, and non-functioning organs replaced, then speech synthesisers or other communication aids may become quite unnecessary. This is the 'bionic option'.

Barriers to Using the Technology

The technology for educating disabled children and adults may well exist by AD 2000, but what are the barriers to using it? Vanderheiden (1982) identifies several.

There is not enough access to standard software. Only small amounts of specially-prepared software are likely to be available for, say, physically-disabled individuals, because of the expense of writing it. Modification of software prepared for able-bodied people is also very expensive, therefore ways must be found for disabled people to use standard software.

Microcomputers for disabled people are not portable enough. The trend is towards lighter and more portable ones, incorporating screens and printers, and perhaps this will cease to be a problem long before AD 2000. At present, portable computers are only capable of a limited range of functions, though some of these happen to be ones useful to disabled people. Demasco and Foulds (1982), at the Tufts-New England Medical Center in Boston, point out that most microcomputers (for example, Apple, Atari, etc.) being used by communication-handicapped people cannot be mounted on a wheelchair and take too much power to be operated by batteries. They have tried to reproduce on a standard Panasonic hand-held computer features available on other machines. Input is available through keyboard or switches, output through visual display or synthetic speech. Storage is somewhat limited at present, but it seems certain that this problem can be solved very soon. Programs can be created on larger computers and transferred to the small machine in the form of a PROM (programmed read-only memory) chip.

Hardware and software become obsolete very quickly, and there is little compatibility between different makes and models. This makes for difficulties in providing disabled people with up-to-date facilities. If hardware is available in compatible modules, which can be replaced in rotation, the problems are reduced.

Profits for the manufacturers of the technology will drop if rehabilitation aids are increasingly made as accessories to standard microcomputers, as seems likely, compared with the period when the manufacturers were supplying purpose-built systems. There is not enough co-ordination of research and development efforts and too little exchange of information. At present, similar 'inventions' occur in many places, a waste of time and (limited) money.

Vanderheiden points out that, on the one hand, there are unrealistically high expectations of technology. For example, microcomputers are powerful in some respects, but they cannot solve all the complex problems faced by many disabled individuals. If they are 'sold' to agencies and people who have these expectations, disappointment is bound to come. On the other hand, there are unrealistically low expectations of technology. Some funding agencies consider that microcomputers are mere toys, and insist on paying far more for specially-built systems when a microcomputer plus aids would do. He thinks that Western society lacks a 'service delivery system', that is, the social infrastructure needed to identify needs and how they can best be met by the technology. In social welfare and education services, suitably qualified staff, who know about disability, the technology and applications of it to disability are few and far between. In particular, disabled people need help in selecting sound applications from among the many mediocre and poor ones. More effort needs to go into understanding what is appropriate and inappropriate. Evaluation of hardware and software for disabled people is badly needed, so that disabled users, teachers, parents and others can be helped to judge what is of high quality.

The Human Element

Whatever happens to bring about advances in new information technology that are of benefit in educating disabled children and adults, the human element in this education will always be paramount. The skill, dedication and patience of professionals who work with and help disabled people is legendary, and no technology can replace it. At best, the technology is a complement, often merely a supplement. By definition, no technology can provide a human caring environment. There can be no question of automating the education of disabled students, any more than there can be for able-bodied ones.

The human element is paramount, and we freely advocate that humans should exploit the technology, to the benefit of disabled humans.

Summary

This final chapter does not provide a detailed picture of what new information technology for education will be like in AD 2000, because that is impossible to predict. We look instead at some possible developments, and at some of the barriers to full exploitation of the technology by the people concerned, the professionals and their disabled students. We end by stressing that the human element, rather than the technological, is paramount.

REFERENCES

Adams, Josephine (1983). World wide appeal. *Learning to Cope '83: An Educational Computing Special.* London: Educational Computing

Adams, Josephine (1983a). A day to remember. *Learning to Cope '83: An Educational Computing Special.* London: Educational Computing

Alpert, D. (1982). Artificial Language Laboratory; Leader in Communication Enhancement Research. *Acronyms,* vol. 12, no. 4

Apple Computer (1981). *Personal Computers for the Physically Disabled: A Resource Guide.* Cupertino: Apple Computer

Arkansas Enterprises for the Blind (AEB) (1980). Arkansas school provides computer training to blind. *THE Journal,* vol. 7, no. 6

Armstrong, Jim and others (1983). *Comparison of Apple, Epson, IBM ... Microcomputers for Applications in Rehabilitation Systems for Persons with Physical Handicaps.* Madison: Trace Research and Development Center for the Severely Communicatively Handicapped, University of Wisconsin

Arnold, P. (1978). The deaf child's written English: Can we measure its quality? *Journal of the British Association of Teachers of the Deaf,* vol. 2

Arnold, P. (1981). Recent research on the deaf child's written English. *Journal of the British Association of Teachers of the Deaf,* vol. 5

Askew, R. (1971). Opportunities for continued education of the deaf in the United Kingdom. *Teacher of the Deaf,* vol. 69

Atherton, Roy (1981). *Structured Programming in COMAL-80.* Chichester: Ellis Horwood

Atherton, Roy (1982). Why COMAL is a quiet revolution. *Phase Two,* vol. 2, no. 1

Bakan, J.D. and Chandler, D.L. (1980). *Access II: the Independent Producer's Handbook of Satellite Communications.* Washington DC: National Endowment for the Arts

Baker, Bruce (1982). Minspeak: a semantic compaction system that makes self-expression easier for communicatively disabled individuals. *Byte,* September

Baker, Bruce (1983). Chopsticks and Beethoven. *Communication Outlook,* vol. 5, no. 2

Barker, Margaret (1983). Computer input devices for physically disabled people. Paper from the Rehabilitation Engineering Center, Children's Hospital at Stanford, California

Barker, Margaret and others (1983). The control evaluator and training kit: an assessment tool for comparative testing of controls to operate assistive devices. In Proceedings of the 6th Annual Conference on Rehabilitation Engineering, San Diego, California

Bate, J. (1983). Personal communication

Behrmann, Michael M. and Lahm, Liz (1983). Technology and handicapped babies. *Communication Outlook,* vol. 5, no. 2

Bell, Daniel (1980). The social framework of the information society. In Forester, Tom (ed.) (1980). *The Microelectronics Revolution.* Oxford: Blackwell

Bennett, Helen (1983). Manpower Services Commission: special schemes for disabled people. Paper presented at a conference on the Computer as an Aid for those with Special Needs, Sheffield

Beukelman, David (1983). Personal communication

Blatt, J. and Sulzer, J.S. (1981). Captioned television and hearing-impaired

246

viewers: The report of a national survey. *American Annals of the Deaf*, vol. 126

Blenkhorn, P. and Tobin, M. (1983). Report on computer hardware in schools and units for the visually handicapped. Research Centre for the Education of the Visually Handicapped, University of Birmingham

Bolton, M.P. and Taylor, A.C. (1981). A universal computer and interface system for the disabled (UNICAID). *Journal of Biomedical Engineering*, vol. 3, October

Booth, Tony (1983). Integrating special education. In Booth, Tony and Potts, Patricia (eds) (1983). *Integrating Special Education.* Oxford: Blackwell

Booth, Tony and Potts, Patricia (eds) (1983). *Integrating Special Education.* Oxford: Blackwell

Bowes, John E. (1980). Mind vs. matter — mass utilization of information technology. In Dervin, Brenda and Voigt, Melvin J. *Progress in Communication Sciences*, vol. II. Norwood, New Jersey: Ablex Publishing

Bowyer, L.R. and others (1963). The relative personality adjustment of severely deaf and partially deaf children. *British Journal of Educational Psychology*, vol. 3

Bramer, M.A. (1982). COMAL 80 — adding structure to BASIC. *Computers in Education*, vol. 6, no. 2

Brawley, R. (1983). Personal communication

Broder, H. and Hinton, G. (1984). Preventive psychotherapeutic measures for use with non-vocal clients. *Communication Outlook*, vol. 5, no. 3

Brooks, J.R. (1984). The evolution of speech synthesis. *Communication Outlook*, vol. 5, no. 3

Bruner, J. (1978). The role of dialogue in language acquisition. In Sinclair, A. and Levalt, W. (eds), *The Child's Conception of Language.* New York: Springer-Verlag

Butler, M. (1978). *Visually Handicapped Students.* London: Royal National Institute for the Blind

Campo, M. (1980). Presentation at the 1980 World Optacon Conference

Carroll Centre for the Blind (1983). Voice output for access by the blind and visually impaired. *Aids and Appliances Review*, Issues no. 9 and 10

Carter, Julia (1983). Expecting too much? *Learning to Cope '83: An Educational Computing Special.* London: Educational Computing

Carver, V. and Hales, G.W. (1974). Tuition and support services for the deaf in the Open University. *American Annals of the Deaf*, vol. 119

Centre for Educational Technology, Israel (1981). Annual report. Tel Aviv: The Centre

Chapanis, A. and others (1972). Studies in interactive communication modes: Effects on the behaviour of teams during co-operative problem solving. *Human Factors*, vol. 14

Chapanis, A. and others (1977). Studies in interactive communication: II The effects of four communication modes on the linguistic performance of teams during co-operative problem solving. *Human Factors*, vol. 19, no. 2

Chapman, B.L.M. (1982). Warnock in the light of the new technology. *Bulletin of the British Psychological Society*, vol. 35, December

Chapman, B. (1983). Personal communication

Chapman, B.L.M. and Wilby, J.F. (1982). Language and silence. *Computers in Schools*, March

Chapman, E.K. (1978). *Visually Handicapped Children and Young People.* London: Routledge & Kegan Paul

Clarkson, T.G. (1981). An eye-controlled communication aid for physically-disabled people. Interim Report (October 1981), King's College, London

Cleveland, Harlan (1984). King Canute and the information resource. *Intermedia*, vol. 12, no. 1

Conrad, R. (1970). Short term memory processes in the deaf. *British Journal of Psychology*, vol. 61

Conrad, R. (1971). The effect of vocalising on comprehension in the profoundly deaf. *British Journal of Psychology*, vol. 62

Conrad, R. (1977). Lipreading by deaf and hearing children. *British Journal of Educational Psychology*, vol. 47

Conrad, R. (1977a). The reading ability of deaf school leavers. *British Journal of Educational Psychology*, vol. 47

Cook, Albert M. (1983). Special uses of electronics and computers in British schools. *Communication Outlook*, vol. 4, no. 4

Cope, N. and King, R.W. (1982). Conversion of teletext and viewdata into braille. IEE Man-Machine Systems Conference, Manchester

Cornett, R.O. (1983). Personal communication

Croft, A.J. and Chaplin, D.M. (1984). Nuffield project for visually handicapped computer programmers. Progress report, Department of Physics, University of Oxford

Cronin, B. (1979). The DAVID system: The development of an interactive video system at the National Technical Institute for the Deaf. *American Annals of the Deaf*, vol. 124

Crosby, D. (1983). Personal communication

Daly, Dennis W. (1983). Information exchange project for special education. *Phase Two*, vol. 3, no. 2

Demasco, P. and Foulds, R. (1982) A new horizon for nonvocal communication devices. *Byte*, September

Deninger, M.L. (1983). Kendall Demonstration Elementary School meets the technological challenge: A comprehensive computer managed education system. Kendall Demonstration Elementary School, Washington DC

Department of Education and Science (1972). *External examinations in schools of the deaf and partially hearing and opportunities for further education*. London: Her Majesty's Stationery Office

Department of Education and Science (1978). *Special Educational Needs*. London: Her Majesty's Stationery Office

Deuchar, M. (1979). The grammar of British Sign Language. *British Deaf News (Supplement)*

Dickson, M.B. (1979). Job seeking skills program for the blind. *Journal of Visual Impairment and Blindness*, vol. 73, no. 1

Dietz, C. (1983). Personal communication

Dineen, M. (1981). Mercury on the right track. *Guardian*, October 25

Dolman, D. (1980). English remediation and the older deaf student: The computer as a tool. *American Annals of the Deaf*, vol. 125

Doorlag, D.M. and Doorlag, D.H. (1983). Cassette braille: a new communication tool for blind people. *Journal of Visual Impairment and Blindness*, vol. 77, no. 4

Drucker, Peter (1969). *The Age of Discontinuity*. London: Heinemann

Duncan, F.G. (1983). Substitutes for speech: experience of applications of artificial voice production in microprocessor-based systems for the disabled. Paper presented at EUROMICRO 83, Madrid, September 14-16

Emmett, Pat and Johnson, Mike (1983). Logo in a special school. Paper presented at the conference on The Computer as an Aid for those with Special Needs, Sheffield, April 14-16

Enell, Nancy C. (1983). Present and future computer applications in special education research, evaluation and planning. Paper presented at the Annual Meeting of the American Educational Research Association, Montreal

Eulenberg, John B. and Rosenfeld, Jan (1982). Vocaid — a new product from Texas Instruments. *Communication Outlook*, vol. 3, no. 3

Eulenberg, John Bryson and Vanderheiden, Gregg C. (1978). We are a community. *Communication Outlook*, vol. 1, no. 1

Evans, Christopher (1981). *The Micro Millenium*. New York: Washington Square Press/Pocket Books

Evenson, R.H. (1981). Cassette braille evaluation. *Education of the Visually Handicapped*, vol. 13, no. 1

Fender, D.H. (1983). Reading machines for blind people. *Journal of Visual Impairment and Blindness*, vol. 77, no. 2

Ferguson, John (1982). Computer applications to school psychological services. *Association of Educational Psychologists Journal*, vol. 5, no. 10

Firminger, Janis (1983). Assessing IT for severely disabled students: new developments at Hereward College. *NATFHE Journal*, December

Flanagan, G. (1983). Personal communication

Flanagan, J.L. and others (1970). Synthetic voices for computers. *IEEE Spectrum*, vol. 7, no. 10

Flather, P. (1983). Preparing for a life without sight. *The Times Higher Educational Supplement*, January

Foulds, R.A. (1980). Communication rates for nonspeech expression as a function of manual tasks and linguistic constraints. Proceedings of the International Conference on Rehabilitation Engineering, Toronto

Foulds, Richard A. (1982). Applications of microcomputers in the education of the physically disabled child. *Exceptional Children*, vol. 49, no. 2

Fountain, Michael (1984). Personal communication

Fox, R. (1979). Media based visual image controlled (Vis-I-Con) instruction delivery system for instruction of deaf and hearing-impaired. *American Annals of the Deaf*, vol. 124

Furth, H.G. (1964). Research with the deaf: implications for language and cognition. *Psychological Bulletin*, vol. 62

Furth, H.G. (1965). *Thinking without Language: Psychological Implications of Deafness*. New York: Free Press

Furth, H.G. (1973). *Deafness and Learning: A Psychosocial Approach*. New York: Wadsworth

Galbraith, G. and others (1979). Interfacing an expensive home computer to the videodisc: Educational applications for the hearing impaired. *American Annals of the Deaf*, vol. 124

Gates, M.Y. (1980). Technological developments in the printing industry from now until 1990. In Maurice, Marcel, Philips, Edward and Scherff, Hans-Ludwig (eds) (1980). *The Impact of New Technologies on Publishing*. London: Saur

Gibbons, J.H. (1982). *Technology and Handicapped People*. Washington, DC: Office of Technology Assessment

Gill, J.M. (1983). Microcomputer aids for the blind. *Computer Education*, November

Glen, Ian (1982). Communicating with a microcomputer. *Learning to Cope: An Educational Computing Special*. London: Educational Computing

Goldberg, L. (1973). The Boston school learning laboratory. *The Convention of American Instructors for the Deaf Newsletter*, vol. 4

Goldenberg, E.P. (1979). *Special Technology for Special Children*. Baltimore: University Park Press

Goldenberg, E.P. and others (1984). *Computers, Education and Special Needs*. Reading, Massachusetts: Addison Wesley

Goodenough-Trepagnier, C. and others (1982). Determinants of rate in communication aids for the non-vocal motor handicapped. Proceedings of the Human Factors Society, Seattle, October

Goodenough-Trepagnier, C. and others (1982a). Derivation of an efficient nonvocal communication system. *Human Factors*, vol. 24

Goodenough-Trepagnier, C. and others (1983). Prespeec: Use of a sound-combination system by non-vocal children. Sixth Annual Conference on Rehabilitation Engineering, San Diego, California

Goodrich, G.L. and others (1977). Training and practice effects in performance with low-vision aids: a preliminary study. *American Journal of Optometry and Physiological Optics*, vol. 54, no. 5

Goodrich, G.L. and others (1979). Kurzweil Reading Machine: a partial evaluation of its optical character recognition error rate. *Journal of Visual Impairment and Blindness*, vol. 73, no. 10

Goodrich, G.L. and others (1980). Preliminary report on evaluation on synthetic speech for reading machines. *Journal of Visual Impairment and Blindness*, vol. 74, no. 7

Goodrich, G.L. and Quillman, R.D. (1978). CCTV's: choices and considerations. *Journal of Visual Impairment and Blindness*, vol. 72, no. 2

Goodyear, Anne (1982). Talking through the computer. *Yorkshire Post*, June 30

Gormley, K.A. and Franzen, A.M. (1978). Why can't the deaf read? Comments on asking the wrong question. *American Annals of the Deaf*, vol. 123

Green, F. and others (1982). *Microcomputers in Special Education*. London: Longmans/Schools Council

Griffin, Penny (1982). A powerful servant, nothing more. *Times Educational Supplement*, September 10

Griffiths, P.A. (1983). The computer in a school for the physically-handicapped. Paper presented at the conference on The Computer as an Aid for those with Special Needs, Sheffield, April 14-16

Groner, G.F. and Savoie, R.E. (1979). Towards a personal speech-output reading machine for blind people. Proceedings (session 6, Microcomputers aid the handicapped learner) of the Wescon Professional Program, San Francisco

Grossner, C.P. and others (1983). An integrated workstation for the visually handicapped. *IEEE Micro*, June

Gumpert, Gary and Cathcart, Robert (eds) (1979). *Intermedia: Interpersonal Communication in a Media World*. New York: Oxford University Press

Gunderson, Jon (1983). A headpointing technique for use with standard computer systems: the long-range optical headpointer. Madison: Trace Research and Development Center for the Severely Communicatively Handicapped, University of Wisconsin

Hales, G.W. (1976). Communicating with the deaf by conventional orthography: the case for a non-verbatim approach. *British Journal of Audiology*, vol. 10

Hales, G.W. (1978). Some problems associated with the higher education of deaf and hearing-impaired students in an open system. PhD thesis, The Open University

Hall, Margery and Turner, Phil (1983). Synthesised speech for the non-communicating pupil. Paper presented at the conference on The Computer as an Aid for those with Special Needs, Sheffield, April 14-16

Hamp, N.N. (1972). Reading attainment and some associated factors in deaf and partially hearing children. *Teacher of the Deaf*, vol. 70

Hanner, B. and others (1971). *Toward the identification of educationally significant traits of post-secondary deaf students*. Rochester: National Technical Institute for the Deaf

Hansen, Per Krogh (1982). Touch sensitive input to computers. Proceedings of the 5th Annual Conference on Rehabilitation Engineering, Houston, Texas

Harley, R.K. and others (1979). *The Teaching of Braille Reading*. Springfield, Illinois: Thomas

Harley, R.K. and Lawrence, G.A. (1977). *Visual Impairment in the Schools*. Springfield, Illinois: Thomas

Harris, Amelia and others (1971). *Handicapped and Impaired in Great Britain*.

London: Her Majesty's Stationery Office

Hawker, P. (1981). Electronic cameras: What now? What next? What then? *Combroad,* June

Hawkridge, David (1983). *New Information Technology in Education.* Beckenham & Baltimore: Croom Helm and Johns Hopkins

Hazen, Paul (ed.) (1982). Proceedings of the Johns Hopkins First National Search for Applications of Personal Computing to Aid the Handicapped. Piscataway, New Jersey: Institute of Electrical and Electronic Engineering

Head, Peter and Poon, Patrick (1982). The enabling microcomputer. *Learning to Cope '82: An Educational Computing Special.* London: Educational Computing

Head, Peter and Poon, Patrick (1983). Communication in an educational setting. *Learning to Cope '83: An Educational Computing Special.* London: Educational Computing

Heber, M. (1977). The influence of language training on seriation of 5-6 year old children initially at different levels of descriptive competence. *British Journal of Psychology,* vol. 68

Hedger, J. (1980). Broadcast telesoftware: experience with Oracle. In Haslam, G. and others (1980). *Viewdata '80.* Northwood, England: Online Conferences

Hicks, David (1984). The trauma of Telidon. *Rehabilitation Digest,* vol. 14, no. 2

Hight, R.L. (1982). Lip-reader trainer: Teaching aid for the hearing impaired. *American Annals of the Deaf,* vol. 127

Hiltz, Starr Roxanne and Turoff, Murray (1978). *The Network Nation: Human Communication via Computer.* Reading, Massachusetts: Addison Wesley

Hinds, R. (1983). Vision stimulation and the home computer. *Computers in Schools,* vol. 5, no. 2

Hine, W.D. (1970). The abilities of partially hearing children. *British Journal of Educational Psychology,* vol. 40

Hobday, Stephen (1983). The PCD Maltron ergonomic keyboard: developments for the disabled. Paper presented at the conference on The Computer as an Aid for those with Special Needs, Sheffield, April 14-16

Hofmann, Anna C. (1983). Senate Bill 1115: funding for communication and sensory aids. *Communication Outlook,* vol. 5, no. 1

Hofmann, Anna C. (1984). Personal communication

Hogg, Robin (1984). *Microcomputers and Special Education Needs: A Guide to Good Practice.* Stratford-upon-Avon: National Council for Special Education

Home Office (1981). *Direct Broadcasting by Satellite.* London: Her Majesty's Stationery Office

Hope, Mary (1983). Jigsaw pieces. *Times Educational Supplement,* November 4

Hope, M (1983a). How can microcomputers help? *Special Education: Forward Trends,* vol. 7

Hope, Mary and Odor, P. (1982). Exploiting the potential and overcoming the problems. *Learning to Cope '83: An Educational Computing Special.* London: Educational Computing

Hubbard, Geoffrey (1981). Education and the new technologies. *Proceedings of the Royal Society of Arts,* vol. CXXIX, no. 5297, April

Humphrey, Mary M. and Kleiman, Glenn M. (1982). Benefits of using computers in special education. Paper for a Workshop at the Rehabilitation Engineering Center, Children's Hospital at Stanford, California

Ince, Darrel (1982). How to make a supercomputer get a move on. *Guardian,* February 11

Innis, Harold (1951). *The Bias of Communication.* Toronto: University of Toronto Press

Irwin, Margaret (1983). Personal communication

Jaffe, David L. (1983). A design/development methodology for rehabilitation

devices using embedded microcomputers. Paper available from the
Rehabilitation Research and Development Center, Palo Alto Veterans
Administration Medical Center

Jampolsky, Arthur and others (1982). *1981-1982 Report of Progress.* San
Francisco: Rehabilitation Engineering Centre, Smith-Kettlewell Institute of
Visual Sciences

Jarrett, Dennis (1980). *The Good Computing Book for Beginners.* London: ECC
Publications

Jenkin, Mark (1982). Preparing for employment. *Learning to Cope: An
Educational Computing Special.* London: Educational Computing

Jenkins, Laurie (1983). Personal communication

Jones, B.W. and Grygar, J. (1982). The Test of Syntactic Abilities and
microcomputers. *American Annals of the Deaf,* vol. 127

Jones, C.F.G. (1983). Deaf people in the 'chip' society: How information
technology may serve our needs in the future. Paper presented to the IX World
Congress of the World Federation of the Deaf, Palermo, Sicily

Jost, M. (1983). Lab I Software Catalog. California School for the Deaf, Riverside

Kaiser, W., Marko, H. and Witte, E. (eds) (1977). *Two-way Cable Television:
Experiences with Pilot Projects in North America, Japan and Europe.* Berlin:
Springer-Verlag

Kincaid, D. Lawrence (1979). *The Convergence Model of Communication.*
Honolulu: East-West Communication Institute

King, R.W. and Omotayo, O.R. (1982). Synthetic speech as a medium for the
output of electronic information services for the blind. IEE Man-Machine
Systems Conference, Manchester

Klimbie, J.W. (1982). Digital optical recording: principle, and possible
applications. In Tedd, Lucy and others (1982). [Proceedings of the] *Fifth
International Online Information Meeting, London 8-10 December 1981.*
Oxford: Learned Information

Koyanagi, K., Shimura, H. and Yamagata, H. (1981). Effects of tactile reading
training of the Japanese language with the Optacon. *NISE Bulletin,* vol. 1

Knott, Jack and Wildavsky, Aaron (1981). If dissemination is the solution, what is
the problem? In Rich, Robert F. (ed.) (1981). *The Knowledge Cycle.* Beverly
Hills: Sage

Kreis, M. (1979). Project Video Language: A successful experiment. *American
Annals of the Deaf,* vol. 124

Larcher, Janet (1983). 'If only time would pass more slowly!' *Educational
Computing,* December

Large, P. (1982). Cable means more to see on TV — and more holes in road.
Guardian, 23 March

LeBlanc, Maurice (1978). Shopping for devices and systems. *Communication
Outlook,* vol. 1, no. 2

Leonard, J.M. (1983). Personal communication

Letterman, Norman (1983). Personal communication

Levine, E. (1960). *The Psychology of Deafness.* New York: Columbia University
Press

Lindenmayer, Graeme (1981). Information and the technologies for handling it.
Programmed Learning and Educational Technology, vol. 18, no. 4

Low, Colin (1983). Integrating the visually-handicapped. In Booth, Tony and
Potts, Patricia (eds) (1983). *Integrating Special Education.* Oxford: Blackwell

Lowenthal, K. and Kostrevski, B. (1973). The effects of training in written
communication on verbal skills. *British Journal of Educational Psychology,* vol.
43

Lunney, D. and Morrison, R. (1981). Microcomputer-assisted laboratory instruction for visually handicapped college chemistry students. Final report, Department of Chemistry, East Carolina University

McConnell, David (1983). Personal report on visits to Scottish schools and research centres

McLaughlin, Donald H. and others (1983). *Coordination and Evaluation of Videodisc and Microcomputer Programs.* Final Technical Report. Palo Alto: American Institutes for Research

McLeod, R. (1981). Toward development of a computer programming ability in deaf pre-high-school students: A pilot study. *American Annals of the Deaf,* vol. 126

MacLeod, Iain and Jackson, J.J. (1979). Computer-based handwriting training for the blind. *Communication Outlook,* vol. 2, no. 1

McLuhan, Marshall (1964). *Understanding Media: the Extensions of Man.* New York: Signet

Machlup, F. (1980). *Knowledge and Knowledge Production.* Princeton, New Jersey: Princeton University Press

Maddox, B. (1981). Cable television: the wiring of America. *The Economist,* 20 June

Mahon, Peter (1983). A personal view. *Learning to Cope '83: An Educational Computing Special.* London: Educational Computing

Mahony, S., Demartino, N. and Stengel, R. (1980). *Keeping PACE with the New Television: Public Television and Changing Technology.* New York: Carnegie Corporation

Markes, M.I.F. (1983). Personal communication

Martin, James D. (1977). *Future Developments in Telecommunications.* Englewood Cliffs, New Jersey: Prentice-Hall

Mason, W.F. (1977). Overview of CATV developments in the US. In Kaiser, W., Marko, H. and Witte, E. (eds) (1977). *Two-way Cable Television: Experiences with Pilot Projects in North America, Japan and Europe.* Berlin: Springer-Verlag

Mayhew, John and Frisby, John (1984). Computer vision. In O'Shea, Tim and Eisenstadt, Marc (eds) (1984). *Artificial Intelligence: Tools. Techniques and Applications.* New York: Harper and Row

Merrill, E.C. (1972). A perspective on higher education for the deaf. *American Annals of the Deaf,* vol. 117

Meyers, Laura F. (1982). Written testimony to a joint hearing on technology and handicapped people, U.S. House of Representatives, Washington DC, 29 September

Meyers, Laura F. (1983). Use of microcomputers to initiate language use in young non-oral children. In Perkins, W. (ed) *Current Therapy of Communication Disorders.* New York: Thieme-Stratton

Meyers, Laura F. (1983a). The use of microcomputers to promote acquisition of beginning language and literacy skills in young handicapped children. In Proceedings of the American Association for the Advancement of Science Conference on Computers and the Handicapped, Trace Center, Madison, Wisconsin. Washington DC: The Association

Meyers, Laura F. (1984). Unique contributions of microcomputers to language interventions with handicapped children. *Seminars in Speech and Language,* vol. 5, no. 1

Millar, W. and others (1983). An intelligent microcomputer keyboard suitable for physically-handicapped children. Paper presented at the conference on The Computer as an Aid for those with Special Needs, Sheffield, 14-16 April

Morgan, E. (1980). *Microprocessors: a Short Introduction.* London: Her Majesty's Stationery Office

Morgan, G. (1980a). Britain's teletext services are a commercial success. In

Haslam, G. and others (1980). *Viewdata '80*. Northwood, England: Online Conferences

Mudge, Robin (1984). CAD within your grasp. *Acorn User*, May

Myklebust, H.R. (1964). *The Psychology of Deafness*. New York: Grune and Stratton

Napier, G.D. (1974). Special subject adjustments and skills. In Lowenfeld, B. (ed.) (1974). *The Visually Handicapped Child in School*. London: Constable

Nash, Ian (1981). Computer link gives new life to Tim. *The Teacher*, 15 May

Nettles, Patricia (1981). Slow-scan: long-distance pictures by phone. *Development Communication Report*, no. 34

Neu, Pat (1983). Personal communication

Newell, Peter (1983). The open door. *Guardian*, 29 March

Nixon, Robin (1983). Programming for disabled users. *Practical Computing*, March

Nugent, G.C. and Stone, C.G. (1982). The videodisc meets the microcomputer. *American Annals of the Deaf*, vol. 127

O'Shea, Tim and Self, John (1983). *Learning and Teaching with Computers*. Brighton: Harvester

Otten, K.W. (1980). Information transfer and the significance of new storage media and technologies. In Maurice, Marcel, Phillips, Edward and Scherff, Hans-Ludwig (eds) (1980). *The Impact of New Technologies on Publishing*. London: Saur

Paisley, William (1980). Information and work. In Dervin, Brenda and Voigt, Melvin J. *Progress in Communication Sciences*, vol. II, Norwood, New Jersey: Ablex Publishing

Papert, Seymour (1977). A learning environment for children. In Seidel, Robert J. and Rubin, Martin (eds) (1977). *Computers and Communication: Implications for Education*. New York: Academic Press

Papert, Seymour (1980). *Mindstorms: Children, Computers and Powerful Ideas*. Brighton, Sussex: Harvester

Papert, Seymour A. and Weir, Sylvia (1978). *Information Prosthetics for the Handicapped*. Artificial Intelligence Memo No 496. Cambridge: Massachusetts Institute of Technology Artificial Intelligence Laboratory

Perkins, W.J. (ed.) (1983). *High Technology Aids for the Disabled*. London: Butterworths

Peterson, E., Silversten, E. and Wang, W. (1958). Segmentation techniques in speech synthesis. *JASA*, vol. 30, no. 8

Pickering, J. (1983). Communication aids and micro-processor technology. A report to the Nuffield Foundation, April

Pickering, J.A. and Stevens, G.C. (1984). The physically-handicapped and work-related computing: towards interface intelligence. Proceedings of the 2nd International Conference on Rehabilitation Engineering, Ottawa

Pierce, J.R. (1961). *Symbols, Signals and Noise*. New York: Harper and Row

Piestrup, Ann M. (1983). Personal communication

Pollan, Michael (1982). The disabled: communications is the great equalizer. *Channels*, February/March

Poulton, A.S. (1983). *Microcomputer Speech Synthesis and Recognition*. Wilmslow, Cheshire: Sigma Technical Press

Quillman, R.D. and Goodrich, G.L. (1979-80). New approaches to low vision services. In Mallinson, G.G. (ed.), *Blindness Annual*, American Association of Workers for the Blind, Washington DC

Raffle, F. (1970). Are you ready, play. *Teacher of the Blind*, vol. 58, no. 3

Rahimi, M.A. and Eulenberg, J.B. (1983). Voice-to-voice and EMG-to-voice systems for speech prosthesis. Department of Computer Science, Michigan State University

Raitt, David (1982). New information technology — social aspects, usage and trends. In Tedd, Lucy and others (1982). (Proceedings of the) Fifth International Online Information Meeting, London 8-10 December 1981. Oxford: Learned Information

Rees, Stuart and Bates, Roger (1982). With a little extra help from his friends. *Learning to Cope '82: An Educational Computing Special.* London: Educational Computing

Rees, Stuart and Bates, Roger (1983). The Lancasterian Project. *Learning to Cope '83: An Educational Computing Special.* London: Educational Computing

Renuk, J. (1982). Communication handicappers. *Communication Outlook,* vol. 4, no. 2

Reynolds, Michael (1980). The production engineering process. *Communication Outlook,* vol. 2, no. 4

Rheingold, Howard (1983). Videogames go to school. *Psychology Today,* September

Rhyne, J.M. (1982). Comprehension of synthetic speech by blind children. *Journal of Visual Impairment and Blindness,* vol. 76, no. 1

Rich, Robert F. (1980). Knowledge in society. In Rich, Robert F. (1980). *The Knowledge Cycle.* Beverly Hills: Sage

Richards, C. (1983). Microelectronics in special education: the essential relationship with the curriculum. A paper from the Special Education Microelectronics Resource Centre, Newcastle-upon-Tyne

Roberts, Oscar and Sarah (1983). Personal report on visit to Speech and Communication Laboratory, University of Southern California, Los Angeles

Roberts, Oscar and Sarah (1983a). Personal report on visit to Cotting School for Handicapped Children, Boston, Massachusetts

Robertson, Joseph (1981). Tomorrow's office automation systems will provide greater productivity gains. *Communication News,* November

Rochester, G.W. (1984). Personal communication

Rogers, Everett M. and Kincaid, D. Lawrence. (1981). *Communication Networks: Toward a New Paradigm for Research.* New York: Free Press.

Rostron, A.B. and Sewell, D.F. (1984). *Microtechnology in Special Education.* London and Baltimore: Croom Helm and Johns Hopkins University Press

Ryan, S.G. and Bedi, D.N. (1978). Toward computer literacy for visually impaired students. *Journal of Visual Impairment and Blindness,* vol. 72, no. 8

Salomon, Gavriel (1979). *Interaction of Media, Cognition and Learning.* San Francisco: Jossey Bass

Sanderson, J. (1983). Personal communication

Sandhu, Jim (1983). Introduction, in *Microfair — Electronic Aids for the Handicapped.* Newcastle-upon-Tyne: Handicapped Persons Research Unit, Newcastle-upon-Tyne Polytechnic

Sandhu, Jim (1984). The question of compatibility — the BARD experience. Paper for a conference on Databases for Disabled People, London

Sargent, D. and Nyerges, L. (1979). A system for the synchronisation of continuous speech with printed text. *American Annals of the Deaf,* vol. 124

Scadden, L.A. (1978). Kurzweil Reading Machine: evaluation of model 1. *Journal of Visual Impairment and Blindness,* vol. 72, no. 10

Schneider, E.W. and Bennion, J.L. (1981). *Videodiscs.* Englewood Cliffs, New Jersey: Education Technology Publications

Schofield, Julia M. (1981). *Microcomputer-based Aids for the Disabled.* London: Heyden, on behalf of the British Computer Society

Schramm, Wilbur (1977). *Big Media, Little Media: Tools and Technologies for Instruction.* Beverly Hills: Sage

Schramm, Wilbur (1981). What is a long time? In Wilhoit, G. Cleveland and de

Bock, Harold (eds) (1981). *Mass Communication Yearbook, vol. 2.* Beverly Hills: Sage

Schubin, M. (1980). An overview and history of video disc technologies. In Sigel, Efrem, Schubin, Mark and Merrill, Paul F. (eds) (1980). *Video Discs: the Technology, Applications and Future.* White Plains, New York: Knowledge Industry Publications

Schweikhardt, W. (1980). A computer based education system for the blind. Proceedings of IFIP-Congress 80, Tokyo

Schwejda, Paul and Vanderheiden, Gregg (1982). Adaptive-Firmware card for the Apple II: alternative input techniques give physically disabled individuals immediate access to standard software. *Byte,* September

Scriven, Michael (1981). Breakthroughs in educational technology. In Cirincione-Coles, Kathryn (ed.) (1981). *The Future of Education: Policy Issues and Challenges.* San Francisco: Sage

Sewell, D.F. and others (1980). Language and the deaf: An interactive microcomputer-based approach. *British Journal of Educational Technology,* vol. 11

Shannon, Claude E. and Weaver, Warren (1949). *The Mathematical Theory of Communication.* Urbana: University of Illinois Press

Shotwell and Associates (1981). *The 1981 Courseware Market Report.* San Francisco: Shotwell and Associates

Sims, D. and others (1979). A pilot experiment in computer-assisted speechreading instruction utilizing the Data Analysis Video Interactive Device (DAVID). *American Annals of the Deaf,* vol. 124

SMDP (1983). Report on the Dunblane Consultative Conference, August. Glasgow: Scottish Microelectronics Development Programme

Smith, R.L. (1981). The birth of a wired nation. *Channels,* vol. 1, no. 1

Smith, S. and Vincent, A.T. (1983). A talking brailler. *Journal of the Association for the Education and Welfare of the Visually Handicapped,* vol. 4, no. 2

Smye, S.M. (1983). A computer based communication aid for the handicapped. Paper presented at a conference on the Computer as an Aid for those with Special Needs, Sheffield

Spychala, Karen (1983). Personal communication

Stevenson, June and Sutton, D.C. (1982). Employment opportunities for physically-disabled people in computing. *Educare,* 15 June

Steward, La V.J. (1983). The relationship between vocational classes in high school and attainment of competitive employment for the visually handicapped. MA thesis, San Jose State University

Stonier, Tom (1979). Changes in western society: educational implications. In Schuller, Tom and Megarry, Jacquetta (eds) (1979). *Recurrent Education and Lifelong Learning.* World Yearbook of Education 1979. London: Kogan Page

Stonier, Tom (1981). A little learning is a lucrative thing. *Times Higher Education Supplement,* May 1

Stonier, Tom (1983). *The Wealth of Information.* London: Methuen

Street, F.P. (1981). To the customer's advantage. *British Telecom Journal,* vol. 2, no. 3, Autumn

Stuckless, E.R. (ed.) (1973). Principles basic to the establishment and operation of postsecondary programs for deaf students. Paper for a Conference of Executives of American Schools for the Deaf, Washington DC

Stuckless, E.R. (1982). Real-time graphic display and language development for the hearing impaired. Rochester: National Technical Institute for the Deaf

Stuckless, E.R. (1983). Personal communication

Stuckless, E.R. (1984). Personal communication

Stuckless, E.R. and Loutrel, L. (1972). Realtime graphic display. Rochester Institute of Technology

Sutter, Erich E. (1983). An oculo-encephalographic communication system. Proceedings of the 6th Annual Conference on Rehabilitation Engineering, San Diego, California

Swann, Will (1983). Curriculum principles for integration. In Booth, Tony and Potts, Patricia (eds) (1983). *Integrating Special Education*. Oxford: Blackwell

Tait, Jean (1983). Redbridge (Special Education Micro-electronics Resource Centre). *Learning to Cope '83: An Educational Computing Special*. London: Educational Computing

Teague, S.J. (1980). Microform publication. In Hills, P. (ed.) (1980). *The Future of the Printed Word*. London: Frances Pinter

Telesensory Systems Inc. (1983). Personal communication

Terzieff, I. and others (1982). Increasing reading rates with the Optacon: a pilot study. *Journal of Visual Impairment and Blindness*, vol. 76, no. 1

Testa, A. and Venturini, B. (1980). Presentation at the 1980 World Optacon Conference

Thibault, M.J. and Foulds, R.A. (1982). The use of diphones in speech synthesis. Fifth Annual Conference on Rehabilitation Engineering, Houston, Texas

Thomas, Lyndon (1983). Personal communication

Tobin, M. (1974). Evaluating the Optacon — and some general reflections on reading machines for the blind. Report on European conference on technical aids for the visually handicapped, Handikappinstitutet, Bromma. Sweden

Toffler, Alvin (1970). *Future Shock*. London: Bodley Head

Tolleyfield (1984). Personal communication

Trachtman, Paul (1984). Putting computers in the hands of children without language. *Smithsonian*, vol. 14, no. 11

Turnbull, S. (1984). Personal communication

Turner, G. (1981). Eliciting spontaneous speech and peer group interaction. *Communication Outlook*, vol. 3, no. 1

Turner, G. (1983). Hermes multi-output communication aid preliminary documentation. Wayne County Intermediate School District, Michigan

US Department of Education (1982). *Progress Towards an Appropriate Education*. Washington DC: Government Printing Office

Uslan, David T. (1983). Computer-generated distress? *The Catalyst*, vol. 2, no. 4

Vanderheiden, Gregg C. (1978). Technically speaking. *Communication Outlook*, vol. 1, no. 1

Vanderheiden, Gregg C. (1981). Practical applications of microcomputers to aid the handicapped. *Computer*, vol. 14, no. 1, January

Vanderheiden, Gregg C. (1981a). Technically speaking. *Communication Outlook*, vol. 3, no. 2

Vanderheiden, Gregg C. (1982). The practical use of microcomputers in rehabilitation. *Bulletin of Prosthetics Research*, vol. 19, no. 1

Vanderheiden, Gregg C. (1982a). Lightbeam headpointer research. *Communication Outlook*, vol. 3, no. 4, June

Vanderheiden, Gregg C. (1982b). Computers can play a dual role for disabled individuals. *Byte*, September

Vanderheiden, Gregg C. (1983). Non-conversational communication technology needs of individuals with handicaps. *Rehabilitation World*, vol. 7, no. 2

Vanderheiden, Gregg C. and Krause, La Vonne A. (1983). *Non-vocal Communication Resource Book*. Baltimore: University Park Press

Vanderheiden, Gregg C. and Walstead, Lottie M. (1983). *International Software/ Hardware Registry*. Madison: Trace Research and Development Center for the Severely Communicatively Handicapped, University of Wisconsin

Vincent, A.T. (1982). Computer-assisted support for blind students: a microcomputer linked voice synthesiser. *Computers and Education*, vol. 6

Vincent, A.T. (1983). Talking BASIC and talking braille: two applications of synthetic speech. *Computer Education*, no. 45

Vincent, A.T. (1983a). Microcomputers and synthetic speech. *The Journal of Blind Welfare*, vol. 67, no. 797

Vincent, A.T. (1983b). A synthetic speech system for schools. 'Computing and the Blind' project, The Open University

Wadsley, P. (1983). Space glasses. *Video Magazine*, July

Wallace, N. (1983). The development of the grunt converter. *Aids, Communication and Electronics*, vol. 2, no. 3

Walker, A. (1982). *Unqualified and Underemployed: the Fate of Handicapped School Leavers*. London: Macmillan

Walker, David D. (1983). Information technology and special education: development centres. *Phase Two*, vol. 3, no. 2

Ward, R.D. (1981). Computer assisted learning for the deaf. MSc thesis, Department of Computation, University of Manchester Institute of Science and Technology

Ward, Robert and Arnold, Paul (1982). Computer assisted learning and deaf children's language. *Journal of the British Association of Teachers of the Deaf*, vol. 6, no. 6

Ward, Robert and others (1983). Interactive computer-assisted learning for the classroom: problems and principles. *Programmed Learning and Educational Technology*. vol. 20, no. 4

Warnock, Mary (1983). Integration in schools. The *Observer*, 3 April

Waters, Peter David (1982). Maximisation of minimum control function and increasing efficiency. *Communication Outlook*, vol. 3, no. 3

Weir, Sylvia (1981). LOGO as an information prosthetic for the handicapped. Report WP-9. Cambridge: Artiticial Intelligence Laboratory, Massachusetts Institute of Technology

Weir, Sylvia, Russell, Susan Jo and Valente, Jose (1982). Logo: an approach to educating disabled children. *Byte*, September

Weiss, M.E. (1976). *Seeing Through the Dark*. New York: Harcourt Brace Jovanovich

Whitehead, R. (1983). Personal communication

Wigley, Ian (1983). A helping hand. *Learning to Cope '83: An Educational Computing Special*. London: Educational Computing

Williams, F. (1982). *The Communications Revolution*. Beverley Hills: Sage

Williams, M.B. (1981). What Emily Post never told me. *Communication Outlook*, vol. 3, no. 2

Williams, M.B. (1982). Confessions of a closet technocrat. *Communication Outlook*, vol. 3, no. 4

Wilson, M. (1981). *The Curriculum in Special Schools*. London: Longmans

Withrow, M.S. (1982). Technology to facilitate language acquisition. Gallaudet College, Washington DC

Wood, S.L. and others (1982). Development of an efficient and versatile speech prosthesis. Veteran's Administration Hospital, Palo Alto, California

Woolfe, R. (1980). *Videotex: the New Television/Telephone Information Service*. London: Heyden

Worcester College for the Blind (1973). *The Teaching of Science and Mathematics to the Blind*. London: Royal National Institute for the Blind

INDEX